Rethinking Ethnicity

ONE WEEK

Rethinking Ethnicity

Second Edition

Richard Jenkins

SAGE Publications
Los Angeles • London • New Delhi • Singapore

First edition published 1997
Reprinted 1998, 2001, 2003, 2006

Second edition published 2008

SAGE Publications Ltd
1 Oliver's Yard
55 City Road
London EC1Y 1SP

SAGE Publications Inc.
2455 Teller Road
Thousand Oaks, California 91320

SAGE Publications India Pvt Ltd
B 1/I 1 Mohan Cooperative Industrial Area
Mathura Road
New Delhi 110 044

SAGE Publications Asia-Pacific Pte Ltd
33 Pekin Street #02-01
Far East Square
Singapore 048763

Library of Congress Control Number: 2007929115

British Library Cataloguing in Publication data

A catalogue record for this book is available
from the British Library

ISBN 978-1-4129-3582-1
ISBN 978-1-4129-3583-8 (pbk)

Typeset by C&M Digital Pvt Ltd, Chennai, India
Printed in Great Britain by The Cromwell Press Ltd, Trowbridge, Wiltshire
Printed on paper from sustainable resources

Contents

Introduction to the Second Edition

A second edition of any book that has 'Rethinking' in its title is vulnerable to two potentially disconcerting responses. The first of these is the expectation that it will offer a re-rethinking of the first rethinking: something strikingly new and original by comparison with its first argument, perhaps, or even a public confession of error. The second is the suggestion that no one took much notice the first time around.

With respect to the first of these, I cannot claim to have changed in any significant way the arguments or proposals put forward in the first edition. There has been a little minor fine-tuning, and a little polishing, but nothing that modifies the central thrust of what I had to say. I hope that this reflects the basic defensibility of my position, rather than intellectual sclerosis. All of the chapters have been comprehensively updated, to situate my arguments with respect to significant additions to the literature over the last ten years or so, and to take account of the changes that have taken place in Northern Ireland, Wales and Denmark, my case studies. A couple of minor factual errors have been dealt with, and some clumsy writing has, I hope, been improved. But the rethinking that I am doing in the second edition is the rethinking that I was doing in the first. I still think that much anthropology, for example, could pay more attention to power and its exercise than it does. I also still think that what I call 'the basic anthropological model of ethnicity' offers the best starting point if we want to understand better how ethnicity works.

With respect to the second point, it is more difficult to offer a convincing response. That the book sold well enough to indicate a second edition, and continued to do so even after eight or nine years, might be taken to mean that someone has been paying attention. However, at least one of the book's original theoretical centrepieces – concerning the routine significance of external definition and categorization – has yet to take the social sciences by storm. If for no other reason, this is sufficient reason to offer a second edition.

On the other hand, much of the rest of what I said in 1997 met more than halfway the arguments of a range of fellow travellers whose works appeared at about the same time, or have appeared since. In particular – and you can look them up in the bibliography – I would like to spotlight Rogers Brubaker, Craig Calhoun, Stephen Cornell, and Joe Ruane and Jennifer Todd. Their work, and in some cases their friendship, is an ongoing inspiration, in many different ways. Although we disagree about many things, we have, it seems to me, converged on the shared central ground of a critical sociological constructionism that is keen to understand why identification matters to people, or not (because it doesn't always). This inspires the hopeful belief that we are basically heading in the right direction. My acknowledgements and thanks go out to them all.

Other acknowledgements are necessary, too. Since 1995, the staff and students of the Department of Sociological Studies at the University of Sheffield have made it a congenial place in which to research, teach and write. More widely, my anthropological friends in Denmark – in Aarhus and Copenhagen – and my social science friends in Northern Ireland – at Queen's and Ulster – continue to keep me on my toes. 'Critical friends' they are, too, which is just as it should be. At the risk of overlooking someone, others who have made the world intellectually more stimulating over the last ten or so years include Thomas Hylland Eriksen, Michèle Lamont, Siniša Malešević, Andy Thompson, and the staff and students in the Novosibirsk group. Rosemary Campbell has been an exemplary editor. Finally, the usual completely inadequate gratitude has to be offered to Jenny Owen.

Richard Jenkins
Sheffield
2 September 2007

Arguments

I have been working on matters to do with social identity in general, and ethnic identity in particular, for nearly thirty years. As a social anthropology student, a post-doctoral researcher, and subsequently as a university teacher in sociology and anthropology, I have always been keenly aware of the intellectual and political importance of these topics, and the difficulties which one faces in trying to research and teach about them adequately, openly, and even-handedly.

The questions and issues that I have encountered during this time are not, however, important only in my professional, academic life. These attempts to understand better social identity – and more specifically ethnicity – are part of an ongoing dialogue with my own history and biography, and are the product of personal experience. Coming from a family that, according to the researches of my amateur genealogist sister, mixes English, Welsh and Irish 'blood', I was born in Liverpool, moving as an infant to a middle-class suburb of Rotherham, in Yorkshire. From there, at the age of eight, I was brusquely transported to a respectable working-class housing estate on the hilly fringes of Larne, a small Northern Irish town. Identified by my peers as English, in the years between eight and twenty-five I had to learn to understand, if not actually fully participate in, the ethnic subtlety and bluntness of Northern Ireland. On the one hand, to negotiate the boundary between English and Northern Irish; on the other to negotiate the distinction between Protestant and Catholic. While it has been very many years since I have been able to see myself as English, I am not, in any straightforward sense, Irish either. And being Protestant in Larne was a very different thing than it had been in Rotherham.

But Larne eventually became – and remains – home. Northern Ireland is certainly where I feel most 'at home'. My children were born there: half me, half their Dutch-Indonesian mother. In the peregrinations that followed, they eventually came to call Swansea, in South Wales, home (and I have come to support the Welsh rugby team). In the court of final demands, they continue to call themselves Irish, by dint of place of birth and sentiment, but they do 'being Welsh' in many important everyday respects. And as their home, and as the home of some of my dearest friends, Swansea has become in large part home to me also. To add to the personal tale, I now live within ten miles of my childhood Yorkshire home; but I have definitely not 'come home'. I could add in further complexities – not least with respect to my relationship to a small town in Denmark, where I have spent a great deal of time over the last ten years – but these are perhaps sufficient to show why I am interested in identity, and ethnicity in particular.

There is another kind of genealogy too, which emphasizes two particular moments, one longer-term engagement, and a consistent thread of indebtedness. The first occasion was in the early 1980s. The SSRC Research Unit on Ethnic Relations in Birmingham, where I was a researcher at the time, was running a taught Master's degree and I ended up doing a few lectures on anthropological approaches to ethnicity. This made me look at issues, concerning anthropology as well as ethnicity, to which – perhaps paradoxically, given the research I was doing at the time and had already done in Belfast – I had hitherto given insufficient attention. Some of what I say in later pages was first said then. The second occasion was ten years on, in March 1992, when I was Visiting Professor in the Institute of Ethnography and Social Anthropology at the University of Aarhus, Denmark. A great deal of the thinking that has gone into Chapters 5 and 6, in particular, dates from then. More generally, over the last ten or more years I have spent a good deal of time as the guest of colleagues in Scandinavia, particularly the anthropologists at the Universities of Aarhus, Bergen, Copenhagen and Oslo. I cannot adequately acknowledge the importance of this 'secondary socialization' into another, perhaps more congenial, anthropological tradition. In all of these contexts I have been enabled – or required – to revisit, and to engage at close quarters with, the work and thought of Fredrik Barth. The subsequent intellectual debt runs throughout this book.

1 Anthropology and Ethnicity

In this book I am trying to understand better how ethnicity works, taking as my starting point an approach that I call the 'basic social anthropological model of ethnicity'. The value and potential of this social constructionist model, which is probably most often identified with the work of Fredrik Barth, have not always been acknowledged as widely as they deserve to be. Many of the discussions of ethnicity under the various signs of postmodernism, post-structuralism and post-colonialism, for example, appear to draw on core themes of this anthropological model, not least its insights that ethnic identifications are negotiable and the boundaries of ethnic groups imprecise, with little or no acknowledgement, or perhaps even knowledge, of their intellectual genealogy. The sound of a wheel being reinvented, often to the accompaniment of vigorous claims to intellectual novelty and radicalism, has been unmistakable. Nor, in fairness, is it the first time that these particular 'new' ideas have been rediscovered. The anthropologists themselves also have a case to answer in this respect, in that their social constructionist model is itself rooted in an earlier sociological literature, particularly Weber and Hughes, that they rarely mention. So there is a lineage to be traced.

As the title suggests, however, I also argue that this basic anthropological approach to understanding ethnicity requires – still, some ten years after the first edition of this book appeared – some rethinking. In particular, we need to recognize, first, that ethnic categorization – the identification of others, in contrast to self- and group identification – is fundamental to how ethnic identification, or indeed any kind of identification, works, and, second, that power and authority are completely basic to how categorization works. Similarly, there is a need to think through ideologies of ethnic identification, and the relationship of ethnicity to cognate identifications such as 'race' and national identity.

There is also something to be said about anthropology. Mine is an approach to social anthropology that would probably be understood by many of my disciplinary colleagues – even at a time when anthropology, certainly in the United Kingdom, may be becoming less narrowly disciplinary – as somewhat heterodox. In fact, I know, because some of them have told me, that my *identity* as an anthropologist is suspect in their eyes. Although formally qualified as a social anthropologist, I have spent most of my teaching career identified – by job title and by most significant others – as a sociologist. I have spent much of that career exploiting and enjoying the creative ambiguities of the intellectual borderlands, doffing and donning disciplinary caps as it suited me. Much of my research has been about topics – class, the labour market, racism – which have been claimed by sociologists and, if they think about them at all, disavowed by most social anthropologists. Theoretically, I owe huge debts to the writings of Max Weber and G.H. Mead, the two great classical theorists who have been most conspicuously neglected by social anthropology. Yet despite this history, and despite occasional moments of irritation with anthropology's intellectual and professional border police, I have never seen myself as anything other than an anthropologist-doing-sociology (and always doing anthropology too). Fortunately sociology is a sufficiently catholic discipline to tolerate this degree of agnostic pluralism (or, to put it another way, sociology has always allowed me to have my cake and eat it).

If the arguments that I offer in this book are plausible, then the anthropological approach to ethnicity – if nothing else – requires rethinking. Or, rather, because in the ten years since this book's first publication its impact has probably been greatest outside anthropology, *still* requires rethinking. Rethinking the topic also might suggest some rethinking, at least, of the discipline. Echoing Edmund Leach's words in his 1959 inaugural Malinowski Lecture (1961: 1), calls to rethink on a disciplinary scale are vulnerable to interpretation as arrogance. They certainly need to be justified. So, first, a few words about anthropology.

Locating social anthropology

The disciplinary question has two dimensions: the intellectual content of social anthropology and its relationship to cognate disciplines. One matter on which I am not going to dwell is the conventional distinction between social anthropology (largely British) and cultural anthropology (largely American). In the first place, the study of ethnicity is one of the areas in which that distinction has been of least moment. In the second, American anthropology has become more complex and diverse, and more difficult to characterize monolithically. In the third, there is every reason to believe that a new global domain of socio-cultural – or, indeed, culturo-social – anthropology is emerging, in which this fault line has ceased to be of particular importance. This is a development in which European scholars and anthropological traditions have been conspicuous. Although my own background and training are in British *social* anthropology, and what I have to say is likely to reflect that in places, too much should not be made of this.

With respect to intellectual content, the primary emphasis in anthropology is still, as it has been since the discipline's inception, upon understanding the cultural Other (defined, historically, from a European or North American cultural viewpoint). Historically, this fascination with the absolute elsewhere is one aspect of the discipline's roots in the colonial encounter. More interestingly, it has always called for an imaginative leap, and an epistemological daring – which some might, ill-advisedly, call a conceit – that is not always present in its nearest intellectual neighbours.

This, perhaps more than anything else, underpins the anthropological emphasis on the personal experience of ethnographic field research. Every academic discipline is grounded in ontological and epistemological axioms that allow knowable *objects* of inquiry, and *how* they are to be known, to be taken for granted as the bedrock of disciplinary reality. The basic epistemological premise of social anthropology is that to understand Others they must be encountered. If the *sine qua non* of history is engagement with primary sources, the equivalent for anthropology is fieldwork. Long-term participant observation is the source of anthropological epistemological authority. An anthropologist's claim to know about her research site and the people who live there is typically, in the first instance, personal and experiential: 'I know because *I* was there'. Her knowledge is grounded in an ordeal of sorts; fieldwork is a professional *rite de passage*, a process of initiation. Without the 'extremely personal traumatic kind of experience' that is ethnographic fieldwork (Leach again, ibid.), she is unlikely to be recognized by other anthropologists as a full member.

This practical ethnographic emphasis on 'seeking quietly the local terms of life', during a 'patient engagement' with the everyday lives of others (Dresch and James 2000: 2) has inclined the discipline towards a focus on the details of face-to-face life. 'Big pictures' may thus be elusive. How to extend the ethnographer's view beyond the immediate realities of everyday social settings has probably been a concern for fieldworkers since Malinowski. During the 1990s this concern hardened up around two issues: how to deal with history, and how to grasp globalization. Each had roots in earlier debates about how, ethnographically, to document social changes that play out over longer periods than fieldwork allows for and are rarely specifically local. With respect to history, anthropology long ago abandoned the notion of an 'ethnographic present', within which non-modern peoples and communities waited patiently to enter modernity. We no longer believe that there are 'peoples without history'. The contemporary ethnographic challenge is how to enter into and understand those ongoing histories from the vantage point of everyday life. With respect to globalization, anthropology has moved away from the notional isolation in which it located the people that it studied, towards an appreciation of physical and virtual interconnections and interdependence that is more appropriate to the age. The challenge for the fieldworker has become how to see the global in the local, and vice versa.

Engagements with history and globalization – and this book is concerned with both – have encouraged new reflections on the pragmatics of fieldwork, in a lively literature about 'anthropological locations', 'shifting contexts' and the 'construction of the field' (Amit 2000; Gupta and Ferguson 1997; Strathern 1995). Placing ethnography firmly in the 'wider world' (Dresch *et al.* 2000), a central theme of these discussions has been how anthropology should respond to a world in which the time-space coordinates of fieldwork are no longer fixed in settled, bounded communities, in which change, if it happened at all, only happened very slowly. The object of anthropology has, it seems, changed (Fog Olwig and Hastrup 1997).

In fact, there are good reasons for insisting that not much has changed at all. It is not, for example, clear that the small communities and 'traditional' cultures of the heroic era of anthropology were, actually, settled, bounded and slow to change. History and archaeology tell us a tale that does not quite match the stereotype. And the modern world is characterized by continuity as well as change, settlement as well as mobility. Perhaps even more to the point, most anthropologists – certainly the overwhelming majority of anthropology graduate students, for whom the ethnographic *rite de passage* remains the passport to professional employment – continue to do something that resembles 'traditional' fieldwork: short- to medium-term participatory engagements with people in relatively compact settings. In other words, anthropological research remains typically 'local'. And two of the most important distinguishing features of the discipline remain that it is empirical, and that data collection is usually done in the first person.

A comparative, essentially relativist perspective on socio-cultural diversity is also central to anthropology. But perhaps the most important foundational assumption of modern anthropology – its crucial ontological premise – is that human beings, regardless of cultural differences, have more in common with each other than not. This 'psychic unity' of humankind allows for the possibility of sufficient cross-cultural understanding for the interpretive and comparative ethnographic enterprises to be epistemologically defensible. Despite a minor failure of epistemological nerve during the last couple of decades, inspired by critiques of ethnographic research practice (e.g. Bourdieu 1977, 1990) and apparently sophisticated engagements with self-consciousness and postmodernism during the 1980s, particularly the debate about the (im)possibility of representation (Clifford and Marcus 1986; Marcus and Fischer 1986), most anthropologists continue to do their field research in the belief that it *can* be done, however imperfectly. Grimshaw and Hart (1995) may have been correct to diagnose a collapse of faith in *scientific* ethnography, but faith in ethnography – as method and as data – remains.

With respect to theory, social anthropology, in addition to its own specialized theoretical concerns, such as kinship, has always participated in general social theory (although, as I have already suggested, the traditions deriving from Weber or Mead have attracted relatively few anthropological adherents). At the beginning of the twenty-first century, anthropology is more theoretically heterogeneous than at perhaps any point in its history: interactionism, culturalist interpretation, structuralism, post-structuralism, feminism, post-colonialism, and postmodern critique all twinkle in the current disciplinary firmament. Although Marxism seems to be in the same regrettable post-1989 quarantine as in other disciplines, there are signs of positive re-engagement with biology and evolution (e.g. Boyd and Richerson 2005; Richerson and Boyd 2004). However, at least one remnant of the structural functionalism that dominated the discipline during much of the twentieth century remains at the heart of the anthropological enterprise. This is the emphasis – which is no bad thing – upon methodological holism: the *aspiration* to study all aspects of a situation or a group's way of life, or as many aspects as possible, in the belief that they are all *potentially*, at least, interrelated.

Allowing for this holistic aspiration – because it is never more than that, if only because of the practical demands of field research – anthropologists have always specialized in studying particular aspects of the human world: symbolism, ritual and religion, myth, kinship and the family, morality, custom and law, micropolitics, and ethnic and communal identification are perhaps the most conspicuous and characteristic. These interests derive partly from the engagement with Other cultures, partly from the experience of data gathering within the give and take of face-to-face interaction, and partly from anthropology's nineteenth-century origins in a fusion of romanticism, exoticism and evolutionism, in the context of European and North American colonialism (Kuper 1988). Taken as a whole, this constellation of interests may be characterized as a bias in the direction of the *cultural* and the *everyday*:

> Anthropologists ... have always derived their intellectual authority from direct experience of life ... That is, they knew the exotic Other and their readers did not. Within that framework of bridging the gap between civilized and primitive, they emphasized the salience of the everyday, the ordinary. (Grimshaw and Hart 1995: 47–8)

The world is, however, changing, as it has always done – if nothing else, that 'gap between civilized and primitive' no longer seems obvious or defensible – and anthropology has, to some extent, changed with it. Additional subjects and issues have been gradually taken on board during the last three or four decades, including urbanization, socio-economic change and 'development', health care and illness, new reproductive technologies, nutrition, tourism, literacy, forced and voluntary migration, nationalism, and even the virtual realities of cyberspace. Allowing for this, however, and, as already suggested, a holistic emphasis on understanding local meanings (culture) using data (about everyday life) gathered via participant observation remains characteristic of the anthropological point of view.

A further important development within the discipline has been a modest shift in its relationship to the exotically Other. This occurred in three phases. First, from as early as the late nineteenth century, and more routinely from the mid-twentieth century onwards, the metropolitan peripheries offered accessible and relatively exotic alterity, in the shape of residual hunters, fishers and nomads, or peasants. Subsequently, second, the exotic Other migrated to the metropolitan homelands of anthropology to become ethnic minorities; anthropologists followed them home. Third, and perhaps most radically, anthropologists have begun to pay more attention to their own ethno-cultural backyards (Forman 1994; Jackson 1987).

These trends – theoretical and topical diversification and a widening of cultural and/or geographical scope – reflect anthropology's attempts to negotiate the post-colonial world and globalization. They have brought with them, however, problems in disciplinary boundary maintenance. It is, for example, not as easy as it might once have been to distinguish anthropology from sociology, its closest sibling and most obvious rival, by reference to method or area. In terms of method, ethnography is a long-standing sociological research tradition – remember the Chicago School? – albeit as part of a varied portfolio of research methods. On the other side of that coin, some anthropologists have been using quantitative and other non-ethnographic methods since at least the 1950s (e.g. Epstein 1967; Pelto and Pelto 1978). And the comparative method – witness Max Weber if no one else – has always been as sociological as it is anthropological.

With respect to area and setting, sociologists have been working in the 'developing world' for a long time, and the two disciplines have always competed in the rural areas of industrial societies. What's more, industrialization and globalization have, between them, conspired to produce a degree of convergence: in some sense *all* societies must now be thought of as industrial societies. Anthropology no longer has a territorial preserve that it can unambiguously call its own (a situation which has been further encouraged by the post-colonial disrepute in which anthropology is held in some places). On top of this – in part in response to it, indeed – anthropologists are, as I have already mentioned, 'coming home' to look at 'their own' societies.

This particular institutional and intellectual fault line has become further confused as sociology, moving now in a fully global arena, has itself engaged with a widening topical agenda. The sociology of culture, in particular, deserves mention in this respect. The blurring of boundaries has been further encouraged by the development of interdisciplinary feminism as a unifying intellectual field of critical discourse, and the debate about, and influence of, postmodernism. Nor is sociology the only problematic boundary: social psychology, social geography and social history might also be mentioned here.

In some other respects, however, anthropology has been moving steadily further away from sociology. As a consequence of the institutional specialization that has encouraged the growth of separate departments within universities and colleges, heightened competition for dwindling resources, the partial abandonment by both disciplines of the shared theoretical heritage of structural functionalism, and the perceived threat posed by the modest convergence of the disciplines in terms of field and topic, boundary maintenance has become more assertive. Competitive or entrepreneurial assertions of the distinctiveness and virtue of anthropological approaches to topics outside the traditional disciplinary spheres of competence have become ever louder. The difference between anthropology and sociology seems to matter more than it did in the 1960s and 1970s (and most anthropologists even then thought that it mattered, and mattered a lot). Despite the fact that personnel and, even more important, *ideas* do cross disciplinary boundaries – most usually, at least in Britain, from anthropology into sociology – those boundaries remain. Sociology – bigger, less specialized, more intellectually promiscuous and pluralist, recruiting from and training within less elitist social and institutional fields – may not be not as sectarian as social anthropology, but *both* disciplines are intellectually impoverished by the communication gap that has opened up between them.

So, where does this leave social anthropology? One analogy which has been used with some success to understand relationships between disciplines – and which is peculiarly appropriate to this discussion – is that of 'academic tribes' (Becher 1989). In this view social anthropology and sociology can be seen as two neighbouring and historically related academic 'tribes' (or, indeed, ethnic groups). With environmental change they are increasingly competing – with respect to limited research and teaching opportunities – in and for the same ecological niches. Bearing in mind that anthropological studies suggest that ethnic identity is often hierarchically segmentary, it is plausible to argue that while social anthropology excludes sociology, sociology includes social anthropology; while sociology embraces all of the methods and many of the concerns of anthropology, the reverse is not true. Social anthropology can thus be analogized as an exclusive and specialized sub-section or clan of the greater tribe that I have elsewhere called 'generic sociology' (Jenkins 2002a: 22–7).

Lest this view be thought too provocative, consider the following definition of sociology, offered by the late Roy Wallis, writing in *The Times Higher Education Supplement* on 18 April 1986, a time when sociology was having to justify itself in an altogether hostile British political climate:

> Sociology is not only about translating the manners and mores of alien life and subculture into the language and sensibility of the rest, it is about making strange and problematic what we already know, questioning the assumptions long held in our community deriving their strength from prejudice and tradition rather than openminded observation. And making the strange, the foreign, obvious, enabling us to see how reasonable people starting from the point they do, could come to live and think this way; and making what has hitherto seemed obvious in our own society problematic, to question how and why it is done, providing the opportunity for reappraisal or greater understanding of our own behaviour, seems to me a socially and morally worthwhile purpose.

This is, admittedly, only one view of sociology, and from 20 years ago. Any such definition, in a discipline famous for differences of opinion, if not discord, must expect to be contested. But it sketches out a broad intellectual enterprise with which most, if not all, social anthropologists would feel utterly at home. In the context of the present discussion, it eloquently emphasizes the essentially sociological character of social anthropology.

This doesn't mean, however, that sociology and social anthropology are the same thing. They clearly are not (quite). The differences of emphasis between them, when taken together, constitute a specifically anthropological point of view:

> Our emphasis on pluralism, our understanding of culture, our appreciation for the informant's perspective … add up to a distinctive perspective. (Blakey *et al.* 1994: 302)

A minimalist disciplinary model of this kind is what I have in mind when I persist in seeing myself as an anthropologist: comparative, epistemologically relativist, methodologically holistic, focusing on meaning, stressing local perceptions and knowledge, and documenting the routines of everyday life. This is the specifically anthropological version of the sociological imagination.

However, if the notion of anthropology as a segment of sociology is right, its continuing vitality will not be nurtured simply by putting sufficient water between sociology and social anthropology to allow the latter a distinct intellectual identity. Despite recent moves in what I think is the right direction, anthropology faces a problem, which the following summarized nicely, more than ten years ago:

> it is not a crisis of *representation* which now threatens our discipline but a problem of *relevance*. Social anthropology as we know it is in danger of becoming marginalized and redundant unless it adapts to the changing world which now threatens to undermine its cherished theories, methods and practices. This means, above all, re-evaluating its conventional objects of study and developing new domains and methods of inquiry that are commensurate with the new subjects and social forces that are emerging in the contemporary world … anthropology's image as a discipline still primarily concerned with exotic, small-scale disappearing worlds must be complemented – perhaps even supplanted – by greater concern with 'emerging worlds', the culture of the 'colonizers' as well as those of the colonized, and on subject areas that cannot be defined by traditional fieldwork methods alone. (Ahmed and Shore 1995: 14–16)

Apart from wanting to insist that the problem of anthropological relevance is not new or even particularly recent – a minority of anthropologists, some of them eminent within the discipline, have been pursuing the approach advocated by Ahmed and Shore for many years now – this, it seems to me, still hits the nail on the head.

The rest of this book should be read, therefore, not only as a rethinking of ethnicity, but also as a contribution to the ongoing rethinking of anthropology. To the development of an anthropology that is unapologetically at home in large-scale, metropolitan, industrialized societies. An anthropology that is sure of its epistemological ground when using survey methods, archival sources, relying on secondary material, or whatever. An anthropology that is not put off its stride by history and globalization. A discipline that is no longer defined by its methods or by its places of work, but by its *concerns* and, above all, by its *point of view*.

Locating ethnicity

So, what do anthropologists mean when they talk about ethnicity? What does anyone mean when they talk about ethnicity? The word comes from the ancient Greek *ethnos*, which seems to have referred to a range of situations in which a collectivity of humans lived and acted together (Østergård 1992a: 32), and which is typically translated today as 'people' or 'nation'. As Ruane and Todd have recently put it, ethnicity is a matter of 'peoplehood' (2004: 216). Since the early decades of the last century, the linked concepts of ethnicity and ethnic group have been taken in many directions, academically (Hutchinson and Smith 1996; Stone 2004) and otherwise. They have passed into everyday discourse, and become central to the politics of group differentiation and advantage, in the culturally diverse social democracies of Europe and North America and, increasingly, globally. With notions of 'race' in public and scientific disrepute since 1945, ethnicity has obligingly stepped into the gap, becoming a rallying cry in the, often bloody, reorganization of the post-Cold-War world. The obscenity of 'ethnic cleansing' stands shoulder to shoulder with earlier euphemisms such as 'racial hygiene' and 'the final solution'.

So it is important to be clear about what our subject – ethnicity – is and what it is not. An early and influential sociological reference to ethnic groups, and the ultimate rootstock of the argument that I develop in this book, can be found in Max Weber's *Economy and Society*, first published in 1922 (1978: 385–98). Allowing for infelicities of translation (Brubaker *et al.* 2006: 11 fn.), an ethnic group is based, in this view, on the *belief* shared by its members that, however distantly, they are of common descent. This may or may not derive from what Weber calls 'anthropological type' (i.e. 'race', embodied difference or phenotype):

> race creates a 'group' only when it is subjectively perceived as a common trait: this happens only when a neighbourhood or the mere proximity of racially different persons is the basis of joint (mostly political) action, or conversely, when some common experiences of members of the same race are linked to some antagonism against members of an *obviously* different group. (1978: 385)

From my perspective, perhaps the most significant part of Weber's argument is that:

> ethnic membership does not constitute a group; it only facilitates group formation of any kind, particularly in the political sphere. On the other hand, it is primarily the political community, no matter how artificially organized, that inspires the belief in common ethnicity. (1978: 389)

Weber seems to be suggesting that the belief in common ancestry is likely to be a *consequence* of collective political action rather than its *cause*; people come to see themselves as *belonging* together – coming from a common background – as a consequence of *acting* together. Collective interests thus do not simply reflect or follow from perceived similarities and differences between people; the active pursuit of collective interests does, however, encourage ethnic identification.

In terms of collective action, this sense of ethnic communality is a form of monopolistic social closure: it defines membership, eligibility and access. Any 'cultural stuff' in common can provide a basis and resource for ethnic closure: language, ritual, kinship, economic way of life, lifestyle more generally, the division of labour, are all likely possibilities in this respect (cf. Ruane and Todd 2004). Shared language and ritual are particularly implicated in ethnicity: mutual 'intelligibility of the behaviour of others' is a fundamental prerequisite for any group, as is the shared sense of what is 'correct and proper' which constitutes individual 'honour and dignity'. By this token, an ethnic group is a particular form of *status group*. Finally, Weber argues that since the possibilities for collective action rooted in ethnicity are 'indefinite', the *ethnic group*, and its close relative the *nation*, cannot easily be precisely defined for sociological purposes.

The next significant sociological contribution to our understanding of ethnicity came in an undeservedly neglected short paper by the Chicago sociologist Everett Hughes, first published in 1948 (1994: 91–6). Hughes had clearly read Weber, and he rejected a commonsensical or ethnological understanding based simply on distinctive 'cultural traits':

> An ethnic group is not one because of the degree of measurable or observable difference from other groups: it is an ethnic group, on the contrary, because the people in it and the people out of it know that it is one; because both the *ins* and the *outs* talk, feel, and act as if it were a separate group. This is possible only if there are ways of telling who belongs to the group and who does not, and if a person learns early, deeply, and usually irrevocably to what group he belongs. If it is easy to resign from the group, it is not truly an ethnic group. (1994: 91)

Hughes's argument can be paraphrased thus: ethnic cultural differences are a function of 'group-ness'; the existence of a group is not a reflection of cultural difference. Furthermore, ethnic groups imply ethnic relations, and ethnic relations involve at least two collective parties, they are not unilateral. Identity is a matter of the *outs* as well as the *ins*. A concomitant of this point of view is the injunction that we should not, for example, study a *minority* group – which is, after all, a relational notion – without also studying the *majority*:

> if the groups in question have enough relations to be a nuisance to each other it is because they form a part of a whole, that they are in some sense and in some measure members of the same body. (1994: 95)

In Weber and Hughes we can see the early sociological emergence of the social constructionist model of ethnicity which anthropologists have so strikingly made their own. From this point of view, ethnic groups are what people believe or think them to be; cultural differences mark 'group-ness', they do not cause it (or indelibly characterize it); ethnic identification arises out of and within interaction between groups.

The notion of ethnicity did not, however, come into widespread anthropological use until the 1960s, beginning in the United States. Within American anthropology, the increasing use of an ethnicity model was part of a long-term, and gradual, shift of analytical framework, from 'race' to 'culture' to 'ethnicity' (Wolf 1994). It can also be interpreted as a change – about which more in Chapter 2 – in the conceptualization of one of the basic units of anthropological analysis, from the 'tribe' to the 'ethnic group'. More recently, the unit of analysis in this respect has widened further, to reflect a growing concern with the 'nation' and the processes whereby ethnic groups and categories are incorporated into states (Baumann 1999; Eriksen 2002; Verdery 1994; B. Williams 1989). It is now anthropological common sense to consider ethnicity and nationalism in the same analytical breath, although 'race', as we shall see, is more problematic. The study of ethnicity – and nationalism – has become one of the major growth areas within the discipline, 'a lightning rod for anthropologists trying to redefine their theoretical and methodological approaches' (B. Williams 1989: 401).

Being a growth area has encouraged a healthy diversity: the anthropological model of ethnicity is a relatively broad church, which allows a wide range of phenomena under its roof. What is more, it remains firmly grounded in empirical research. In this field as in others, social anthropologists remain most concerned to get on with writing in detail about everyday life in specific local contexts. This is what most anthropologists see themselves as doing best (and in this they are probably right). At the level of meta-theory, however, it is perhaps worth noting that these detailed ethnographic texts about particular places and people contribute, even if only by default, to the perpetuation of an axiomatic view of the human world as a mosaic of discontinuous and definite cultural *difference*, rather than a seamless web of overlapping and interweaving cultural *variation*.

The empirical ethnographic tradition notwithstanding, there is social anthropological theory and there are definitions. Perhaps the most general is the notion of ethnicity as the 'social organization of culture difference' originally proposed by Fredrik Barth's symposium *Ethnic Groups and Boundaries* (1969b), the seminal text from which stems much current anthropological conventional wisdom about ethnicity. In his 'Introduction' to that collection, Barth (1969a) outlined in detail a model of ethnicity that was intended as a corrective to the structural functionalist understanding of the human world – which was at that time still dominant within anthropology – as a system of more or less unproblematic, more or less firmly bounded, societies or social groups, which existed as 'social facts', and were, *pace* Durkheim, to be treated or understood as 'things'.

Barth began with what actors believe or think: ascriptions and self-ascriptions. He focused not upon the cultural characteristics of ethnic groups but upon relationships of cultural differentiation, and specifically upon contact between collectivities thus differentiated, 'us' and 'them' (Eriksen 2002: 11–13). Barth's emphasis was not so much upon the *substance* or *content* of ethnicity, what he called the 'cultural stuff', as upon the social processes which produce and reproduce – which organize, if you like – boundaries of identification and differentiation between ethnic collectivities:

> we can assume no simple one-to-one relationship between ethnic units and cultural similarities and differences. The features that are taken into account are not the sum of 'objective' differences, but only those which the actors themselves regard as significant ... some cultural features are used by the actors as signals and emblems of differences, others are ignored, and in some relationships radical differences are played down and denied. (Barth 1969a: 14)

In emphasizing boundaries between groups, and their production and reproduction, Barth immediately shifted the analytical centre of gravity away from this or that settled, bounded group – or 'society' – and towards complex universes of relationships between groups and their members.

In doing so, Barth emphasized that ethnic identity is generated, confirmed or transformed in the course of interaction and transaction between decision-making, strategizing individuals. Ethnicity in *Ethnic Groups and Boundaries* is, perhaps before it is anything else, a matter of political manoeuvring, and individual decision-making and goal orientations. This provided the ammunition for the consistent criticism that Barth's view of humans is materialistic, individualistic, narrowly instrumental and neglects 'structural constraints' (Evens 1977; Kapferer 1976; Paine 1974; for a response, see Barth 1981: 76–104).

Shared culture is, in this model, best understood as generated in and by processes of ethnic boundary maintenance, rather than the other way round: the production and reproduction of difference *vis-à-vis* external others is what creates the image of similarity internally, *vis-à-vis* each other. Barth and his collaborators ushered in an increasing awareness on the part of many anthropologists that 'culture' is a changing, variable and contingent property of interpersonal transactions, rather than a reified entity, somehow 'above' the fray of daily life, which produces the behaviour of individuals. As Barth has more recently suggested, this point of view can be seen to anticipate the postmodern view of culture (Barth 1994: 12). Whatever one might make of that idea – and, as I have already implied, it is not absurd – his understanding of ethnicity has been central to pretty much all subsequent anthropologizing about ethnicity.

Like Hughes, Barth had clearly read Weber. Having been a student at the University of Chicago in the late 1940s, he was probably also familiar with Hughes's work (and he acknowledges the influence of Erving Goffman, one of Hughes's students). Whatever the source – because intellectual lineages are never straightforward – the above quotation from Barth illustrates the striking affinities between the model of ethnicity that was elaborated in *Ethnic Groups and Boundaries* and earlier sociological discussions of ethnicity. It can, in fact, be understood as their development and elaboration.

Barth's arguments had more strictly anthropological antecedents, too. Leach (1954), for example, talked about Kachin identities in Highland Burma as flexible rather than fixed over time, questioning the general utility of the notion of the 'tribe'. Later, Moerman's (1965) discussion of the situational variability of ethnicity in Thailand implicitly anticipated much of Barth's model, and Yehudi Cohen's apparently independent discussion of 'social boundary systems' (1969) is a good example of the extent to which the contributors to *Ethnic Groups and Boundaries* were part of a wider intellectual *Zeitgeist*. Thus, although his was arguably the most systematic model in depth and detail, the most securely grounded in wider theoretical arguments about social forms and social processes (e.g. Barth 1959, 1966, 1981), and has certainly been the most influential, Barth was not alone in establishing the current anthropological understanding of ethnicity.

And Barth's is not the only influential anthropological model of ethnicity to have been influenced by Weber. Reflecting, on the one hand, the practical ethnographic concern with the everyday lives of real people – their 'actually existing' social relationships (Radcliffe-Brown 1952: 190) – and, on the other, the pursuit of *verstehen* ('understanding') advocated by Weber and Simmel, Clifford Geertz has elegantly defined ethnicity as the 'world of personal identity collectively ratified and publicly expressed' and 'socially ratified personal identity' (1973: 268, 309). In this view, which does not clash with Barth's approach at all, ethnicity has to mean something – in the sense of making a difference – not only to *the people* one is studying, but also to individual *persons*. I will return to Geertz in subsequent chapters.

What I have called the 'basic social anthropological model of ethnicity' can be summarized as follows:

- Ethnicity is a matter of cultural differentiation – although, to reiterate arguments I have explored in detail elsewhere (Jenkins 2004), identification always involves a dialectical interplay between similarity and difference.
- Ethnicity is centrally a matter of shared meanings – what we conventionally call 'culture' – but is also produced and reproduced during interaction.
- Ethnicity is no more fixed or unchanging than the way of life of which it is an aspect, or the situations in which it is produced and reproduced.
- Ethnicity, as an identification, is collective and individual, externalized in social interaction and the categorization of others, and internalized in personal self-identification.

Some cautionary words about 'culture' are appropriate before going further. First, the implicit understanding of culture upon which this model of ethnicity depends is considerably narrower than the general-purpose model of culture – as the definitive characteristic of human beings, the capacity for which unites us all in essential similarity – to which neophyte anthropologists are quickly introduced, often in the shape of Tylor's famous and time-honoured omnibus definition. Here, instead, is a model of different *cultures*, of differentiation based in variation of language, religion, cosmology, symbolism, morality, ideology, and so on. It is a model that leads occasionally to the problematic appearance that culture is different from, say, politics or economic activity (when, in fact, they are all 'cultural' phenomena in Tylor's sense). In this, the model is revealed as the analytical analogue of everyday notions of ethnic differentiation. This should be borne in mind in reading the discussions of the 'cultural stuff' in subsequent chapters.

A second, more awkward, point about the notion of culture follows from this. 'Culture' is, at best, a cumbersome concept, difficult to define in any rigorous manner and difficult to distinguish in any sensible fashion from its conceptual close cousins 'society' and 'the social' (Jenkins 2002a: 39–62). Ideally, I would like to discard these words altogether. However, not only is 'culture' a lively presence at large in the human world, but the entire social science debate about ethnicity is couched in terms that, explicitly or implicitly, refer to it. So consigning it to the bin is not an option. The reader should, therefore, bear in mind that the notion of 'culture' in what follows is at best a general-purpose and somewhat vague word drawn from the social science vernacular, referring to equally vague analogous notions in the everyday conversations of the human world.

Returning to ethnicity, the general model that I have outlined above is accepted, to some degree, by most social anthropologists who work with the topic. I will elaborate upon it in subsequent chapters, and introduce some important qualifications and modifications. However, it is not my intention to provide a comprehensive survey of the enormous anthropological literature about ethnicity. Several, generally complementary, essays into this territory are already available (Banks 1996; Baumann 1999;

Cohen 1978; Eriksen 2002; B. Williams 1989) and little would be served by repeating, or competing with, them. However, the fact that lots of anthropologists are talking to each other about ethnicity, combined with the disciplinary enthusiasm for prioritizing detailed ethnographic studies, may lead to some things being taken for granted. Among these things are the definition of anthropology, and, more important, the definition of ethnicity, both of which have already been discussed.

A further problem, however, is the perpetual need to struggle against our tendency to reify ethnicity (and, indeed, 'culture'). Although they are talked about endlessly in these terms, neither ethnicity nor culture is 'something' that people 'have', or, indeed, to which they 'belong'. They are, rather, complex repertoires which people experience, use, learn and 'do' in their daily lives, within which they construct an ongoing sense of themselves and an understanding of their fellows. Ethnicity, in particular, is best thought of as an ongoing *process* of ethnic identification.

One possible consequence of this reification, particularly given anthropology's history, is the construction of ethnicity as typically – or even only – an attribute of the Other. Ethnicity thus becomes a phenomenon that characterizes other people, rather than ourselves. We need to remind ourselves all the time that each of *us* participates in an ethnicity – perhaps more than one – just like *them*, just like the Other, just like 'the minorities'. Some of us, members of those 'ethnic minorities', perhaps, or who come from ethnically marked peripheries – such as, in the British Isles, Wales, Ireland, or Scotland – may know this only too well. However, for others it can be difficult to appreciate. Yet its appreciation is arguably the first step towards understanding the ubiquity and the shifting salience of ethnic identification. Recognizing that ethnocentrism is routine and understandable, as routine and understandable as the invisibility of one's own identity, does not absolve us from the need either to struggle against it, or to make ourselves more visible (to ourselves).

Although, as good social scientists, we may, and probably should, pooh-pooh its reality, or distance ourselves from it by recourse to irony, our national identity or 'national character' may be easier to perceive than our ethnicity. Nationalism and the construction of national identity are, after all, explicit projects of the state. If nothing else, we have passports. The contours and contents of national identity are likely to be more visible, as are the contexts of its uses and justifications. And even if, as good anthropologists, we may not have to remind ourselves of the socially constructed character of national identity and sentiment, there is certainly a job to be done in keeping that idea as firmly in the public eye as possible.

And that idea is undoubtedly important. Although it is welcome, we should not really *need* Eric Wolf's reminder (1994) that 'race', 'culture' and 'people' are 'perilous ideas'. We *should* know this. Newscasts if not history should have taught us it long ago. Which makes anthropological research and teaching about ethnicity both urgent and troublesome. Because of its combination of a comparative global reach and a local-level research focus, its emphasis upon shared meanings as well as social construction, and its capacity to see individual trees as well as the collective wood, anthropology offers a promise to the world beyond the academy: to relativize notions about ethnicity and to resist the naturalization or the taking for granted of ethnic identity and nationalist ideology.

No less than when I wrote the first edition of this book, more than ten years ago, there is still some way to go, however, and some conceptual clarification, before we can live up to that promise. This book is offered as a contribution to that clarification. It should be read as part of an ongoing enterprise. It is, hence – and perhaps all theoretical texts should declare themselves in this way – self-consciously provisional (which doesn't mean that it is merely tentative). I hope that the fact that it is a computer-age *bricolage* – a rewriting and collage of an existing body of papers – has not resulted in too much repetition or overlap in the arguments, and that the reader will bear with me where they occur.

2 From Tribes to Ethnic Groups

Until the 1960s, and in many cases later, social anthropologists studying ethnicity and inter-group relations typically concentrated upon ethnicity as a corporate social phenomenon. They oriented themselves to the identification and understanding of substantial ethnic groups, conceptualized as distinct-from-each-other, culture-bearing collectivities. This approach still tacitly characterizes the working practices of many anthropologists. As an ontology of the human world it emerged from the social anthropological preoccupation – itself a legacy of the long-standing and disproportionate theoretical sway exercised by structural functionalism during the discipline's formative years – with social structure, social groups and their systematic interrelationships, and social order and integration.

To an audience that has, perhaps, allowed itself to become over-impressed by the postmodern fluidity and evanescence of the human world and its conventions, these concerns may appear to be *passé* or quaint. However, they continue to inform many of the presumptions and foundational axioms of anthropology as a generalizing study of human social life. Nor are they necessarily ill-founded. The human world is, among other things, a world of institutionalized social groups, that world is to some extent, at least, ordered, and integration is not insignificant. It is the preoccupation with, and the taking for granted of, these dimensions of the human world, to the exclusion or marginalization of other things – non-corporate collectivities, transient and heterodox improvisation, disorder, disintegration, conflict – which is problematic. These preoccupations, and the taking for granted, were what Barth was writing against in the 'Introduction' to *Ethnic Groups and Boundaries*.

During the colonial and immediately post-colonial periods, social anthropology's theoretical preoccupation with corporate groups and integrated social systems was manifest in an orthodox assumption that the subject matter of the discipline – 'primitive' peoples (Firth 1958: 6) – was most commonly organized into tribal groups. Indeed, as in the following quotation from one of the founders of the ethnographic method, the notion of the 'tribe', as a real, substantial social entity, was central to the theoretical and the methodological development of social anthropology:

> [The modern ethnographer] with his tables of kinship terms, genealogies, maps, plans and diagrams, proves the existence of an extensive and big organisation, shows the constitution of the tribe, of the clan, of the family ... The Ethnographer has in the field, according to what has just been said, the duty before him of drawing up all the rules and regularities of tribal life; all that is permanent and fixed; of giving an anatomy of their culture, of depicting the constitution of their society. (Malinowski 1922: 10, 11)

In one move, the concept of the tribe accomplished two important things: first, it distanced tribal society from civilized society, in both common-sense and analytical discourses; second, it provided the anthropologist with a theoretical model of 'non-civilized' social organization which could serve both to organize ethnographic data and function as a framework for the cross-cultural comparison of 'primitive social organization'. Thus, while on the one hand the difference between 'them' and 'us' was firmly established, on the other, the basic similarity between different sorts of 'them' was proclaimed.

One of the earliest anthropologists to question the usefulness of the notion of the tribe was Edmund Leach, in his study of inter-group relations in northern Burma. Leach argued that tribes as discrete bounded entities were essentially analytical models – developed by anthropologists or other outsiders, for their own purposes – rather than locally meaningful principles of everyday social organization in practice:

> the mere fact that two groups of people are of different culture does not necessarily imply – as has nearly always been assumed – that they belong to two quite different social systems. (Leach 1954: 17)

Leach argued that although locals might sometimes talk about themselves *as if* there were clear-cut collective identities and entities, everyday interaction and organization revealed a more complex pattern of overlap and variation, the reality of which was *also* recognized by locals. While hinting at a more general theoretical problem (ibid.: 281–2), Leach attributed his conceptual difficulty in the first instance to local ethnographic specifics: anthropology 'in the classic manner which treated culture groups as social isolates' was impossible in the Kachin Hills, due to the fact that 'named groups culturally or partly distinct' were often 'all jumbled up' (ibid.: 60).

By the 1960s the notion of the tribe was beginning to be replaced by the, perhaps less embarrassingly colonial, 'ethnic group'. However, the underlying presumptions had not necessarily changed. The event that most clearly marked an anthropological paradigm shift, from the study of 'tribal society' to the social constructionist model of 'ethnic groups' which is current today, was the publication of *Ethnic Groups and Boundaries* (Barth 1969b). For Barth, the issue was not whether local ethnography fitted the model. The problem was inherent in the presumption of 'distinct named groups'. In saying this his argument was in harmony with a growing body of critique which, *contra* structural functionalism, had begun to explore the important place of non-corporate collectivities in social life: 'networks' (Barnes 1954; Mitchell 1969), 'non-groups' (Boissevain 1968), and 'action sets' and 'quasi groups' (Mayer 1966), for example.

Barth identified four theoretical features of the conventional, taken-for-granted model of the corporate, culturally distinct ethnic group (1969a: 10–11). First, such a group was biologically self-perpetuating; second, members of the group shared basic cultural values, manifest in overt cultural forms; third, the group was a bounded social field of communication and interaction; and, fourth, its members identified themselves, and were identified by others, as belonging to that group:

> This ideal type definition is not so far removed in content from the traditional proposition that a race = a culture = a language and that a society = a unit which rejects or discriminates against others ... we are led to imagine each group developing its cultural and social form in relative isolation ... a world of separate peoples,

each with their culture and each organized in a society which can legitimately be isolated for description as an island to itself. (Barth 1969a: 11)

It would be wrong to present the 'tribe-group' model that Barth was criticizing as an explicit analytical framework. It was implicitly embedded in most ethnographic studies, without being examined or seriously questioned. But it was there, and the kind of problem that this taken-for-granted understanding of collective identity has bequeathed to latter-day interpreters of the classic ethnographies is well illustrated by the well-known controversy, which has been utterly overtaken by recent events in the region, surrounding the question of whether the Nuer of the southern Sudan – as documented by Evans-Pritchard (1940) – are, in fact, really the Dinka (Newcomer 1972), or whether they are both distinct components of a single plural society (Glickman 1972).[1]

In Barth's model, ethnicity and the boundaries of ethnic groups – and hence their ontological status as collectivities – should not be treated as 'hard' or accepted uncritically as fixed aspects of the social reality in question. Barth insisted that ethnic identity, and its production and reproduction in routine social interaction, must be treated as essentially problematic features of social reality, emergent properties of everyday life. The ethnographer must examine the practices and processes whereby ethnicity and ethnic boundaries are socially constructed. And the starting point for such an examination must be an acknowledgement that 'ethnic groups are categories of ascription and identification by the actors themselves' (Barth 1969a: 10).

To make use of a distinction first developed by Raymond Firth (1961: 28), Barth and his colleagues shifted the theoretical emphasis, from the evocation of tribal identity as a defining feature of *social structure*, to a recognition of ethnic identity as an aspect of *social organization*. In addition, as Ronald Cohen pointed out (1978: 384), while the earliest anthropological notions of ethnic groups still typically implied that such groups were isolated, primitive-atavistic, or non-Western, the shift of emphasis signalled by *Ethnic Groups and Boundaries* involved 'fundamental changes in anthropological perspectives', from a Western interest in the uncivilized peoples of the colonies and ex-colonies, to a more equitable concern with the routine heterogeneity of all societies.

Returning to Barth's critique of the traditional model, several features of the emergent alternative framework are worth highlighting. In the first place, the analysis of ethnicity starts from the definition of the situation held by social actors. Second, the focus of attention then becomes the maintenance of ethnic boundaries in the interaction between 'us' and 'them' that takes place across the boundary. Third, ethnic identity depends on ascription, both by members of the ethnic group in question *and* by outsiders. Fourth, ethnicity is not fixed, it is situationally defined. Fifth, ecological issues are particularly influential in determining ethnic identity, inasmuch as competition for economic niches plays an important role in the generation of ethnicity.

The origins of this understanding of ethnicity can be traced as far back as Max Weber, as argued in the previous chapter. In laying it out as explicitly as he did, introducing it to a new audience, and developing it within an anthropological context, Barth sketched out the essentials of the model of ethnicity that has dominated discussion of the topic within European and North American anthropology in subsequent decades:

there is little doubt that Barth's introduction to *Ethnic groups and boundaries* holds a special place. More than any other text, it has become the symbolic marker of the changes to which it contributed substantially ... The shift from a static to an inter-actional approach was accomplished by differentiating the notion of ethnicity from that of culture. Barth presented ethnicity or ethnic identity as an aspect of social organization, not of culture. (Vermeulen and Govers 1994: 2)

In British social anthropology, the development of the ethnicity model can be exemplified by looking at the work of Michael Banton and Sandra Wallman. In his original formulations Banton (1967) argued that 'race'[2] is used as a role sign. Social groups are unities that appear in response to various stimuli to alignment, and 'race' is a visible marker of status and role as functions of group membership. The notion of ethnicity is here combined with a status-attainment model of stratifica-tion. The emphasis is upon inter-ethnic behaviour as transactional, albeit within a social context of stratification and/or coercion. Subsequently, Banton developed a 'rational choice' model of inter-ethnic relations (1983), which sought to integrate the study of ethnicity and nationalism with the study of 'race relations'. This ana-lytical framework is founded on four premises: one, human beings act in order to maximize their net advantage; two, social action has a cumulative effect, inasmuch as present actions limit or constrain subsequent actions; three, actors utilize phys-ical or cultural differences to generate social groups and categories; and, four, when relationships between groups which are held to be physically distinctive are deter-mined by an imbalance of power, 'racial' categories are created.

Banton's ideas shared some of the same assumptions as Barth's, and presumably some of their Weberian roots. However, the relation between the analyses of Barth and Wallman was a good deal closer (Wallman 1978, 1979, 1986). Locating herself explicitly within the Barthian framework, Wallman argued that:

ethnicity is the process by which 'their' difference is used to enhance the sense of 'us' for purposes of organisation or identification ... Because it takes two, ethnicity can only happen at the boundary of 'us', in contact or confrontation or by contrast with 'them'. And as the sense of 'us' changes, so the boundary between 'us' and 'them' shifts. Not only does the boundary shift, but the criteria which mark it change. (Wallman 1979: 3)

By this definition ethnicity is transactional, shifting and essentially impermanent. Ethnic boundaries are always two-sided, and one of the key issues becomes the manipulation of perceived significant differences in their generation. Furthermore, Wallman considered that it is 'useful to set the ethnic/racial quibble aside and to consider simply how social boundaries are marked' (1978: 205); having once done so, there is an effective concentration in her work upon the mobilization of social (ethnic) identity as a resource with respect to social support, solidarity, communi-cation and economic cooperation.

Moving away from the narrow orbit of specifically British social anthropology, the ethnicity paradigm was usefully developed by Don Handelman (1977), in an article that spoke to a number of the issues with which this book is concerned. While Handelman acknowledged the Barthian importance of boundaries and the situational negotiability of ethnic membership, he criticized Barth for confusing 'the idea of "group" with the ascription of social categories which are everpresent features of the process of interaction' (p. 187), a comment which echoed an earlier sceptical assessment of Barth by Abner Cohen: 'At most, what we are establishing ... is the simple fact that ethnic categories exist' (1974: xiii). Handelman further suggested that Barth, in assuming or overstressing the necessity of 'group-ness' to ethnic identification, failed to appreciate that:

> 'Cultural stuff'... and ethnic boundary mutually modify and support one another. The former establishes and legitimizes the contrast of the boundary; while the latter, often in response to external conditions, modifies or alters the relevance to the boundary of aspects of the former. (1977: 200)

Thus, for Handelman, the cultural content of ethnicity was an important aspect of its social organization: a crude dichotomy between the cultural and the social is misleading. Acknowledging the influence of Boissevain's discussion of 'non groups' (1968), Handelman argued further that ethnicity is socially organized or incorporated in differing degrees of intensity and territoriality – differing degrees of group-ness, if you like – on which depend its salience and importance in individual experience. Moving from 'the casual to the corporate', Handelman distinguished the *ethnic set*,[3] the *ethnic category*, the *ethnic network*, the *ethnic association* and the *ethnic community*. Ethnic identities can, for example, organize everyday life without ethnic *groups* featuring locally as significant social forms.

Handelman was also concerned with the relationship between ethnicity and other identities. He distinguishes 'lateral' from 'hierarchical' arrangements of categorical membership. Laterally arranged identities are of more or less equal significance and individuals may be categorized in different ways in different situations: their occupation or class may be most important in one situation, their religion in another, and their ethnicity in another. In a hierarchical arrangement, however, one category will tend to dominate or colour all others. 'Race' is a potent example of a hierarchically dominant ethnic category set (p. 193).

The understanding of ethnicity that was ushered in by *Ethnic Groups and Boundaries* has had valuable consequences. Inasmuch as it stresses social processes and the practices of actors, the approach has encouraged a move away from various strands of determinism that were influential during the 1970s and early 1980s. Similarly, its emphasis upon the social construction of ethnic or 'racial' categories discourages the intrusion of biologically based conceptions of 'race' into social analysis. Finally, the importance that it attaches to the views and self-perceptions of social actors themselves – the 'folk view' of ethnic identity – should lead us away from the taken-for-granted ethnocentrism of much social science. These are all important gains, which remain valuable today.

However, the ethnicity paradigm – the 'basic social anthropological model of ethnicity' outlined in Chapter 1 – seems often to have suffered at the hands of those who have most wholeheartedly embraced it. Pursuing a theme similar to Handelman's, Ronald Cohen (1978: 386–7) argues that, by stressing concepts such as 'group', 'category' and 'boundary', and processes of 'maintenance', Barth unintentionally contributed to the further reification of the ethnic group as an enduring, substantial corporate entity. In particular, the notion of the 'boundary', with its spatial and physical overtones, allows the superficial or the careless to celebrate the situational flexibility of ethnicity without taking on board the more difficult

questions – about the nature of collective social forms – in which Barth is interested. In their enthusiasm for processes of boundary maintenance, negotiation and
strategizing, many of those whose analyses owe much – if not everything – to Barth
have taken for granted, and continue to take for granted, what he did not, the
'group' that is the object of their research.

Two other major criticisms are worth brief consideration. First, there is the
apparent difficulty experienced by many anthropologists in handling the distinction between the ethnic and the 'racial'. Banks suggests (1996: 97–100), that the
most typical anthropological response to this problem is either to ignore it or just
to mention it in passing. It is certainly not sufficient to adopt Wallman's solution
and simply dismiss the distinction as 'a quibble'. John Rex has argued, for example, that we must pay attention to the importance and significance of folk 'racial'
categorizations, because:

> a far wider set of situations are based upon cultural differentiation of groups than
> those which are commonly called racial and ... few of them have anything like the
> same conflictual consequences that racial situations do. (Rex 1973: 184)

Since Rex wrote that, events have somewhat caught up with the second part of his
argument: Northern Ireland, the Balkans, southern Sudan, Iraq, one could doubtless cite other ethnic conflicts which seem to give it the lie. But it is really only
somewhat and only *seem*. Ethnicity is still a wider classificatory or organizational
principle than 'race', and it remains true that few ethnic conflicts are as bloody as
'racial' ones (and the genocide in Rwanda is depressingly instructive here).[4]
Furthermore, the boundary between 'race' and ethnicity is historically variable;
what was 'racial' before 1945 may be more publicly acceptable as 'ethnic' today.

The second critical point is that anthropologists are reluctant to acknowledge
and 'deal with' power. This apparent lack of enthusiasm is the basis for what sometimes appears a disciplinary predilection to treat ethnicity as a positive social
resource. This criticism is related to the first, in that 'racial' categories and racism
are characteristic of situations of domination. It is also bound up with the relative
lack of theoretical attention which has been given by anthropologists to relationship between ethnicity, on the one hand, and class and stratification, on the other
(Eriksen 2002: 49–51). Despite the important contributions made by political
anthropologists to our understanding of how humans dominate each other (e.g.
Gledhill 2000), and recent heterodox anthropological contributions to debates
about power (e.g. Rapport 2003), there is still, at least, a case to be answered here.
However, if there is a disciplinary 'blind spot' about power, it is not an inherent
theoretical incapacity. The same is true of the post-Barthian approach to ethnicity:
one of the papers in the *Ethnic Groups and Boundaries* collection was, for example, concerned with ethnic identity as a social stigma (Eidheim 1969).

These criticisms do not reflect fatal, unavoidable shortcomings in the anthropological model of ethnicity. They reflect aspects of social anthropology – its preoccupation with social integration, and an ontology of the human world framed in
terms of corporate groups – that have long been contested within the discipline
itself[5] and were precisely the problems that led Barth to formulate his arguments
in the first place. As I shall discuss below, these shortcomings, if such they can be
called, are not peculiar to anthropology, either: they have re-emerged recently, in

Brubaker's critique of contemporary conceptualizations and studies of ethnicity (Brubaker 2002; 2004: 7–27), as general *sociological* problems. An answer to both criticisms can, I suggest, be found in the distinction between groups and categories, a distinction which is elided in bald assertions, by Barth and Wallman, that ethnicity depends on ascription from *both* sides of the group boundary. It is important to distinguish in principle between two analytically distinct processes of ascription: *group identification* and *social categorization*. The first occurs *inside* and across the ethnic boundary, the second *outside* and across it.

Social categorization, in particular, is intimately bound up with power relations and relates to the capacity of one group successfully to impose its categories of ascription upon another set of people, and to the resources which the categorized collectivity can draw upon to resist, if need be, that imposition. To acknowledge the significance of the distinction between group identification and categorization is to place relationships of domination and subordination on the theoretical centre-stage.

Similarly, the distinction between groups and categories may help to clarify the contrast between ethnicity and 'race'. Banton has argued that ethnicity is generally more concerned with the identification of 'us', while racism is more oriented to the categorization of 'them' (1983: 106). From this point of view ethnicity depends, of necessity, upon group identification, while 'race' or racism is most typically a matter of social categorization. Such an understanding is, however, only helpful if it is heavily qualified. First, group identification and social categorization are inextricably linked, logically, inasmuch as similarity entails difference (and inclusion exclusion) and processually, with respect to individual as well as collective identification (Jenkins 2008). Furthermore, on the one hand, hostile categorization with reference to putative ethnic or cultural criteria is common, and, on the other, groups may come to identify themselves positively in 'racial' terms, as in the more or less supremacist ideologies of societies such as Imperial Britain, National Socialist Germany, Imperial Japan, or the South Africa of apartheid.

So although group identification and social categorization are analytically distinct, each is bound up with, and makes no sense without, the other. Ethnicity may, for example, be strengthened or generated as a response to categorization; similarly, an aspect of a group's ethnic identification may be – indeed is likely to be – the categories with which it labels other groups or collectivities. In each of these cases the centrality of power relationships – a centrality that many ethnicity theorists have been reluctant to include in their analyses – must be acknowledged.

To return briefly to the quotation from John Rex, above, ethnicity is a more general social phenomenon than racism or 'racial' categorization. It is equally clear that ethnicity, although its emphasis may conventionally be thought to fall upon group identification, is routinely implicated, through the signification of cultural or ethnic markers, in processes of categorization. Bearing these considerations in mind, racism may be understood as a historically specific facet of the more general social phenomenon of ethnicity. As such, it characterizes situations in which an ethnic group (1) dominates, or attempts to dominate, another set of people and (2) seeks to impose upon those people a categorical identity that is primarily defined by reference to their purported inherent and immutable differences from, and/or inferiority to, the dominating group. Viewed from this perspective, the distinction between ethnicity and 'race' is more than a quibble, and demands the most serious attention (Miles 1982: 44–71; Rex 1986: 18–37; M.G. Smith 1986: 188–94). This is not least the case because 'race', as a generic concept and in its local versions, is nothing but socially constructed (Wade 1993, 2002).

Groups and boundaries revisited ...

In its generic emphasis upon social construction, its recognition of fluidity as well as solidity, and its refusal to naturalize ethnic identification in the face of powerful essentialist discourses, the post-Barth 'basic anthropological model of ethnicity' remains arguably the best approach to the topic. It has survived a fair amount of criticism to become the increasingly comfortable intellectual furniture of several generations of anthropologists interested in ethnicity and analogous collective identifications. From Cohen's analysis of the 'symbolic construction of community' (1985), to Baumann's multi-layered exploration of 'discourses of identity' in west London (1996), to Balzer's study of the historical and contemporary twists and turns of 'indigenous' identification in Siberia (1999) – and these are necessarily invidious personal choices – its influence is wide-ranging.

This influence is also obvious in research, across disciplines, which does not explicitly mention Barth. Good examples are Lentz's historical anthropology of ethnic identification in northern Ghana since initial colonization (1994, 2000), a loosely related set of studies of the ethnic complexity of contemporary Miami (Grenier and Pérez 2003; Grenier and Stepick 1992; Portes and Stepick 1993; Stepick *et al.* 2003) and Lamont's sociology of the 'boundary work' of class and 'race' in France and the United States (1992, 1995, 1997, 1999; Lamont and Molnár 2001). In these cases, and many others that I could have selected, the apparent oversight – if, indeed, fairness permits me to describe it as such – is not a matter of ignorance, conceit or carelessness. I have taken care to choose examples where these are not conceivable. Nor are these authors making the claims to radical novelty that I criticized in Chapter 1. The explanation is, I think, more simple: once a set of ideas becomes sufficiently accepted and influential, it simply passes into the axiomatic common sense of the field and becomes common property.

Although the intellectual genealogy of the ideas about ethnic identification that I am exploring in this book reaches back to the sociology of Weber and Hughes, there seems little doubt that Barth's *Ethnic Groups and Boundaries* was 'particularly germinal' (Lamont and Molnár 2002: 174) in providing the stimulus for their eventual widespread acceptance. As Malesevic has put it:

> Barth's *Ethnic Groups and Boundaries* provided nothing short of a Copernican revolution in the study of ethnicity. Barth turned the traditional understanding of cultural difference on its head. He defined and explained ethnicity from the outside in: it is not the possession of cultural characteristics that makes social groups distinct but rather it is the social interaction with other groups that makes the difference possible, visible and socially meaningful. (2004: 2–3)

Accepting this, the previous sociological history of these ideas reminds us that the 'basic anthropological model of ethnicity', as I have called it, is but one version of a long-standing and wide-ranging interactionist sociology of identification (Jenkins 2008; Malešević, 2004: 61–77).

Very recently, that interactionist sociology has provided the context for Rogers Brubaker's influential, and sceptical, revisiting of the conceptualization of 'ethnic groups' in particular, and 'identity' more generally. Inspired not least by Barth, and by the perspective that sees groups as somewhat indeterminate, in that their boundaries and membership are changeable and uncertain, Brubaker insists that ethnic groups, as he believes they are most generally understood within social science and elsewhere – as definitely bounded, internally more or less homogeneous, and clearly differentiated from other groups of the same basic kind – don't actually exist. They are not, in fact, real. It is only a shared sense or image of 'groupness' that is real; the participants in ethnic conflicts are thus actually individuals and organizations, not ethnic groups (Brubaker 2002; 2004: 7–27). Ethnicity, for Brubaker, is a point of view of individuals, a way of being in the world (2004: 64–87; Brubaker *et al.* 2004). Employing similar logic, Brubaker further argues that identity more generally is not real, either, in the sense that it is not a 'thing' that people can be said to have or to be (2004: 28–63; Brubaker and Cooper 2000). Instead we should talk about ongoing and open-ended processes of identification. By this logic, identity does not impel people to do anything; it is, rather, people who engage in identification.

Up to a point, Brubaker is right, in both of these respects. It is certainly true, as I argue in this book, for example, that whatever reality can be attributed to groups depends on people thinking that groups exist and that they belong to them. It is also certainly true that identity depends on processes of identification and does not determine, in any mechanistic or causal sense, what individuals do (Jenkins 2008). Individual behaviour is a complicated outcome of conscious decision-making, habit, emotion, health and well-being, access to resources, knowledge and world-views, the impact on them of what others do, and probably several other factors besides. Neither (ethnic) group membership nor (ethnic) identity can be said to *determine* anything.

Brubaker is, however, right only up to a point (and for a further supportive critique of his position, which is complementary to that which I offer here, see Ruane and Todd 2004). In contrast to the definition of groups that Brubaker presents as wrong-headed, conventional social science wisdom – that is, as clearly demarcated and bounded, homogeneous collectivities – there is another, more minimal definition, which simply says that a group is a human collectivity the members of which recognize its existence and their membership of it (Jenkins 2008: Chapter 9). There are no implications of homogeneity, definite boundaries, or, crucially, coordination of collective action. This is the definition that informs my arguments in this book, and it commands considerable support across a broad social science spectrum. Viewed from this perspective, which is also Brubaker's own position, his distinction between apparently non-existent groups and real 'group-ness' doesn't make much sense, in that groups are constituted in and by their 'group-ness' (see also the debate between Brubaker [2003] and Calhoun [2003a, 2003b]).

In a hard-nosed, almost puritanical, search for unambiguous analytical categories – which, in the search for the *really* 'real', have more than a whiff of both materialism and positivism about them – Brubaker's is a sensible argument that, driven to a logical extremity, ends up somewhere less sensible. He is attempting to impose conceptual order on a human world that is not a straightforward place, in which fuzziness, ambiguity and paradox are part of everyday life. While social scientists must strive for maximum conceptual clarity, our concepts must also be grounded in the observable realities of the human stuff with which we deal. If we attempt to impose concepts that are too straight-edged on this messy reality we risk divorcing ourselves from it, and, in Bourdieu's words, substituting the 'reality of the model' for a 'model of reality' (1977: 29).

These critical comments notwithstanding, it is important to acknowledge that the social theoretical model of unitary, homogeneous groups at which Brubaker aims his darts is not a mirage. John Urry, for example, argues that the impacts of globalization mean that it no longer makes sense for the basic unit of sociological analysis to be the spatially and socially bounded set of locally focused institutions that we call 'a society' (Urry 2000a, 2000b). He argues, instead, that, entering a new epoch in which the old rules no longer apply, we must shift our focus away from boundaries and towards individual and collective patterns of spatial and social 'mobilities'. He is, in effect, arguing that there are no more 'societies'.

Despite his own argument, however, Urry remains a prisoner of the social theoretical conventional wisdom that is the focus of Brubaker's critique, which overstates the unitary solidity and boundedness of 'societies' – and of groups in general – and, in the process, misunderstands them. Urry's argument about social change only makes sense if societies as he understands them – as largely self-regulating, possessing definite boundaries, culturally unified if not uniform, different in important respects from other societies, and self-reproducing – have, historically, been the norm of human collective organization. However, viewed in the light of the historical and ethnographic records, this 'formal organization' or 'nation-state' model of human groups does not correspond particularly well to the long-run observable realities of the human world. It has probably never been the only, or even the dominant, form of collective human organization. That the last two or three centuries or so have witnessed increasingly determined *efforts*, in some regions of the world – and, increasingly, everywhere – to formalize and exert control over the boundaries of collective identification and territory and the 'cultural stuff' within them, does not mean that fixed, definite boundaries or cultural homogeneity are universal human collective patterns. If they were, less determination and effort might be required to maintain and police them, and they might not, as in Urry's account of the present state of globalization, be threatened today. His argument is an exemplary illustration of social theory's need to reflect upon and transcend its axiomatic modernism.

Urry's work, in raising the issue of the territoriality of modern nation-states, offers a bridge into the last topic that I wish to consider here. Where Barth emphasized that interaction across group boundaries produces and reproduces group identifications, a more recent body of literature, taking its lead from Sahlins's pioneering historical research on the Pyrenees (1989), has begun to explore border regions as distinctive locations, worthy of research in their own right (Donnan and Wilson 1999; Lamont and Molnár 2002: 183–5; Wilson and Donnan 1998). In addition to their role in dramatizing and underlining the national state identities that meet on their ground, territorial borders – and I suspect that this is an argument with wider applications – are revealed as imprecise zones that may, to at least some degree, be independent of, or different from, the states in question. They offer possibilities for the emergence of distinctive 'border identities' and ways of doing things. Similar, perhaps, to the ways in which social control encourages deviance, formality informality, and power resistance (Jenkins 2008: Chapter 16), the official policing of borders may foster unofficial alternatives.

At several points in this chapter, I have mentioned in passing the possibilities for developing the 'basic anthropological model of ethnicity'. Before exploring some possible avenues for this development, other matters require further introductory attention. These are, in particular, the interrelationship of different ethnic identities within one 'society', the relationship of ethnicity to other kinds of social identity with which it might be thought to have affinities, and, following on from these, the 'nature' of ethnicity.

3 Myths of Pluralism

The development of the notion of the 'plural society' was, much like anthropology's gradual abandonment of the 'tribal' model, an adjustment to a changing world. It, too, emerged out of the discipline's theoretical investments in social groups, as the basic unit of analysis, and processes of social integration. The notion of pluralism or the 'plural society' was a response to two distinct, if not dissimilar, problems.

Some colonial territories, for example many British possessions in Africa and elsewhere, were governed by means of a system of indirect rule, through native courts and chiefs. In these situations different collectivities – 'tribes' – were integrated into the colonial administrative framework through different sets of institutions and administered according to localized and conflicting bodies of custom and law. How was one to conceptualize the convergence of these separate institutional systems – one (or more than one) for the tribespeople, another (or others) for the Europeans and the urbanized intermediate groups – into a coherent and integrated social system?

A different situation pertained in those colonial territories that were, by contrast, basically unitary institutional systems for the purposes of politics and government. In these systems the indigenous peoples, although contained within and controlled by the state, were rarely, if at all, considered to be jurally adult members of the polity. As the twentieth century drew towards its mid-point this situation began increasingly to exhibit signs of change. The 'natives', in short, were increasingly moving from subjection to citizenship. The meek, it appeared, were about to (re)inherit their particular bits of the earth. But what would be the political structure of the resultant new nation-states?

Both of these questions spoke to the same history: the creation, by the European powers, of colonies or other dependent territories – and, later, emergent new states – whose internationally recognized boundaries bore little or no resemblance to the local spatial arrangements of ethnic identity or cultural variation. As such, they lacked the clear-cut homogeneous national identities which at that time still seemed to characterize the established states of the Old World. Social anthropologists had to develop a new analytical model in order to understand the changing situation.

In fact, they didn't develop a new model. They turned to political science instead. The notions of 'pluralism' and the 'plural society' have their origins in Furnivall's analysis of colonial policy in South East Asia in the 1940s (Furnivall 1948). The social anthropologists who are perhaps most closely associated with the elaboration of his ideas are M. G. Smith, in the context of West Africa and the Caribbean (Smith, 1965; 1974), and Leo Kuper, in his studies of South Africa and other African states (Kuper, 1971; Kuper and Smith, 1969). A number of sociologists have also found the plural society model attractive and useful: Schermerhorn (1978: 122–63) and van den Berghe (1967, 1981) are perhaps deserving of particular mention in this respect.

When these writers talk about pluralism, they mean the institutional incorporation of different ethnic groups or collectivities into one societal or state system. In other words, as opposed to the homogeneous nation-state, there is the heterogeneous plural society. Even though the model's initial formulation significantly predated *Ethnic Groups and Boundaries*, the concept of pluralism, as Barth (1969a: 16), Cohen (1978: 398) and Eriksen (2002: 48–9) have recognized, sits reasonably comfortably alongside the basic anthropological model of ethnicity. Logically and theoretically, the progression from an awareness of the importance of ethnicity to the identification of a pluralist social system is an obvious, although not a necessary, step to take. Although relatively few social scientists have been concerned with the theoretical elaboration of formal models of pluralism, the word 'pluralism' has carelessly passed into the everyday vernacular of many social anthropologists and other social scientists, as a loose and apparently useful descriptive term for labelling all multi-ethnic societies.

There are, however, those who have been concerned with precision in the concept's usage. M.G. Smith (1974: 108–10, 205–39, 341–2) distinguished three types of pluralism. The first of these is *cultural pluralism*, in which, although a society is composed of different ethnic groups, these are not relevant in the political sphere or as a criterion of citizenship. Examples of such a situation are Brazil or, arguably, the United Kingdom. Second, there is *social pluralism*; in this situation, although ethnicity is relevant in terms of political organization, it does not affect citizenship, the incorporation of individual members of ethnic groups into the state. Here one can point to the West Indies, the USSR as was, or Belgium, as examples. Finally, Smith talks about *structural pluralism*, where ethnic identity directly affects citizenship and the incorporation of collectivities into full membership of the state, as in the South Africa of apartheid, Israel, the USA (with respect to native Americans), and Burundi. These different kinds of pluralism correspond in an approximate fashion to what Smith describes as different *modes of incorporation*, the principles through which individuals or collectivities are incorporated into membership of the society: uniform or universalistic, equivalent or segmental, and differential (1974: 333–7). In a later discussion (1986: 194–8), he identifies differential incorporation with *hierarchic plurality*, equivalent/segmental incorporation with *segmental plurality*, and the mixture of both modes of incorporation with *complex plurality*. Finally, to complicate – or confuse – the matter further, Smith also talks about *the* plural society as a generic type, in which cultural diversity is associated with the rule of a dominant minority through the medium of a state system (e.g. 1974: 214).

R.A. Schermerhorn has also attempted to conceptualize pluralism and its varieties with a degree of rigour (1978: 122–5). He distinguishes between *normative pluralism*, which is a political ideology in its own right, *political pluralism*, which describes a society with a multiplicity of political interest groups, *cultural pluralism*, which relates to a multi-ethnic society, and *structural pluralism*, a society which is institutionally internally differentiated in a manner which reflects the differentiation of its population. Although cultural and structural pluralism are analytically distinct, 'they have a dialectical relation of mutual implication in the empirical world' (p. 127). Since Schermerhorn understands ethnic relations as intimately bound up with relationships of integration and conflict, and with processes of group identification and categorization, cultural and structural pluralism are, from his point of view, necessarily interconnected. In adopting this position his debt to social anthropology is plain; his attempt to analyse conflict in a framework which also explicitly emphasizes an integrative dimension owes something to Max Gluckman's analyses of 'custom and conflict' (Gluckman 1956; 1965).[1] It remains important, however, to distinguish between the models of pluralism put forward by Schermerhorn and Smith; for Smith there is no necessary association 'in the real world' between structural pluralism and cultural pluralism.

Such differences notwithstanding, Smith and Schermerhorn are clearly working within a broad theoretical framework of shared understandings about 'plural societies'. As such there are a number of general criticisms to which they – and other authors such as Kuper and van den Berghe – are equally vulnerable. The most basic of these, following Ronald Cohen (1978: 399), is that the notion of pluralism implies that cultural or political homogeneity – 'monoism', to coin an unlikely neologism – is the social norm. This, of course, harks straight back to the anthropological atom of comparative analysis, the bounded tribal society, which was discussed in the previous chapter. In fact, it is poly-ethnic collectivities, with fluid and permeable boundaries, which appear to have been, and still to be, the norm. Neither the isolated tribal group nor the ethnically homogeneous nation-state, to take the extreme 'monoist' theoretical alternatives, is much in evidence in the historical or the contemporary sociological and anthropological records.

A second criticism is that, at the end of the day, the notion of pluralism is theoretically vapid. The best that can be said is that it is merely profoundly descriptive, going no further than the extensive cataloguing of concrete situations by reference to a classificatory scheme of ideal-typical plural societies, an approach exemplified by van den Berghe (1967: 113–15, 132–48). The classificatory quagmire into which this approach can beguile the analyst is clear from my account of Smith's work, above. A further, related, criticism is that the model resists the incorporation of other principles of stratification – such as class – or of international relations.

Finally, there is a set of trenchant criticisms of the pluralist model made by Heribert Adam, a sociologist who has written extensively about the South Africa of apartheid (Adam 1972; Adam and Giliomee 1979: 42–50). Although not all of these criticisms need detain us here, three are particularly serious. First, Adam argues that the pluralism approach overestimates the autonomy of the segments of a supposedly plural society. In the process it neglects to examine the necessary degree to which they are all reciprocally implicated in a societal framework of common political, social and economic institutions. This implicit criticism of the pluralism model also emerges from a reading of Gluckman's analysis of inter-ethnic relationships in South Africa (1956: 137–65). Second, the emphasis on cultural and political diversity as the primary sources of heterogeneity ignores the role and importance of economic disparities and inequalities – from Adam's point of view, capitalism – in the production of social cleavages. Finally, with respect to Smith's general notion of *the* plural society, Adam denies that there is a necessary association between cultural diversity within the political boundaries of one state and domination by a cultural minority; he argues that such a condition could, in theory, lead just as easily to a system which granted each cultural segment equality of representation.

These criticisms amount to a heavyweight challenge to the pluralist perspective, so substantial that there seem to be no compelling reasons for insisting upon its continued usefulness in the analysis of ethnicity and 'race relations'. This is particularly the case with respect to the 'strong' version of the pluralist model, as articulated by Smith or Kuper, for example. Even with respect to the 'weak' version of the notion, however – the everyday, almost casual, usage which equates plural societies with multi-ethnicity – if the above criticisms are admissible there are irresistible grounds for removing the word from the social science vocabulary altogether: if, in this sense, all societies are to some extent plural societies, from what is pluralism actually being distinguished?

And there is another reason, not yet discussed, for dismissing altogether the plural society model. Schermerhorn, as we have already noted, recognizes the ideological or normative uses of the notion; similarly, Adam has highlighted the uses to which the South African state during the apartheid years put the notion of pluralism in legitimizing its 'separate development' and 'homeland' policies (Adam and Giliomee 1979: 45). This is all the more reason for treating the concept with caution in academic discussions of inter-ethnic relations. If we cannot talk about pluralism without potentially importing into our discourse ideological baggage of this kind, then perhaps we are better not talking about it at all. At the very least, the word deserves to live out its days in the inverted commas which, as with 'race', denote a degree of dissension or controversy.

This does not, however, seem to be about to happen. If for no other reason, this is because some anthropologists[2] continue to talk about pluralism or 'plural societies' when they appear to mean nothing more than multi-ethnicity (e.g. Doornbos 1991; Grillo 1998; Maybury-Lewis 1984; Rapport 1995). But there is another – frequently implicit – notion of pluralism increasingly afoot in current debates. This quasi-analytical and normative model, different to the one I have been talking about so far, has enjoyed a vogue under the sign of various strands of postmodern critique. The word 'pluralism' may not always be used, but the impulse and the concerns are unmistakable.

The key to this new discourse of 'pluralism' is a celebration of *difference*: as the site of resistance to Eurocentric and androcentric meta-narratives of history and progress; as the basis for imagining a new world of mutual recognition and tolerance; as a bulwark against fundamentalist images of the world; as an assertion of the rights to autonomous (co-)existence of peripheralized, marginalized, minoritized peoples; as the inspiration for ethics and politics of representation and diversity which challenge the centralization, the homogenization, the integration, and the domination of the nation, or more particularly the nation-state; and as the inspiration for new analytical models of the complexity of the human world (e.g. Benhabib 1996; Gutmann 1994; Irigaray 1993; Rutherford 1990; Seidman 1997; Woodward 1997).

In social theoretical terms, this multi-faceted and heterogeneous strand of argument and debate acknowledges that the world is a less straightforward place than – with the naïvety of a post-war generation which (mis)took the particular world in which it grew up to be the norm rather than the historical exception – we perhaps once thought it was (Baumann 1999; Eriksen 2002: 143–61). This acknowledgement was a reaction to the material and political uncertainties of the post-1989 world – which were to be followed by the further uncertainties of the post 9/11 world – and an attempt to read new meanings into the apparently unravelling intellectual project of the Enlightenment. It is a response to the ambiguities and contradictions of relativism, in postmodernism no less than in its immediate ances- tor, liberal humanism. It is, finally, a recognition – whether belated or timely is a matter of viewpoint – that culture is definitively socially constructed and arbitrary (Barth 1994: 12).

All of which is welcome. Viewed from such a point of view, cultural and ethical pluralism is a humane and attractive aspiration. But this particular understanding of it is not without problems. Stuart Hall has been among the debate's most char- acteristic and consistent voices. To pay him a doubtful compliment by treating him as an exemplar of key features of a (post)modern discourse with which he may not wholly identify, let us look at his position (see also Hall 1990, 1991, 1996). The topic he is addressing is the resurgence of nationalism, apparently against the grain of history:

> Since cultural diversity is, increasingly, the fate of the modern world, and ethnic absolutism a regressive feature of late-modernity, the greatest danger now arises from forms of national and cultural identity – new or old – that attempt to secure their identity by adopting closed versions of culture or community, and by the refusal to engage with the difficult problems, that arise from trying to live with difference. (Hall 1992: 8)

A couple of paragraphs later, Hall describes the peoples of the diasporas of 'the South' as:

> products of the cultures of hybridity. They bear the traces of particular cultures, tra- ditions, languages, systems of belief, texts and histories which have shaped them ... They are not and will never be unified in the old sense, because they are inevitably the products of several interlocking histories and cultures, belonging at the same time to several 'homes' – and thus to no one, particular home.

He finishes with a rousing declaration of the need to recognize, and to meet the challenge of, the fact that: 'in the modern world identity is always an open, com- plex, unfinished game – always under construction'.

Running through all of this is the strong suggestion that negotiable, socially con- structed identities and cultural diversity – difference, pluralism – are somewhat new phenomena, 'the fate of the modern world'. The mirror image of this is a vision of the past as homogeneous: 'unified in the old sense'. Although he refers approv- ingly (p. 6) to Welsh Nationalist politician Dafydd Elis Thomas's view that the 'old' nation-states of the West have always been 'ethnically hybrid – the product of con- quests, absorptions of one people by another', what Hall actually appears to offer is a historicism that imagines a pre-modern world of stable culturally unified soci- eties being progressively replaced by a shifting, culturally plural modernity. The image of primordial, original 'cultural purity' is further emphasized by Hall's use of 'racial' metaphors such as 'hybridization' and, borrowed from Salman Rushdie, 'mongrelization'.

The arguments against ideas of this kind are in some respects pretty much the same as the critique of the more analytically formal model of pluralism offered ear- lier. Once again, a model of ethnicity as socially constructed sits easily alongside an understanding of societies as culturally plural. And the reality of 'monoism' that the latter assumes – a human world which is, or was, an archipelago of discrete, bounded, culturally distinctive and homogeneous units – is no more plausible here than it was there. What is more, the account of modernity that is on offer seems to be blinkered with respect to the past and cross-cultural variation; unsupported by the historical or ethnographic records, it appears to have more rhetorical than analytical power.

South and west Wales as a case in point[3]

The Stuart Hall paper that I have just discussed was originally given in Cardiff, as the 1992 Raymond Williams Memorial Lecture. There is, therefore, a tidy appropriateness in looking at the issues in a Welsh context. It is even more appropriate given that Wales has actually been characterized, by Giggs and Pattie (1992), as a 'plural society' in terms of ethnicity and class. They argue that this long-standing pluralism is the result of four 'tidal waves' of in-migration from England and elsewhere, beginning in the early Middle Ages. The implication is that before that time Wales was culturally and socially relatively homogeneous. Taking as my particular focus south and west Wales, the geographical bottom half of the Principality, which is in many respects distinct from north Wales, I want to argue that the *region* – because to talk about 'Wales' as an entity becomes more and more anachronistic the further back in time one looks – has always been culturally and ethnically heterogeneous, always a 'plural society'.

It has been a very long time since the people of south and west Wales have been able to live their lives solely within the horizons of their local preoccupations and concerns, if indeed that has ever been the case. During the extensive period to which archaeology and history allow us access, the inhabitants of this small part of the world have been in regular contact with the inhabitants of other small parts of the world. Isolation, whether cultural, political or economic, has not been the Welsh lot; nor has cultural homogeneity. As far back as it is possible to look with any clear-sightedness, one finds unambiguous evidence of migration, trade, and extensive cultural diffusion or assimilation.

Following the gradual recession of the glaciers of the last great Ice Age, some time before 12,000 BP (10,000 BC), the area must have been gradually colonized from the south to the north in the first of many successive waves of immigration. These processes of migration have, over the subsequent millennia, resulted in the present-day population of Wales. Perhaps the first immigrants to single out for mention, insofar as they loom so large in the national consciousness of all the peoples of western Britain and Ireland, are 'the Celts'. Current archaeological opinion about these people is divided, and ethnicity is precisely the point in question. The long-established view is that they were Iron Age farmers from continental Europe – and originally further east – who settled in Wales in successive waves between the seventh century BC and the period immediately before the arrival of the Romans (Cunliffe 1997; Megaw and Megaw 1996, 1998). Alternatively, upstart revisionists – and the debate has taken on something of this tone – argue that the notion of 'the Celts' is a modern anachronism, an 'imagined community' with its origins no earlier than the seventeenth century, which does not correspond to any of the ethnic realities of the earlier period, that there was no relatively homogeneous pan-European Iron Age culture, and that 'Celtic' cultural innovations in places like Wales may not have been the result of immigration (Chapman 1992; Collis 2003; James 1999).

Whoever they were, and wherever they came from, their mark has perhaps most strikingly been left in the great hill forts and promontory forts of this era: Llanmelin (Gwent), Y Bwlwarciau (Mid Glamorgan), Cil Ifor (West Glamorgan) and Carn Goch (Dyfed) are among the better known examples. In this period may also be found the deepest roots of the modern Welsh language. In south and west Wales, 'Celtic' groups called the Silures and the Demetae resisted the Roman campaigns of AD 74 and 78, the second stage of the Imperial subjugation of Britain. Southern Wales was successfully Romanized to a degree unknown in the north. Caerwent, Caerleon, Cardiff, Neath, Loughor and Carmarthen were Roman centres of differing degrees of importance; the mines at Dolaucothi, Dyfed, provided Welsh gold for export to the Imperial heartland. Here and there one can still follow a Roman road; in other places the modern road does so. The linguistic influence has perhaps been most enduring and most significant: more than a thousand modern Welsh words have their origins in the Latin of the Roman occupation.

From the late third century AD, Roman Britain was increasingly under pressure from the barbarians of the east and the north. A process of gradual Roman withdrawal culminated in 410, when the Emperor Honorius finally abandoned the pretence of Imperial dominion – the last Roman troops had departed for Gaul in 407 – and bade Britain see to its own defences against the Anglo-Saxons. And with the Anglo-Saxons lay much of the future of Britain. Romano-British culture and society – the civilized 'Celts' and their descendants – survived only on the western and northern margins. To the victorious barbarian immigrants went the spoils in the shape of the fertile English lowlands; the mountains of the west were the refuge and the punishment of a defeated population. They were also the anvil upon which a distinctly Welsh identity was to be forged, in the creation and consolidation of kingdoms such as Dyfed, Brycheinlog and Glywysing (later known as Morgannwg, the present-day Glamorgan), and in the persistence of a distinctly 'Celtic' Christianity. That religious distinctiveness survives, still significant, today (Harris 1990).

Early medieval Welsh society – beginning in the period we somewhat misleadingly call the 'Dark Ages' – was neither isolated nor safe. Anglo-Saxon Mercia was a particular threat, its raiding forces regularly sallying forth from behind the safety of Offa's Dyke to devastate Welsh land, livestock and settlements. But there were also alliances – of convenience, or necessity, or simple self-interest – to be struck with the English. The border zone became an extensive and imprecise area in which Welsh and English lived beside and among each other. There were contacts, particularly religious contacts, to be maintained with Ireland and the wider Christian communion of the north Atlantic seaboard. And there were also the Norse sea-raiders, the people whom we today call 'the Vikings', to be traded with and defended against. The ecclesiastical settlement of St David's, Dyfed, was particularly vulnerable in this last respect, but it was not the only local object of the northern pirates' attentions.

The Normans, the next major invaders and originally of course Scandinavian raiders themselves, conquered England between 1066 and 1070. Wales took a little longer. Starting in 1067, Norman control was not finally established until Edward I's second campaign against the kingdoms of Gwynedd and Deheubarth in 1282–3. The earliest (and easiest) Norman gains, however, had been made on the border and in the southern coastal areas of Gwent, Glamorgan, Gower and Pembroke. These are still the most Anglicized parts of Wales, replete with the family names of its conquerors, and with their castles: Caerphilly, Cardiff (built right on top of a Roman fort), Kidwelly and Pembroke are now prime sites on the 'heritage' trails of tourism.

The overlordship of England was to prove no less permanent than the stones with which these castles were constructed and no more glorious. Despite the best efforts of Owain Glyndŵr between 1400 and 1408, Wales was henceforth to be an integral part of its more powerful neighbour. The political ties binding the two countries together were only tightened further when a Welsh noble, Henry Tudor, took the English throne in 1485 after his victory at Bosworth Field, founding a dynasty which has coloured many of our basic expectations of the British monarchy.

The Norman conquest and subsequent political incorporation into England of Wales did not mark the end of large-scale migration into or out of south and west Wales. The nineteenth century saw population movements in both directions: Welsh folk going to work in the industrial heartlands of England or joining the drive to populate the Empire with white settlers; people from England, Ireland and as far away as Spain coming to the industrial valleys of south Wales, with their promise of employment in mining and metal manufacture. Irish migration has continued throughout the twentieth century and there was, early on in that century, an equally distinctive wave of Italian settlement. The size of the Irish community is easy to gauge from a Swansea or Cardiff telephone directory: O'Sullivans, Murphys, Maloneys, Flynns, they are all there. As for the Italians, they are now sufficiently established to have provided, since 1990, at least two members of the Welsh national rugby union team of Italian descent, Mark Perego and Robert Sidoli.

In this brief overview of a rich and complicated history, I have so far tried to make three points. First, the region that is now south and west Wales has been part of the ebb and flow of cultural, economic and political relations between the peoples of the western maritime margins of Europe, and further afield, for a very long time. Second, as a consequence, there is no point in searching, ever further back in time, for a period when Wales *was* Wales, free from outside influence and interference.[4] Not only was there never such a time, but what we know today as 'Welsh culture' has its roots in a past which is as Roman as it is 'Celtic' (British). And neither 'Celts' nor Romans can be identified as anything approaching autochthonous. Third, the development of Welsh society – whatever that might *mean* – continues to be a definitively plural and international process, enriched internally and externally by contacts with other cultural traditions. It is only within those plural and international contexts that a defensible sense of 'Welshness' – whatever *that* might mean – is likely to be articulated.

To bring the story up to date, a view of south and west Wales during the last two decades continues to illuminate the themes of this discussion. With respect to culture, perhaps the most salient thing upon which to focus is the Welsh language. Without wishing to pre-empt the discussions of subsequent chapters, there are two trends to bear in mind (Aitchison and Carter 1999; C.A. Davies 1990; Day and Rees 1989). On the one hand, the language has been, and continues to be, in long-term decline in *y fro Cymraeg*, the traditionally Welsh-speaking rural areas of the west and north; on the other, however, as a consequence of a complex of educational, labour-market and political factors, Welsh is experiencing a modest but not insignificant resurgence in the Anglicized south-east. In different ways, and with strikingly different connotations, both areas are becoming more 'pluralized'.

Looking at 'external' factors, the United Kingdom's membership of the European Union (EU) and other European organizations is increasingly a significant factor in the constitution of everyday life in south and west Wales. The pressure of European competition has been an important factor in the restructuring – or devastation, each word contains more than a grain of a complicated truth – of the local steel industry (Mainwaring 1990). Llanwern, Ebbw Vale, Port Talbot and Llanelli are communities that bear painful witness to the various meanings of 'rationalization' in steel-making. Nor is agriculture beyond the reach of the EU (Hutson 1990). The Common Agricultural Policy has had enormous consequences: the imposition of milk quotas, following a long period of subsidized expansion in milk production, brought many small farmers to absolute ruination or close during the 1980s. In the mid-1990s many farmers in the region suffered further from the EU's ban on British beef, due to scientific and public concern about BSE; even after the partial easing of the prohibition in 1999, and its complete lifting in 2006, the export market for Welsh beef has remained weak. And it is not just the EU or beef: the USA has yet to lift its beef ban, and Welsh farming more generally – disproportionately small-scale family businesses – is vulnerable to the eddies and currents of decision-making within a global arena (Day 1999; Hutson 2003; Midmore *et al.* 1994).

Being 'in Europe' is not wholly to the region's detriment, however. There is, for example, the important role that various relationships with European institutions have played in the promotion of equality of opportunity and enhanced employment rights, particularly for women workers (Charles 1990). The EU has also contributed, via regional aid, the European Social Fund and, most recently, Structural Funds, to the improvement or development from scratch of a range of projects from bypass roads to theatres. No less significant, perhaps, was the availability, prior to limited legislative devolution in 1999, of an alternative – if perhaps relatively ineffective – forum within Europe for publicizing and articulating Welsh concerns and grievances, and promoting local interests.

But why, pre-1999, was such an alternative political forum seen to be necessary? After all, south and west Wales was an integral part of one of the oldest democracies in the world, a pioneer welfare state, and a land in which individual liberties were said to be so firmly enshrined in the common law as to render a written constitution nearly unthinkable. The answer is that government from Westminster, Whitehall and the Welsh Office, was increasingly seen and experienced as an alien imposition by many south and west Walians. During the late 1980s and early 1990s the legitimacy of the then existing constitutional arrangements for the government of Wales was regularly called into public question.

There were at least two related reasons for this (Stead 1990). First, there was a long spell of government – 1979 to 1997 – by a party, the Conservatives, which was a minority party, by a very long head, within Wales. The difficulties of this situation are strikingly exemplified in the appointment of several Secretaries of State for Wales who had no Welsh connections at all. And although, of their number, Peter Walker, for example, was locally seen to have Welsh interests at heart, as a conscious demonstration on his part, perhaps, of the continuing virtues of left-of-the-party 'wet' Conservatism, that party and its leader were emphatically not seen in the same light. His replacement, David Hunt, was indeed Welsh by birth – but it was the same party, the same leader and the same problem. About *his* replacement, John Redwood, perhaps the only thing of which I need to remind the reader is the wonderful spectacle of his gallant attempt to mime *Mae hen wlad fy nhadau, yn annwyl i mi* – the (unofficial) Welsh national anthem – at a Welsh Conservative Party Conference.

Second, the late 1980s saw the imposition of a new system of local government finance – first, the poll tax or Community Charge, and subsequently the present Council Tax – which may suit a relatively affluent electorate in areas with high rateable values, but does not suit a great many Welsh people, whose property values, for the most part, continue to lag behind those in many other areas of Britain. Nor was Wales seen to have provided an electoral mandate for the new system. And this is to say nothing, for reasons of space, about local perceptions during this period of other Conservative policies, such as the privatization of public utilities.

Since 1997, and the coming to power of New Labour in Westminster, we may be witnessing an incipient 'internationalization' of the politics of the United Kingdom, even if not necessarily the 'break-up' about which Tom Nairn speculated (1981). Leaving the particular situation of Northern Ireland aside for the moment, the Scots now have their own Parliament, and, following a narrow referendum result in Wales, the National Assembly for Wales – admittedly with weaker legislative powers than its more robust equivalent in Edinburgh – opened for business in 1999. Cardiff continues to gain in significance as regional power centre, and does direct political business with the European Union.

Spheres of activity other than politics must also be taken into account. Inward investment – particularly, but by no means exclusively, from the United States and Japan – has been important in replacing some of the jobs lost in the traditional extractive and manufacturing industries. However, the investment decisions of Ford, Hitachi, Hoover, Sony or whoever are taken in the context of a global complex of economic and political factors within which the needs and priorities of Wales – or of any region within Wales – have (at best) to take their place alongside a host of competitors. Much the same can be said about the strategies of British companies. Nor is it simply the financing of manufacturing employment that has been internationalized. Cardiff has become an important financial centre in the United Kingdom. The prosperity that is in part attendant upon this transformation is locked into the international telecommunications networks of global markets. Similarly, much of the capital required for major civil engineering programmes such as the Cardiff Bay project was found neither in the local arena nor in the public purse (although this has not been insignificant, particularly since devolution), but in those same international markets.

Telecommunications and information technologies are important in other respects as well. While Sianel Pedwar Cymru (S4C, the Welsh Channel Four television station) provides the Welsh language with a new and resolutely non-traditional forum – and promotes an increasingly busy Welsh cultural industry sector – the wonders of cable and the satellite dish mean that it is now possible to watch dozens of different television channels, from all over the world, offering a varied fare of movies old and new, sport (everything from Sumo wrestling to professional ten-pin bowling), and news commentary. In homes, social clubs and pubs, and whether for good or ill, television and satellite technology have made a difference. Over Christmas and New Year 1989–90, for example, Welsh audiences sat down to watch a revolution in progress in Romania, at one end of the world, and the US invasion of Panama, at another. When the World Trade Center Towers came down in New York on the 11 September 2001, Wales, along with rest of the word, was watching. It is a trite cliché to observe that television has made the world smaller, but it is only trite and clichéd because it is true. The mobile phone and internet revolutions have similarly transformed experiences of the wider world (and myspace.com works as well in Welsh as in English).

Other things, too, have simultaneously narrowed and broadened horizons in south and west Wales, as elsewhere. It is no longer the case, for example, that the emigration of daughters and sons means a *de facto* final farewell. Where forty years ago a holiday for a family from Bargoed might have been, at best, a week at Barry Island, it is now more likely to start with a journey to Rhoose, to Cardiff-Wales International Airport. From here or from Bristol, there is a choice, summer and winter, of package tour destinations in the Mediterranean, the Balkans, North Africa, and North America. It is no longer an object of local comment to hear of somebody going for a holiday to Florida; quite the reverse, Disney World is now an ordinary destination, not much to shout about, even if it remains out of the economic reach of many. What's more, using the latest generation of mobile phones, photographs of the holidaymakers, and their antics, can be back in Wales before they are.

The cutting edge of tourism cuts both ways, of course. The development of an organized tourist industry in the region – not just the marketing of existing 'traditional' resources, but the creation and promotion of 'heritage', the manufacture of attractions and facilities in post-industrial areas such as the Valleys, the recognition of the central significance of tourism to the Welsh economy as a whole – may turn out to be one of the most diagnostic local trends of the current times. Despite the doubtful contribution such ventures have made to the prosperity of most Valleys' people, it seems likely that they are here to stay. Those who can no longer mine or make must, if they are lucky, serve.

Neither travel nor television necessarily liberates the imagination or undermines local chauvinism and parochial smugness. The reality of the low-cost Mediterranean resort, or, for example, the Sky television channels, is different. Mean-minded, crass, lowest-common-denominator commercialism is unlikely to be the best vehicle for improving – even if it were transparently clear what that word might mean in this context – understanding and relations between people internationally. Nonetheless, there are two sides to this story: on the one hand, McDonald's and Coca-Cola in Russia, on the other, many thousands of people sitting round their televisions in Welsh households on a Sunday afternoon in February 1990, waiting to see Nelson Mandela walk out of imprisonment (and, just as significant, millions more in households around the world). It has become increasingly difficult *not* to acknowledge that the women and men on the streets of Saõ Paulo, Warsaw, Soweto or Llandysul share many similar fears, basic needs and aspirations. In a sense, the fact of their obvious – and equally important – differences only serves to make their similarities clearer.

Many of those fears, needs and aspirations are no respecters of international boundaries, and nor are the problems to which they relate. The environmental movement is, by definition, global in its concerns and in its activities and organization. Global warming, the depletion of the rain forests, whale hunting, marine pollution, Chernobyl and Sellafield, toxic waste, food additives, etcetera, etcetera – the list is long and all of it matters to Wales. Much of it – such as radiation from Chernobyl, oil spills and climate change – ends up, quite literally, on Welsh doorsteps. These are issues that local politicians, whether their new green hue is dyed in the wool or merely a superficial tint, can no longer afford to ignore. Welsh concerns entail global issues. They are issues in the pursuit of which the narrow focus of local self-interest must, of necessity, combine with a wider perspective.

The last three decades have seen south and west Wales become ever more firmly tied into a widening international context. Although this is neither new nor a radical departure from a parochial past, it is gathering speed and momentum and shows no signs of slowing down. And the context has broadened and deepened to the point where it is genuinely global. Whether in terms of national identity, culture and language(s), the popular view of the world, the economic realities of trade and employment, the preservation or improvement of the environment, or the institutional framework of politics, the future is one in which what it means to be Welsh, and what it is to live in Wales, will reflect, to some large degree, what goes on in the outside world. And it really will be the outside *world.*

Modernity and globalization

There is an obvious affinity between social constructivist approaches to ethnicity and models of society as culturally plural, heterogeneous and diverse. It is a pity, therefore, that both the formal theorists of 'pluralism' and the recent (post)modern celebrants of 'difference' suggest – if nothing stronger – that plural diversity is a relatively modern phenomenon, presumably a development and progression from previous conditions of bounded cultural homogeneity. This essentially historicist model – from simple to complex, closed to open, absolutist to relativist, static to dynamic – is, if only on the evidence of south and west Wales, implausible. This chapter raises two questions. Can 'pluralism' be a defensible analytical – rather than a simply commonsensical or descriptive – category? And if, as I am arguing, it is routine, everyday, and nothing more than the expected state of social affairs, should we continue to talk about 'difference' as if it were something distinctive or special, worthy of comment or in need of explanation? My own answer is 'no' to both: emphatically in the first case, more equivocally in the second.

Cultural and ethnic diversity (pluralism) is nothing new. The secure hermetically bounded group is an imaginative, somewhat romanticized, retrospect. But, as the excursion to south and west Wales also illustrated, the human world of the early twenty-first century *is* different in some respects from what went before. It is different in the *scale* of the meaningful arenas within which people see themselves and others. To draw on a set of notions from the work of Alfred Schutz (1967; Schutz and Luckmann 1973), the 'life-world' has widened and deepened. The immediate everyday world of our 'fellows' has expanded because of improved communications of all sorts: it is now possible for people to remain in immediate and intimate contact at enormous distances – globally – and travel over global distances is no longer difficult or impossibly expensive. As Giddens has argued (1984: 110ff.) time and space are no longer bound up with each other to the degree that they used to be. The more abstract and socially distant world of our 'contemporaries' has changed too.

These changes are, before they are anything else, *quantitative*: we know about many more people we do not know personally than we did even as recently as a generation ago, and we know more about them. We also know about them more immediately: telecommunications, in particular, have been responsible for a blurring of the distinction between our fellows and our contemporaries that is one aspect of globalization. The spreading ripples of globalization are enlarging the scale of the social arenas in which identities are forged and maintained. The amount of information about Others is expanding and becoming more immediate. But these changes do not represent discontinuity and radical novelty; they are differences of degree and of emphasis. The difference between our fellows and our contemporaries remains. We should not lose sight of the fact that most of us, most of the time, continue to live in practical life-worlds that are primarily what they have always been: small-scale arenas peopled largely by those whom we know face to face (which is not the same thing as knowing them well or intimately). This is not to deny the significance or reality of globalization, merely to put it into everyday perspective.

Taking seriously the ongoing behemoth of globalization can also put another spin on the ball. It is plausible that globalization – which I take to mean a very real set of changes, albeit one with deeper historical roots than is often supposed (Frank and Gills 1993; Raudzens 1999) – has had an impact on the pluralism and diversity of the human world. Due to the vastly increased speed and availability of movement and communication, a wider array of cultural possibilities and differentiations may be on offer today. This is central to Stuart Hall's argument, discussed earlier, and also, perhaps, fairly obvious. There are, however, at least two reasons for suspecting that it may not be as significant as authors such as Hall insist.

First, if there has been a historically recent global efflorescence of difference, this tells us nothing about the meaning of diversity in the past or the meaning of diversity now. Then, as now, diversity was experienced in many different ways, had many different consequences, and had many different meanings in people's lives, depending upon their historical, local and personal circumstances. The simple fact of diversity – and, of course, it is anything but a simple fact – may in itself not mean very much, so more or less of it may be neither here nor there.

Second, one of the consistent themes in the literature about globalization is that globalization produces not just diversity but also greater sameness. So, if anything, we might plausibly insist that the modern world is in some respects becoming ever *more* homogeneous. Step off the plane in New York, the New Hebrides or Novaya Zemlya, and, increasingly, the similarities may be as striking as the differences. Nor is it simply a matter of technology: the global convergence of business, tourism and, to some extent, culture and politics is a phenomenon to be reckoned with. In terms of values – particularly with the apparent triumph of capitalism – the cultures of the world are now at least as much divided by what they hold in common as by their differences. One version of this thesis has become famous in the work of George Ritzer as the *McDonaldization of Society* (2004) and, despite the criticisms that can be levelled at it (e.g. Smart 1999), it has an obviousness that speaks vividly to a widespread experience of human life at the beginning of the twenty-first century.

But homogeneity may not be all that it seems, either, and we should not deny the realities of diversity and fragmentation: they are certainly no *less* real than they ever were. As Ulf Hannerz has argued, for example, the impact of being homogenized or globalized – whether economically, politically or culturally – often calls forth local responses that in all sorts of ways and for many different reasons re-emphasize and reimagine difference and diversity: the 'global ecumene' involves convergence *and* polycentric variety (Hannerz 1992: 217–67). This, to borrow a word from the new-speak of international business, via Roland Robertson (1992: 173–4; 1995), is 'glocalization'. The global and the local are always in bed together, and the same is true of similarity and difference.

Between the global arena and the everyday world there arise tricky questions about scale and categories of identification. What, for example, is the relationship, and how do we distinguish, between local identities and ethnic, regional and national identities? These issues, among others, are broached in Chapter 4.

4 Ethnicity Etcetera

In Chapter 1 I outlined a basic social constructionist anthropological model of ethnicity, made up of four elements:

- in ethnicity the emphasis falls on cultural differentiation (although identification is always a dialectic between similarity and difference);
- ethnicity is based in shared meanings – 'culture' – but is produced and reproduced during interaction;
- ethnicity, rather than being fixed or unchanging, is, depending on situation and context, to some extent variable and manipulable; and
- ethnicity, as an identification, is both collective and individual, externalized and internalized.

That this is the basic anthropological model, and that it is widely agreed upon, does not mean – as indeed we have already seen – that it is uncontroversial. Some of the most interesting controversies bear upon questions about how ethnicity is to be differentiated from, or related to, other bases of communal attachment or identification with which it appears to have much in common. Hence the 'ethnicity etcetera' of this chapter's title. Looking at these issues leads almost inexorably to questions, which are probably always lurking somewhere in the background, about what ethnicity actually *is*, about the *nature* of ethnicity in some kind of basic ontological sense.

The communal, the local, the national, the global

Inasmuch as it is situational, ethnic identity is also likely to be segmentary and hierarchical. Although two groups may be differentiated from each other as A and B in one situation, in a different context they may combine as C in contrast to D (with which they may combine in yet other circumstances). One of the best illustrations of this model can be found in Moerman's classic paper dealing with Thailand (1965). The model is straightforward to communicate, and easy to relate to on the basis of one's own experience. But it does precipitate an interesting problem. When does an identity in the segmentary hierarchy of comparison and contrast become 'local' or 'communal' rather than 'ethnic'? Consider Figure 4.1, a very incomplete classificatory sequence, which harks back to the case study of south and west Wales in the previous chapter (for another example, based on Sicily, see Jenkins 2002b: 122):

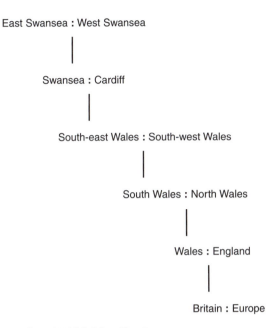

East Swansea : West Swansea

Swansea : Cardiff

South-east Wales : South-west Wales

South Wales : North Wales

Wales : England

Britain : Europe

Figure 4.1   A hierarchy of Welsh identifications

This scheme is, of course, incomplete: with what, for example, might one contrast Europe? It is also only one way to cut this particular cake. Most obviously,
whether Swansea is south-east or south-west Wales, or whether it lies on the border between the two, might, for example, be a matter of local disagreement.

Precisely where, in Figure 4.1, does an identity that is based on community or
locality become an identity that is based on ethnicity? Is the difference between,
for example, a South Walian and a *Gog* (an epithet for a North Walian, derived from
the Welsh *gogledd*, meaning 'north') an ethnic difference? And where does ethnicity become national identity? And why? And what, indeed, is the difference? After
all, each of these identificatory contrasts reflects 'the social organization of culture
difference' (Barth) and involves 'socially ratified personal identities' (Geertz).

One way to understand the Welsh illustration, above, is as a hierarchy of *nominal* identifications, which overlap and intermesh with each other in complicated
ways, depending upon the *virtualities* of each. Nominal identification is a matter
of name and classification; virtual identification encompasses the consequences of
name and label, what the nominal *means* in terms of experience (Jenkins 2008:
Chapter 8). From this perspective, the difference between, say, the communal and
the local, or the local and the ethnic, lies in the consequences of each: in terms, for
example, of rights and responsibilities, or access to social and economic resources,
or social recognition. Shared locality does not entail the same kind of mutual interpersonal recognition that is ideally presupposed in communality. In terms of administration and bureaucracy, locality involves political rights and responsibilities – the
payment of local taxes, the right to vote in local elections – which are not entailed
in ethnicity. And so on.

Questions about the relationship between ethnic and other identities are thrown into sharp relief by the work of Anthony Cohen on cultural identity and the symbolic construction of community and communal boundaries (Cohen 1982, 1985, 1986). There is a great deal of similarity between the ideas of Cohen and his collaborators and the Barthian, social constructionist view of ethnicity. Indeed, many of the contributors to Cohen's edited volumes (1982 and 1986) make the connection explicit, as does Cohen himself. What is more, the subtitles of both of the edited collections invoke the idea of 'British cultures', a minor reification which hints that each of the local research sites documented by the ethnographers concerned can be conceptualized, anthropologically at least, as a distinct domain of bounded cultural difference. Perhaps not quite ethnic groups or tribes, but almost:

> 'Community' thus seems to imply simultaneously both similarity and difference. The word thus expresses a *relational* idea: the opposition of one community to others or to other social entities ... the use of the word is only occasioned by the desire or need to express such a distinction. It seems appropriate, therefore, to focus our examination of the nature of community on the element which embodies this sense of discrimination, namely, the *boundary*. (Cohen 1985: 12; original emphasis)

Substitute for 'community' the words 'ethnicity' or 'ethnic group', as appropriate, and this would be a perfectly sensible set of propositions, that would not look out of place in Barth's 'Introduction' to *Ethnic Groups and Boundaries*. Cohen's further emphasis upon the role of symbolism in the social construction of community boundaries is, suitably modified, a powerful contribution to our understanding of ethnicity.

But this still leaves the question of whether, and how, we can distinguish the ethnic from the communal or the local. Ruane and Todd's notion of 'peoplehood' might be one way (2004: 216), even if it merely shifts the definitional question to what is a 'people'? When does a 'community' become a 'people'? Nor is the question confined to locality or community. Heading in the other direction, towards the more macro and the more abstract, when does ethnic identity become national identity, and what is the relationship between them? This question is also posed by the Welsh illustration, above. From a different angle, Eriksen (1993b, 2002: 115–18) draws upon his Mauritian ethnography to raise the possibility of a 'non-ethnic nationalism'. Which turns the argument somewhat on its head: when does nationalism *cease* to be ethnic? Does it, indeed, make any sense to talk about a non-ethnic nationalism? Two things seem to be in need of conceptual clarification here. The first has to do with the scale of our abstraction and analysis, the second with the developing character of nationalism in the modern world. These are matters to which I will return in subsequent chapters.

Talking about the nature of the modern world raises again some of the issues that I discussed in the previous chapter. Regardless of what we decide to call the historical juncture at which we presently find ourselves – 'postmodernity', 'high modernity', 'late modernity', or whatever – one consistent theme, about which there is a broad consensus among academics and other commentators alike, is that something called 'globalization' is happening or has happened. The nation-state economies of the world are becoming ever more interdependent and ever more subject to the eddies and currents of a thoroughly internationalized economic system. New technology has facilitated a shift in the nature, amount and communicative immediacy of information that is available to us. Cultural homogenization and creolization seem, in some respects, to be the order of the day, alongside diversity and 'pluralism'. International travel, whether it is migratory or temporary, occupational or recreational, has become an accepted part of the way of life of ever larger sections of the world's population. The result – globalization – is believed by some to be a qualitative break with the past (Robertson 1992), while others locate the present situation firmly within a much more long-term evolution of a world social and economic system (Frank and Gills 1993; Raudzens 1999). Whichever option we choose, a range of commentators agree that globalization has consequences, one way or another, for ethnicity as a social phenomenon (Friedman 1990, 1994; Hall 1991; Hannerz 1990, 1992; Waters 1995: 133–9).

It is, however, painfully clear that globalization doesn't necessarily broaden the mind. Globalization and heightened localization, far from being contradictory, are interlinked: the world is becoming smaller and larger at the same time; cultural space is shrinking and expanding. Localism and ethnicity are conceptualized as inseparable sides of the same coin, and each may (re)assert itself either as a defensive reaction to, or a result of, the increasingly global context of social life.

The debate about globalization raises a number of concerns. Perhaps the most important is whether the 'global' can ever be an appropriate or useful unit of analysis, particularly with respect to identity and culture. Is it possible to say anything about it other than the glib or the superficial? Another concern is the way in which the local and the global are juxtaposed. There are a number of mediating contexts of identification in between, which require considerable attention as well: nations, regions, and ethnic groups have not diminished in importance. The notion of globalization also seems to take for granted more than it should the close implication of the ethnic in the local. The jury is still out with respect to the shape which all of these issues will assume in the medium term, but, in the anthropological here and now, the discipline is still only beginning to formulate a response with respect to either theory or method (Baumann 1999; Eriksen 2002: 143–61; MacClancey 2002; Marcus 1992; Miller 1995; G. Smith 1999).

Globalization notwithstanding, I find it difficult to imagine a future in which the notion of ethnicity does not continue to be necessary as a way of talking about one of the most general and basic principles of human 'sociality' (Carrithers 1992): collective identification, a sense of 'us' and 'them', socially constructed with some reference to cultural similarity and difference. By this token, the communal, the local, the national and the 'racial' are to be understood as historically and contextually specific social constructions on the basic ethnic theme, allotropes of ethnic identification. We can also talk about ideologies of identification such as communalism, localism, nationalism, racism and ethnicism. Whether or not we can look forward to talking about globalism remains to be seen (although, in the shape of the dream of socialism, it may already be something about which we can, regrettably, only be nostalgic). Unresolved for the moment, these issues remain on the table, questions which must be broached in our research and theorizing and in our teaching. Fundamentally concerned with the theoretical constitution of the topic and the pragmatic definition of the field for research purposes, they could not be more important.

The primordial versus the instrumental

Over the years this opposition has generated a perennial and argumentative debate about the nature of ethnic identity (Cornell and Hartmann 1998: 39–71; Fenton 2003: 73–90). Is ethnicity a fundamental, primordial aspect of human existence and self-consciousness, essentially unchanging and unchangeable in the imperative demands it makes on individuals and the bonds that it creates between the individual and the group? In other words, is ethnicity an irresistible aspect of human nature? Or is it, to whatever extent, defined situationally, strategically or tactically manipulable, and capable of change, both individually and collectively? Is it socially constructed?

This argument takes its place alongside a range of theoretical controversies about the capacity of humans to intervene in their own lives, to determine or to be determined. But the primordial model also has deep historical roots in the Romantic reaction to Enlightenment rationalism. Finding some of its more respectable voices in the work of Herder and Hegel, this is more than an academic point of view, providing the intellectual charter for a great deal of terrible – to the point of murderous – ethnic chauvinism and nationalism. The ideology of primordialism naturalizes ethnic groups and justifies chauvinistic ethnic sentiments. It can, for example, be identified at play in the ongoing debate about the modernity and nature of nationalism (Bauman 1992; Smith 1994).

Within anthropology, the name that has most often become identified with a primordial model of ethnicity is that of Clifford Geertz (1973: 255–310). Drawing upon the work of Edward Shils (1957), Geertz, writing originally in 1963, was concerned to understand the obstacle that 'primordial attachments' – deriving mainly from kinship, locality and culture and encompassing much more than ethnicity – posed to the development of the modern political sentiment of citizenship, in the emergent post-colonial 'new states', in particular:

> [the] crystallization of a direct conflict between primordial and civil sentiments – this 'longing not to belong to any other group' – ... gives to the problem variously called tribalism, parochialism, communalism, and so on, a more ominous and deeply threatening quality than most of the other, also very serious and intractable, problems the new states face. (1973: 261)

If nothing else, this quotation provides a neat bridge between the present discussion and the issue of contexts of identification that was raised in the previous section. It is also a timely reminder that the problem is not new.

In opposition to this position one is generally offered the 'instrumentalist' or 'situationalist' perspective, deriving in the main from Barth. As we have already seen, this model of ethnicity emphasizes a degree of plasticity in ethnic identification and in the composition of ethnic groups: that people (and peoples) can and do shift and alter their ethnic ascriptions in the light of circumstance and environment. The pursuit of political advantage and/or material self-interest is the calculus which is typically held to inform such behaviour.

The dispute is, however, not as clear-cut as it seems, and it is hard to resist the conclusion that more heat than light has been its outcome. To begin with, both positions arguably have at least as much in common as not (Bentley 1987: 25–7; Hale 2004: 459–62). Whether that is the case or not, the protagonists are certainly usually misrepresented, sometimes to a remarkable degree. For example, as Eriksen reminds us (2002: 53–6) even Barth has been accused, by Abner Cohen, of the sin of primordialism:

> Barth ... [sees] ethnic categories as classifying persons in terms of their 'basic most general identity '... Some writers attribute primordiality to this basic identity.
>
> Ethnicity tends to be conceived by this school of thought as an essentially innate disposition. Barth goes so far as to attribute to it an existence of its own, separate from any social 'content'. (Cohen 1974: xii)

Geertz, too, has often been widely caricatured, as the purveyor of:

> a picture of underived and socially-unconstructed emotions that are unanalysable and overpowering ... A more unintelligible and unsociological concept would be hard to imagine. (Eller and Coughlan 1993: 187)

However, turning to what he actually wrote, Geertz explicitly recognizes not only the role of culture in defining the primordial 'givens', but also that the:

> strength of such primordial bonds, and the types of them that are important, differ from person to person, from society to society, and from time to time. (1973: 259)

Further, Geertz is perfectly clear that what matters analytically is that ties of blood, language and culture are *seen* by actors to be ineffable and obligatory; that they are *seen* as natural. This is, in fact, 'constructed primordiality' (Cornell and Hartmann 1998: 89–90; see also Gil-White 1999; Hale 2004). Geertz is concerned with the terms in which attachments are understood and mobilized locally, with what people *believe*. Later in the same piece (1973: 269–70) – making a point which, in all its essentials, has been echoed by Anthony Cohen (1985: 117), with respect to the effect of national integration on local, communal identities – Geertz further argues that, in some respects, these putative 'primordial attachments' are actually likely to be stimulated and quickened by the political modernization of nation-building.

Barth, for his part, has never neglected the power and stability of ethnic identifications, the 'organizing and canalizing effects of ethnic distinctions' (1969a: 10). As much concerned with the persistence of ethnic boundaries as with their flux, his argument was that under certain, not uncommon, circumstances ethnic change *can* happen, not that it *must*. More important perhaps, Barth's point of view is often presented fossilized in its 1969 *Ethnic Groups and Boundaries* incarnation. Since then he has explored the importance of ongoing and historically relatively stable 'streams of tradition' or 'universes of discourse', within the constraints of which ethnic identities are produced and reproduced in practice (Barth 1984, 1989). Most recently, in a discussion which explicitly refers to the 'privacy of ... hearts and minds' (1994, 29), he acknowledges the need to add micro and macro levels of analysis to the intermediate level upon which his original arguments concentrated. This means looking at what ethnicity means for individuals.

There are other reasons for becoming impatient with the debate between instrumentalism and primordialism. In the evocative words of one recent text, it offers a contrast between 'ethnicity in the heart' and 'ethnicity in the head' (Banks 1996: 185–7). While this may alert us to the need to acknowledge affect and emotion in our considerations of ethnicity (Epstein 1978), it offers an unreal choice: calculation and emotion are not alternatives. There is no necessary contradiction between instrumental manipulation, on the one hand, and powerful ethnic sentiment, on the other (Cornell and Hartmann 1998: 39–71; Ruane and Todd 2004: 228). They may, in fact, go hand in hand. They may also, of course, conflict. But so may different sentiments, or opposing instrumental goals. And when they do, difficult decisions – of precisely the kind that are the staple of political manoeuvre and manipulation – are the result.

Taking another tack, there is good cause to reject totally any strongly primordialist view. Too much ethnographic evidence exists of the fluidity and flux of ethnic identification, and of the differing degrees to which ethnicity organizes social life in different settings. The theoretical argument in favour of the constructionist view is also well founded. As the discussion in Chapter 1 showed, Barth did not 'invent' the constructionist understanding of ethnicity and its utility is not confined to a limited range of cultural contexts. Leach's classic study of Shan and Kachin in highland Burma (1954) is an ethnographic precursor of the social constructionist position in important respects, and many other studies could be cited to make the point: a wide range of work about pastoralists in East Africa, for example, has offered a similar view (Forster *et al.* 2000; Schlee 1989; Spear and Waller 1993).

However, we cannot deny the longevity and stubbornness, in certain circumstances, of ethnic attachments (Hale 2004). Pondering the relative failure of the project of social and cultural 'integration' with respect to 'ethnic minorities' in Britain – and, in the seventeen years since these remarks the situation has, if anything, become more marked – John Rex comments that:

> despite the very strong pressure in complex societies for groups to be formed on the basis of congruence of interest, many individuals do in fact stubbornly continue to unite with those with whom they have ties of ethnic sameness, even though such alliances might run contrary to patterns of group formation determined by shared interests. (Rex 1991: 11)

But to acknowledge this point doesn't necessitate embracing an unreconstructed notion of primordiality or abandoning the social constructionist perspective. It is not stretching the point to regard ethnic differentiation – the social construction of 'us' and 'them', marked in cultural terms – as a ubiquitous feature of human sociability, and hence of all human societies. The only possible exception to this might be an imaginary and altogether unlikely society existing in total isolation. The debate about whether or not ethnicity is 'situational' or 'primordial' has confused the *ubiquity* of a social phenomenon such as ethnicity with 'naturalness', implying fixity, determinism and some kind of pre-social power of causation. To suggest that ethnicity is ever-present as one of the 'givens' of human social life – or that group identification, for example, is simply part of the human species-specific repertoire, and, thus, 'human nature' – is *not* to endorse any of the arguments of the primordial point of view.

An individual's sense of ethnic membership may – depending upon context – be internalized during early primary socialization, along with many of the markers of ethnicity such as language, religion, non-verbal behaviour, etc. (Bentley 1987; Fenton 2003: 88). During this period the primary, deep-rooted identities of selfhood, gender and humanness are entered into (Jenkins 2008: Chapter 7). In these senses, identification is an aspect of the emotional, psychological and cognitive constitution of individuality; it is, correspondingly, bound up with the maintenance of personal integrity and security, and may be extremely resistant to change. In a social setting where ethnic differentiation is sufficiently salient and consequential to intrude into the early world of children – over and above the routine acquisition of the 'cultural stuff' – ethnicity may be entered into self-consciously, as an integral part of the individually embodied point of view that is selfhood. Thus ethnicity may, depending on local circumstances, be a *primary*, although not a primordial, dimension of individual identity.

Internal or self-identification – whether by individuals or groups – is, however, not the only 'mechanism' of ethnic identity formation. People are not always in a position to 'choose' who they are or what their identity means in terms of its social consequences. Power differentials are important here. As will be explored in later chapters, external categorization is an important contributor to ethnicity, not least during primary socialization, but also in a range of other, lifelong settings. Categorization is, furthermore, related to my earlier distinction between the nominal and the virtual: the consequences of ethnic identification across a range of settings – not least whether these are mutually reinforcing or not – are likely to have an important influence on how much ethnicity *matters*. To put this in another way:

> How is intense ethnic solidarity and resistance to change constituted ...? The answer does not lie in any essential feature of ethnicity – none exists – but in a particular set of interrelations of elements which form systematic feedback patterns, or a 'path dependent' system. (Ruane and Todd 2004: 224)

So the salience of ethnicity within primary socialization, for example, is likely to be a product of local contingencies of place and time. Growing up in Denmark in 2007, for example, is not the same as growing up in Northern Ireland in 2007. And – to return to the distinction between the nominal and the virtual – growing up in Denmark in 2007 is not the same as growing up in Denmark in 1944. Ethnicity, or at least an awareness of it, is likely to figure in different ways, with different social costs and benefits (consequences) attached, in each place and at each time. Other processes of ethnic categorization – which is, after all, what is going on in primary socialization: children know who they are, in large part, because others *tell* them – also vary with context in their effectiveness and intrusiveness. Thus, although ethnicity *may* be a primary social identity, its salience, strength and manipulability are situationally contingent (to say which is to come very close to Geertz's position, outlined above). No matter how apparently strong or inflexible it may be, ethnicity is *always* socially constructed, in the first instance and in every other.

If the primordial position is so unconvincing, that may be because, as an analytical model, it is largely something of a straw man. The debate about instrumentalism and primordialism has exaggerated the differences between, for example, Geertz and Barth, and does neither justice. It is tempting to agree with Eller and Coughlan (1993) that the notion of 'the primordial' should be banished from the social science lexicon. However, the debate remains important and it would be irresponsible to forget it altogether. Crude primordialism is essentially a common-sense view, with enormous power in the world. In sheep's clothing it occasionally makes an academic showing, indirectly in the guise of sociobiological arguments about kin-based nepotism (van den Berghe 1981, 1995) and, more explicitly, in a recent paper about territoriality (Grosby 1995). Even though these views are not widely supported they cannot simply be ignored. In response, an anthropological perspective, rooted in social constructionist assumptions, has much to offer as a critique of the naturalization of chauvinism and ethnic conflict.

Culture and biology

The controversy about the relationship between culture and biology is in many respects homologous to the debate about instrumentality and primordiality. It is at least as important, and for largely similar reasons: common sense continues to assert the reality and significance of 'race' and racism blights human lives. Building upon the example set by Boas (1940), social and cultural anthropologists have long offered an important challenge to dubiously scientific notions of 'race' (Benedict 1983 [1942]; Lévi-Strauss 1952). Unfortunately, an ironic consequence of the ascendance of the social constructionist model of ethnicity as – to borrow a notion from Kuhn – a normal science paradigm within the discipline has been that the problem of 'race', of the relationship between biology and culture, has tended to recede from the anthropological agenda. Sandra Wallman, as we saw earlier, dismisses the debate about the distinction between 'race' and ethnicity as a 'quibble' (1978: 205). Elsewhere (1986: 229) she argues that phenotype or physical appearance is just one potential ethnic boundary marker among many. A strikingly similar position is taken by Thomas Hylland Eriksen in his recent textbook: 'Ideas of 'race' may or may not form part of ethnic ideologies, and their presence or absence does not seem to be a decisive factor in interethnic relations' (2002: 6).

Adopting this position amounts, at least in part, to a laudable refusal to risk inadvertently validating biological models of ethnic difference. Interestingly, however, the naturalization of ethnicity within a sociobiological framework can lead to a similar position. In van den Berghe's terms, for example, ethnicity is an extension of kinship, a manifestation of an adaptive nepotism between kin that has essentially genetic foundations. Van den Berghe argues that 'race' has become nothing more than a 'special marker of ethnicity', a visible folk test of likely common ancestry (1981: 240). By this token, it is racism rather than 'race' that matters, as an adaptive stratagem of 'biologically-rooted nepotism' (although it is instructive to observe the later conflation of 'race' and racism in his writing: see van den Berghe 1995).

There are, of course, anthropologists who neither gloss over the relationship between 'race' and ethnicity nor submerge the one in the other. As illustrated by the discussion in Chapter 2, one such is Michael Banton, who has written at length about the history of theories of 'race' (1998), and consistently explored and theorized the two concepts and the relationship between them. His basic argument is that 'race' is a categorical identification denoting 'them', based on physical or phenotypical characteristics, while ethnicity is the cultural group identification of 'us' (Banton 1983: 1–14; 1988: 1–15). Ethnicity is thus voluntarily embraced, while 'racial' identifications are imposed. Although Banton is clear that both – albeit perhaps with different force – are socially constructed, Wade (1993, 2002: 18) has criticized him for taking phenotypical variation somewhat for granted, neglecting the social processes of categorization which denote and signify the differences which make a difference. In Wade's view, physical differences of 'race' are always highly – if not *completely* – socially constructed.

A closely related issue is the anthropological perspective on racism, most particularly the typical anthropological celebration of ethnicity as a 'good thing', as a cultural and social resource rather than a liability. Anthropology has also concentrated on minority rather than majority ethnicities. Each of these biases derives in part from the anthropological romance with exotic Otherness, in part from the interpretive cross-cultural advocacy role assumed by many anthropologists, and in part from the continuing legacy of structural functionalism and the theoretical underplaying of conflict. There is an increasing number of exceptions to these generalizations, and clear evidence that world events – in the Balkans, Amazonia, Indonesia … the list would have to be a very long one – in tandem with the developing anthropological concern with nationalism, are finally effecting shifts in these respects within the discipline that are likely to prove durable.[1] Nonetheless, racism remains an aspect of the social construction of ethnic differentiation that is relatively little discussed by anthropologists; when it is, it is not always done well (see the exchange between La Fontaine [1986] and Jenkins [1987]).

The arguments about the spurious nature of 'race' are too well known to require rehearsal here. The complexities of how one might theorize the relationship between 'race' and ethnicity are discussed in subsequent chapters. Here all I want to do is to suggest that the issue of 'race' is currently underplayed by anthropologists – even though there are indications of a revival of critical interest, particularly in the United States (Gil-White 2001; Harrison 2002; Wade 2002: 3) – and that adopting a social constructionist model of ethnicity neither requires nor entitles us to indulge in this neglect. Anthropology has, after all, for many years specialized in the study of classificatory systems. To reiterate Wade's key point (1993, 2002), whatever else it is, 'race' is a set of classificatory social constructs of considerable historical and contemporary significance. Exemplary studies of the social construction of 'racial' categorization, by non-anthropologists, can be found in Dikötter's monograph about modern China (1992) and his edited collection about China and Japan (1997). Racism, as an ideology of ethnic identification and a folk cosmology, is also socially constructed, an everyday version of the primordial view. It, too, is an appropriate object for the anthropological attention that, at the moment, it receives all too infrequently.

Redrawing the boundaries

A social constructionist approach to ethnicity and cultural differentiation involves, of necessity, an appreciation that ethnic identification is situationally variable and negotiable. It also involves recognizing the central emphasis that must be placed on the points of view of actors themselves, if we are to understand how processes of social construction and negotiation work. None of the reservations about the anthropological model that have been expressed cast doubt in any way on these basic points of departure. However, the criticisms and reservations suggest that some qualifications to these foundational principles are necessary. These qualifications are, in large part, restatements or developments of the original arguments of Weber, Hughes and Barth.

For example, with respect to cultural differentiation, the arguments of Chapter 3 must be re-emphasized: diversity – with respect to ethnicity – is nothing new, it is altogether the 'norm'. It is an expected dimension of human sociality. Inhabited social arenas are routinely multi-ethnic: as far as the archaeological, historical and anthropological records can tell us, bounded, homogeneous 'societies' or 'cultures' are exceptional (if they can be said ever to have existed at all). This is what ethnicity – collective identification that is socially constructed in the articulation of purported cultural similarity and difference – is all about. The increasing scale, density and extensiveness of modern social life, allied to rapidly evolving technologies of the intellect – to borrow a useful expression from Jack Goody – *may* have upped the tempo of, and increased opportunities for, differentiation. But, even if this is so, to suggest that this represents something qualitatively new or radical is probably to fall victim to one of the many conceits of modernity.[2]

Thus we should neither problematize difference *in itself*, nor celebrate it as a departure – and a liberation – from the past. It simply *is*, and there is no reason to expect that matters could ever be otherwise. Adopting this sceptical position does not, of course, prevent us from critically and systematically investigating either *how* difference is socially constructed, or the relative *salience* of difference from one context to another. The key Barthian theme that seems to have been most comprehensively forgotten by anthropologists who have written about ethnicity in the wake of *Ethnic Groups and Boundaries* requires emphatic reiteration here: 'group-ness' is not to be reified, and 'groups' are not distinct 'entities' or 'things' in any sense (and nor, *pace* Durkheim, are they to be treated *as if* they are things). They are contingent and immanently changeable, an emergent product of interaction and of classificatory processes (the definition of 'us' and the categorization of 'them'). Human society – and here we return to the issues raised in the discussion of Brubaker's recent work in Chapter 2 – is best seen as an ongoing and overlapping kaleidoscope of 'group-ness', rather than a 'plural' system of distinct and separate groups.

There is more to difference, of course, than the simple fact of diversity: there is also temporal and situational difference, the flexibility and negotiability of ethnic identity. One of the central lessons of the anthropology of ethnicity is that there is nothing new or distinctively modern – let alone *post*-modern – about the possibility of a degree of shape-shifting, whether collective or individual, with respect to ethnicity (and a similar point could be made about other identifications). There is, however, a further point that should be underlined here. To say that ethnic identity is transactional and changeable is really to say that it *may* be; it doesn't mean that it *always* is, or *has* to be. This is perhaps the one sensible point that emerges from the debate about instrumental versus primordial ethnicity. The recognition that ethnicity is neither static nor monolithic should not be taken to mean that it is definitively and perpetually in a state of flux. It isn't. There are, however, important questions to be asked – and they should always be asked – about how and why ethnicity is more or less flexible, or more or less imperative, in different places and at different times (Ruane and Todd 2004).

In the chapters that follow, these arguments will be given shape and direction through the exploration of three interrelated themes. The first of these is the role of *social categorization* in the construction of ethnic identifications. This directs our attention away from the 'group' as the atom of ethnicity, and also highlights relationships of power and domination. Second, there is the relationship between ethnicity and other analogous or homologous principles of identification. This involves looking not only at *classificatory* models such as 'race' or nationality (or, indeed, class and religion), but also at the role of *ideology*. Finally, I want to begin to address the *individual* or personal aspects of ethnicity. To turn Geertz's definition on its head, this is to problematize the processes whereby social identity becomes personally ratified. Why does ethnicity seem to matter to some people(s) – in some situations – but not to others? And why, when ethnicity matters, does it seem to *really* matter?

5 Categorization and Power

One of the most important insights offered by the basic social anthropological model of ethnicity is that ethnicity is not an immutable bundle of cultural traits, which it is sufficient to enumerate in order to identify a person as a member of this or that ethnic group, or to locate the boundary between ethnic collectivities. As Barth has consistently argued, ethnicity is situationally defined, produced and reproduced in the course of interactions that occur at or across – and in the process help to constitute – the ethnic boundary in question. Ethnicity is thus fundamentally political, at least with a small 'p', and ethnic boundaries are to some extent permeable and osmotic, existing despite the flow of personnel across them (and because of the interaction across them). Criteria of ethnic ascription and subscription are variable in their nature and salience.

Although Barth's overall concerns have remained grounded in the theoretical concerns of his 1966 *Models of Social Organization* project – how to theorize 'the constraints and incentives that canalize choices' and the ways in which social 'patterns are generated through processes of interaction and in their form reflect the constraints and incentives under which people act' (1966: 1, 2) – his point of view on ethnicity has not remained static since the publication of *Ethnic Groups and Boundaries*. His later discussions of the routine cultural pluralism of complex societies emphasize, for example, the importance of history, as well as the interactional immediacy of everyday life and its negotiations (Barth 1983, 1984, 1989). He invokes history in two different senses: as the ongoing progress of events which constitutes the context and content of the here-and-now, and as 'streams' of 'tradition' – the reference to Redfield is explicit – within which people are to differing degrees located and of which they differentially partake. Stressing history has produced a shift of emphasis away from the individualistic voluntarism of his earlier writings, for which he has been so consistently criticized, and towards a Weberian acknowledgement of the unintended consequences of action. Further, recognizing the centrality of history entails a search for pattern, influence and effect within a wide social and geographic arena; attention must be given to factors both within and without the social setting, local community or region that is the object of analytical attention.

In all important respects, however, Barth has remained true to the original perspective of *Ethnic Groups and Boundaries*, not least in according primacy to the perceptions, definitions and behaviour of actors themselves. I shall concentrate upon this in what follows, focusing on the question of *which* actors? Rather than offer an alternative that pretends to radical novelty, I shall draw out some elements of the anthropological model of ethnicity, interpreting their implications in the context of a set of general arguments about the production and reproduction of social identity (Jenkins 2008).

Groups and categories

If ethnicity is interactional, those interactions are of two basic kinds. First, there are processes of *internal definition*: members of a group signal to fellow group members or others a self-definition of who they are, their identity. This can be an individual process or a collective, group process (although when we are talking about an individual, it only makes sense to talk of ethnicity when the identification in question and its expressions refer to a recognized collectivity and draw upon an appropriate repertoire of shared practices). Although conceptualized in the first instance as 'internal', these processes are necessarily interactional and social – even in the individual case – because they presuppose an audience, without whom they make no sense, and a shared framework of meaning.

On the other hand, there are processes of *external definition*. These are other-directed processes, during which one person or set of persons defines the other(s) as 'X', 'Y', or whatever. This may, at its most consensual, be a validation of the others' internal definition(s) of themselves. At the conflictual end of the spectrum of possibilities, however, there is the imposition, by one set of actors on another, of a name and/or characterization that the categorized do not recognize, which affects in significant ways their social experience(s).

This process of external definition may, in theory, be an individual act, in which person A defines person or persons B as, say, 'X' or 'Y'. For two reasons, however, it is difficult to think about external definition as solely an individual act. In the first place, more than an audience is involved: the others here are the object(s) of the process of definition, and implied within the situation is a meaningful intervention in their lives, an acting upon them. Thus external definition can only occur within active social relationships, however distant or at however many removes. Second, the capacity to intervene successfully in other people's lives implies the capacity – the power or the authority – to do so. The exercise of power implies competitive access to and control over resources, while authority is, by definition, only effective when it is legitimate. Power and authority are necessarily embedded within active social relationships.

This distinction between internal and external definition is, of course, primarily analytical. In the complexity of day-to-day social life, each is chronically implicated in the other in an ongoing dialectic of identification. The categorization of 'them' is too useful a foil in the identification of 'us' for this not to be the case, and the definition of 'us' too much the product of a history of relationships with a range of significant others (Hagendoorn 1993). Which was, of course, one of Barth's original claims. Ethnicity – the production, reproduction and transformation of the 'group-ness' of culturally differentiated collectivities – is a two-way process that takes place across the boundary between 'us' and 'them'. At the individual level, in the ongoing production of personal identities, much the same can be said. Individual identity is located within a two-way social process, an interaction between 'ego' and 'other', inside and outside. It is in the meeting of internal and external definition that identity, whether collective or individual, is created.

It may be objected that the suggested homology between collective identity and individual identity is misleading, in that the boundaries of the self are secure and unproblematic in a way that is not, for example, true of social groups, particularly inasmuch as selfhood is embodied. There are, however, a number of reasons for persisting with an approach that treats individual and collective identities as similar in important respects. First, it seems clear that a relatively secure sense of the boundaries of individual selfhood is *acquired*, as the infant separates itself psychologically from the significant other(s) in its life through an early interactive process of being defined and defining (Cicchetti and Beeghley 1990; Dunn 1988; Kaye 1982; Stern 1985). Second, there is a well-established understanding of adult personal or self-identification that understands its content(s), boundaries, performance and, most critically, security as *variable* over time, given changing circumstances (Giddens 1984: 41–92). Finally, even if the boundaries of the self are, most of the time, stable and taken for granted, this is only true as long as it *is* true. When it is not, when the boundary between the self and others weakens or dissolves, the result is a range of more or less severe, and not uncommon, disruptions of secure selfhood which, in Western cultures, are conceptualized as psychiatric disorder (for one understanding of which, within a model which is analogous to the distinction between external and internal definition, see Laing 1971). To extend the logic of this last point, the boundaries of collective identity are also taken for granted until they are threatened.

Drawing upon concepts from social research methodology may help to illuminate further these internal and external processes of identification. The classification of human collectivities is basic to sociology and anthropology. One useful way to do this is to distinguish between *groups* and *categories*: a group is a collectivity which is meaningful to its members, of which they are aware, while a category is a collectivity that is defined according to criteria formulated by the sociologist or anthropologist. A group is a self-conscious collectivity, rooted in processes of internal definition, while a category is externally defined. This distinction is, in the first instance, concerned with the procedures that sociologists and anthropologists employ to constitute the human world as a proper object for systematic empirical inquiry and theorization. As such, it is relevant beyond the study of ethnicity and ethnic relations. Debates about social class, for example, are often characterized by disagreement about which principle of definition is most appropriate for the adequate constitution of classes as objects of/for analysis.

However, social groups and social categories can also be understood as different kinds of collectivities *in the actual human world*, and not just in the abstracted human world conjured up by social scientists. A vivid example of this can be found in Marx's famous contrast between 'a class in itself' (a category) and 'a class for itself' (a group). In this understanding of the development of class consciousness, the working class(es) – a social category that was initially defined, with reference to their immiseration and alienation from the means of production, and to their threat to the established order, by others such as capitalists, agencies of the state, socialist activists, etc. – becomes a social group, the members of which identify with each other in their collective misfortune, thus creating the possibility of organized collective action on the basis of that identification.

What this suggests is that social categorization – the identification of *others* as a collectivity – is no less a routine social process than the collective self-identification of the group. Whereas social groups define themselves, their name(s), their nature(s) and their boundary(ies), social categories are identified, defined and delineated by others. All collectivities can be conceptualized by reference to processes of group identification and social categorization: each side of the dichotomy is implicated in the other and social identification is the outcome of a dialectical process of internal *and* external definition. Whether, in any specific instance, one chooses to talk about a group or a category will depend on the balance struck between internal and external processes in that situation. It is a question of degree.

Which may be a good point at which to address a criticism of this model of categorization, and to look at another, more general, way in which the word is used in connection with ethnicity. Levine has argued that my use of 'categorization' is 'conventionally psychological' and, more significantly perhaps, that it leaves us unable to distinguish between groups and categories, in that people A will be a group in their own eyes and a category in the eyes of others: 'Can categories become groups and groups become categories?' (Levine 1999: 168). The answer, to rephrase what I have said above, is that a category can certainly become a group, and groups are – always – categories as well. What's more, a group may define itself in one way, but the Other's alternative categorization of them may turn out, in the local context of power relationships, to carry more weight and be more consequential (to the degree that the original group in question may, in fact, eventually come to see itself in terms that have been defined by the Other). The point that Levine misses is that my focus is on two different *processes* – group identification and categorization – and how these are implicated in each other in the production and reproduction of ethnic identifications and collectivities. And my point is also that categorization, *as I define it*, has been neglected, not just by anthropologists, but certainly also by anthropologists.

The 'as I define it' in the last sentence is important. The conventional psychological use of the term 'categorization' refers to what anthropologists, equally conventionally, tend to call 'classification': the process of dividing the world up into classes of phenomena on the basis of criteria of similarity and difference. While in the psychological literature this is fundamental to understandings of stereotyping (Hogg 2004; Oakes 2004), it also applies to what psychologists call 'self-categorization'. This seems to be very close, if not identical, to what Levine has in mind in his cognitive 'reconstruction' of ethnicity: 'ethnicity is that method of classifying people (both self and other) that uses origin (socially constructed) as its primary reference' (1999: 168). Brubaker's notion of 'ethnicity as cognition' (2004: 64–87; Brubaker *et al.* 2004) also offers essentially the same understanding of ethnicity, and of categorization.

And I do not doubt that ethnic identifications are classificatory processes – *done* by people – that produce and reproduce shared meanings. They also, necessarily, produce and reproduce collectivities, as meaningful social phenomena. The major difference between Levine's position and mine, and also mine and Brubaker's, seems to be largely a matter of how we use words: I am distinguishing between classification and categorization, reserving the latter – in a very different sense to the 'conventionally psychological' usage – for the external definition of identity.

Although social anthropology, inasmuch as it has considered *individual* identity at all, has privileged social or external knowledge over self- or internal knowledge (A.P. Cohen 1994), the emphasis of the post-Barthian anthropology of ethnicity and *communal* identity has tended to fall on the other side of the internal–external dialectic: on processes of group identification rather than social categorization (e.g. A.P. Cohen 1982, 1985, 1986; Eriksen 1991, 2002; Wallman 1978, 1986). To go over some old ground, there are at least three reasons why this is so. First, anthropology, in its enthusiasm for 'Otherness' and its powerful residual model of the human world as, essentially, non-conflictual – regardless of internal theoretical debates or the impact of various threads of postmodernism – tends to celebrate ethnicity as a positive social resource. This is often at the expense of paying sufficient, or indeed any, attention to ethnicity as a social liability or stigma. Second, this is reinforced by the fact that enthusiasm for an interactional model of social life – ethnicity as *process* – has typically been accompanied by a view of social relationships as rooted in reciprocation, exchange and relatively equitable negotiation. Finally, anthropology's continued emphasis on participant observation as the discipline's methodological *sine qua non* has led its practitioners to concentrate on the collection of data during face-to-face encounters or through direct observation. Processes of collective internal definition may be easier to study using such an approach than their external counterparts. This bias is, however, entailed neither by the Barthian model nor, indeed, by anthropology. The exploration of processes of ethnic and other forms of categorization is an extension, refinement and development of the anthropological model rather than an alternative to it.

There is one important further point that has so far only been implicit. In talking about the names, characteristics and boundaries of groups and categories, there is a strong suggestion that identity is 'made up' of a number of distinct strands, even if they are only analytically distinguishable. Two of these strands, in particular, are significant here. Social identity, whether it be ethnic or whatever, is both *nominal*, i.e. a name, and *virtual*, a practical meaning or an experience. This contrast is implicit in the distinction between boundaries and their contents, and very approximately analogous to the well-worn distinction between 'status' and 'role' (Jenkins 2008: Chapter 13). It is an important contrast because one can change without the other doing so; similarly one can be the product of internal processes of identification, the other of categorization. For example, although categorization may not necessarily change the name or boundary of an identity, it may have considerable potential to define what it means to bear it, the consequential experience of 'being an X'. I will explore the implications of this below.

Social categorization

Distinguishing between internal and external definitions, between group identification and social categorization, allows us to think about ethnic identification from a number of different points of view within a unified analytical framework. The basis for this framework is what I have called, elsewhere, *pragmatic individualism*: the recognition that the human world is constituted in and by embodied individuals (Jenkins 2002a: 57–8, 2008: Chapter 4).

Taking inspiration, *inter alia*, from Erving Goffman (1969, 1983) and Anthony Giddens (1984: 1–40), I have elsewhere proposed a model of the human world that begins from the proposition that embodied individuals are no less central to any sociological understanding of the human world than collectivities (Jenkins 2002a: 68–76). Viewed in this light, it is possible to talk about whatever it is that we call society as a set of relationships within and between three orders of phenomena:

- The *individual order* is the human world considered as made of embodied individuals and 'what-goes-on-in-their-heads'.
- The *interaction order* is the human world as constituted in the relationships between embodied individuals, in 'what-goes-on-between-people'.
- The *institutional order* is the human world seen as pattern and organization, as established 'ways-of-doing-things'.

This scheme is only a way of *thinking about* the human world. It simply says that the experiential world that is produced and reproduced by humans can be thought of as constituted in and by individuals, the interaction between individuals, and institutions. It also says that it cannot be thought of as constituted in and by any of these in isolation from the other two. This an ideal-typical model of a complex actual reality: it is not meant to suggest that there are *really* three separate social domains, analogous, for example, to ecological zones or different states of physical matter.

Each 'order' is constituted in and by embodied individuals. Thus embodiment is one of the keys to understanding this model. Each of the three orders is *distinctively* materialized: in individual bodies; in the collective space of 'set and setting' and the interactional practices that take place between embodied individuals; and in the institutionalized appropriation of space in buildings, territories, visible symbolism, etc. The use of the word 'order' is meant to indicate both distinctive 'domains of activity', and the ordered, if not always orderly, nature of the human world (Goffman 1983: 5). But words such as 'world' and 'domain' are apt to mislead: the orders overlap completely. Each is irredeemably implicated in each of the others, and none makes sense without the others. The word 'order' also indicates that these are classificatory devices that should not be confused with the actual phenomena and localities of the human world to which they refer. They are different ways of apprehending the same observable realities, and amount to an act of ordering in their own right.

The internal–external dialectic of identification can be seen at work in each of these orders. Before looking at each one in greater detail, a number of basic points of departure need to be outlined. The most fundamental of these is that internal and external identification do not exist in isolation from each other. Identification is never a unilateral process: at the very least there is always an audience. This principle can be established in a number of ways. First, categorization – external definition – is a basic dimension of internal definition. The process of defining 'us' demands that 'they' should be split off from, or contrasted with, 'us'; group identification is likely to proceed, at least in part, through categorizing others, whether positively or negatively. Second, external definition – by others of us – undoubtedly has an impact on our internal definition(s). Finally, pre-existing established internal definitions may provide a defence against the imposition of external definitions. The experience of categorization may strengthen existing group identity through a process of resistance and reaction. Thus, the experience of being categorized as 'A' may, only apparently paradoxically, contribute to the reinforcement, or even perhaps the formation, of group identity as 'B' (although the ways in which it will do so are a matter for empirical investigation rather than theoretical prediction). Arguments analogous to all the above can also be offered with respect to individual identity.

To talk about the *individual order* is to talk about mind, selfhood and embodiment. I will leave the issue of the social constitution of mind for discussion elsewhere (Jenkins 2008: Chapter 5) and concentrate on embodied selfhood here. A concept that is well known in this respect is the distinction between *I* and *me*. Inspired by William James, it derives its sociological formulation from G.H. Mead (1934: 173–226), a theorist who has been 'curiously unacknowledged' by social anthropology' (A.P. Cohen 1992: 226; see Morris 1994 for a good example of this neglect). To paraphrase Mead, the 'I' is that active aspect of the self which responds to others, whereas the 'me' comprises the attitudes and responses of significant others, as they are incorporated into the self. Mead's 'me' is intimately bound up with what he called the 'generalized other', the voice of the individual's community of membership. Mead's self is embodied, not in a crude physiological sense, but in the notion that selfhood is the social organization of individual consciousness. To put this another way, the self fills the space between embodied mind and (embodied) social interaction, and is inextricably a part of each. Hence *Mind, Self, and Society*, as the building blocks of Mead's theoretical framework (1934).

The distinction between the 'I' and the 'me' is homologous in many respects to Freud's formulation of the 'ego' and 'superego' as fundamental aspects of individual personality. And it shares at least one of the Freudian model's major shortcomings: the ongoing embodied unity of selfhood is vulnerable to misrepresentation as an assembly of more or less separate bits: 'as if an ordinary person is really some sort of committee or team of persons, all laced together inside one skin' (Ryle 1963: 181). That criticism aside, however, Mead's model of the self is suggestive here, particularly because it leaves no room for doubt about the social character of selfhood, or the centrality to selfhood of an internal–external dialectic of identification (Jenkins 2008: Chapter 6).

In the course of earliest socialization each human being develops a unique personality, a 'sense of self' that, although it may not always be available to us consciously, is one of the bedrocks of our 'ontological security' (Giddens 1984: 50 ff.) Much of this 'sense of self' is located in that embodied hinterland of routine and unreflexive habit – neither conscious nor unconscious – that is the generative site of practices which Bourdieu calls the *habitus* (Bourdieu 1990: 53–97). This 'sense of self' is not simply a 'mental' phenomenon but is intimately bound up with the physical integrity of the individual. Selves are located within bodies, and that embodiment is one of the sources of the unity of selfhood. A sense of self is created in the course of the early verbal and non-verbal dialogue – a complex interaction of separation *from* and identification *with* – between the child and significant others. Typically parents in the first instance, the voice of these others becomes internalized as what Mead calls the 'me', and Giddens (1984: 8) the 'moral conscience'. A voice which tells the child both who it *is* and what it should *do*, each being an aspect of the other.

We know who we are because, in the first place, others tell us. This is the interactional learning process of primary socialization, which works consciously and less-than-consciously, and which creates an internal relationship – whether harmoniously 'adjusted' or not – between the individualized demands of the self and its internalized social expectations (which may also be thought of in this context as representing 'culture'. It is in the initial and continuing dialectic between the internal and the external that basic selfhood – the individual's sense of who she is, and her embodied point of view on the 'rest of the world' – is constituted.

It is easy to imagine how primary socialization may – depending on local circumstances and the salience of ethnicity – include an ethnic component. Cognitively, if nothing else, the child will develop a point of view on a world that is axiomatically organized in terms of ethnic classifications. She will learn not only that she is an 'X', but also what this means: in terms of her esteem and worth in her own eyes and in the eyes of others; in terms of appropriate and inappropriate behaviour; and in terms of what it means *not* to be an 'X', what it means to be a 'Y' or a 'Z' perhaps (Epstein 1978). This is emphatically the case, for example, in social contexts where 'racial' categorization is a powerful principle of social organization and stratification (Goodman 1964; Milner 1975; Troyna and Hatcher 1992; van Ausdale 2001).

The *interaction order* is where *self-image* meets *public image*. Self-image is the way we see ourselves and, perhaps even more important, the way we would *like* to be seen by others. The starting point for any attempt to understand how this works in interaction is Goffman (1969). In the context of this discussion, Goffman's most important arguments about the 'presentation of self' are: first, that identity is a matter of performance; second, that, in interactional terms, there is no necessary consistency in selfhood, but rather a range of partial aspects or *revelations* of self, depending on the situation; third, that management of the awkward relationship between the desired presentation of self and other, countervailing aspects of one's biography and present situation is of great importance; and fourth, that validation of the performance by others, if not their complicit collaboration, is central to successful impression management. The homology between Goffman's view of social selfhood as performative and processual and Barth's model of ethnicity as interactional is obvious.

The third and fourth points, above, direct our attention to public image, the vexed question of how others see us. It goes without saying that there is no necessary equivalence between self-image and public image. What is more, it is not always easy to know how others see us anyway. Apart from the obvious epistemological issue – the old philosophical problem of 'other minds' – there are a number of reasons why this should be so. The audience may attempt to conceal its opinion of both actor and performance. The actor may, for various strategic or tactical reasons, attempt to present something other than their 'true' self-image. There may be poor communication between the two sides, for various individual, interactional, institutional or other external reasons. The unique personal psychology that is integral to selfhood may, in the event of major disagreement between self-image and public image, block acknowledgement of the threatening public image.

However, allowing for these qualifications, there will usually be at least *some* interaction between self-image(s) and public image(s), some process of conscious or unconscious adjustment in the ongoing process of the making and re-making of social identity. An example may clarify the point. Occupational identities are among the most important of social identities. For many people they provide the basis on which their livelihood is secured. They are also closely connected to social status. This was so in the pre-modern world and it remains so today. In modern industrial societies, there is an element of election involved in the assumption of an occupational identity. Choice, however, only operates within strict limits and is generally bilateral: other people, gatekeepers of one sort or another within the education system and the labour market, play a crucial role in validating (or not) occupational aspirations. In order to pursue occupational goals and ambitions, qualifications must be obtained, jobs must be applied for and the cooperation of more powerful others obtained. In the process, there is for many young people, first in school and subsequently in the world of employment and unemployment, a gradual convergence of aspiration and outcome, self-image and public image, which is recognized culturally as 'realism' and is one source of stability in a visibly inequitable system (Jenkins 1983; MacLeod 1987; Willis 1977).

It is not just aspirations that are adjusted because of their public reception and evaluation; identity is also variable and vulnerable. For example, the labelling perspective in the sociology of deviance suggests that deviant identities can become internalized as a consequence of the individual concerned being publicly categorized as a law/rule breaker and treated accordingly (Becker 1963; Lemert 1972; Matza 1969). Similarly, identities are imposed upon individuals in school (Cicourel and Kitsuse 1963; Rist 1977) and in the labour market, in a dialectical process of internal and external definition. The individual is identified in a particular way by significant others, who by virtue of their power or authority are in a position to make their definition of the person and the situation count, and thus to constitute that person's subsequent career in terms of the identity in question. That individual's experience of the consequences of being categorized may, over time, lead to an adjustment in her self-image in the direction of the stigmatizing public image. For example, an individual who is defined as 'unreliable', and is not only distrusted but *publicly* distrusted and denied access to occasions where reliability is expected and could therefore be demonstrated, may, as a consequence, become as unreliable as she is purported to be. The notion of unreliability may then become an important dimension of her self-image.

A point that is made less often is that similar self-fulfilling processes are likely to operate with respect to positive or socially valued categorizations. Labelling is not just a negative phenomenon. Inasmuch as the external world is at least as much a source of self-esteem as it is a threatening environment of hostile labelling, this basic model can also be applied to the incorporation of positive public images into self-imagery.

The implications of these examples for ethnicity are apparent if we look at discrimination in the labour market and the depression or encouragement of aspiration – either effect being possible – among those ethnic minorities who find themselves on its receiving end. The cumulative outcome of this kind of situation, if left unchallenged by currents of resistance within the ethnic community(s) concerned, may, at best, be the development of ethnic occupational niches and a communally and individually accepted ceiling on occupational mobility. At worst, the self-image of a stigmatized and discriminated-against minority will interact with discrimination and exclusion in a vicious circle of cumulative decay and disadvantage, as documented in a series of classic studies of black urban neighbourhoods in North America (Anderson 1978; Hannerz 1969; Liebow 1967). 'Realism' becomes, in part at least, constitutive of 'reality'. This general process is not in any sense peculiar to 'race': a similar argument can be made, for example, with respect to class.

Ethnic disadvantage in the labour market may seem far removed from the micro-interactional concerns of Goffman. A better example for our purposes might, perhaps, be the subtlety with which people in Northern Ireland purport to 'tell' the difference between Catholic and Protestant in social interaction (Burton 1978: 37–67; Jenkins 1982: 30–1; Lanclos 2003: 127–9, 146–7). However, the principles involved are essentially the same. The 'labour market' is, after all, nothing more than an abstraction from a myriad of encounters in which the strategies of job-seekers are subject to categorizing decisions about who should get which jobs (Jenkins 1986a). Although, for the moment, a question is begged here – that of *who* is authorized to make the decisions and to make those decisions count – the example serves to connect the micro-interaction of self-image and public image with the *institutional order* of groups and categories.

The important thing to emphasize is that ethnic groups, indeed all groups, are institutions: patterns of social practice identifying persons that have become established over time as the 'way things are done' in a particular local context, and of which people in that context are conscious. Institutions are aspects of local social reality in terms of which and with reference to which decisions are made and behaviour is oriented. Social categories may not be institutions – although they may be – but ethnic categorization is likely to be, at least in part, institutionalized.

Most discussions of ethnicity are pitched in terms of *social groups,* the emphasis being on collective internal definitions of distinctiveness: 'ethnic groups are categories of ascription and identification by the actors themselves' (Barth 1969a: 10). While it is clear from Barth's discussion that the 'actors themselves' can signify actors on both sides of the ethnic boundary, it is equally – if implicitly – clear that explanatory or analytical priority is accorded to identification *within* the ethnic boundary. And there is a sense in which this is as it should be. A claim to ethnic identity must be validated by an audience of outsiders or Others – because without such an audience the issue would not arise – but it seems to make little sense to talk about an ethnicity which does not, at some point, and no matter how weakly or tenuously, recognize itself as such.

When the issue is expressed thus, the anthropological emphasis upon internal group identification becomes apparent. Leaving aside the massive body of work on caste and hierarchy in India and elsewhere, because it is arguably not concerned with ethnicity as such – although there is a discussion to be had about this – there are relatively few examples in the anthropological literature on ethnicity of an explicit concern with processes of *social categorization*. Those examples that can be found, however, testify to the value of such an approach. For the reader who wishes to survey the diversity of ways in which it can be done, these include: Hugh Brody (1986) on relations between the Beaver Indians of the Canadian sub-Arctic and white trappers; Bernard Cohn on the impact of colonial censuses in South Asia (1988: 224–54); Elizabeth Colson (1953) on Makah native Americans and reservation life; the theoretical arguments of Jean and John Comaroff (Comaroff and Comaroff 1992: 49–67); Frederick Erickson (1976) discussing gatekeeping encounters and 'race' in the schools of Chicago's West Side; Ralph Grillo (1985) on encounters between French bureaucrats and (im)migrants; my own work (Jenkins 1986a) on racism and employment recruitment in England; Carola Lentz (1994, 2000) on the colonial and post-colonial creation of ethnic identities in Ghana; and

Jill Nash and Eugene Ogan (1990) on mutual categorization in Papua New Guinea. To this list I would also want to add anthropologically informed studies of the historical and recent categorization of the Ainu by the Japanese, by David Howell (1994) and Richard Siddle (2002a), respectively, and Siddle's study of the Japanese categorization of Okinawans (2002b).

For the purposes of illustration, looking at one such example in a little detail will do (Stuchlik 1979). During European colonial expansion into Chile, the Spaniards came into contact relatively early – in the sixteenth century – with an indigenous people known today as the Mapuche. Milan Stuchlik, using documentary sources, identifies five distinct ways in which the Spanish, and subsequently the Chileans, categorized the Mapuche in the course of the centuries which followed: as 'brave and fearless warriors', 'bloodthirsty bandits', 'lazy drunken Injuns', 'the white man's burden' and 'gentle savages who lack education', in historical sequence. The main thrust of this analysis – which, while it does not tell us directly about the impact of categorization on Mapuche group identity, does suggest some of its consequences for Mapuche life – is that these categorical models of the Mapuche are not a reflection of 'factual' knowledge about the Mapuche. Rather, they tell us about native policies, the goals of the Spanish and the Chileans with respect to the Mapuche. Hence they tell us about the *categorizers* – how they see themselves and their objectives – more than the *categorized*. It is Spanish and Chilean ethnic identifications that are under construction as much as anything else.

A more general point can perhaps also be made about the anthropological enterprise itself, particularly with respect to notions of 'primitiveness' as a categorization of other cultures (Boon 1982; Kuper 1988). The constitution of individual Others as sufficiently *similar* to us to be comprehensible human beings has been one of modern anthropology's greatest achievements. It has, however, proceeded, much of the time, hand in glove with powerful assumptions and discourses about collective *difference*. Fortunately, unlike Spanish colonizers or Chilean administrators and politicians, the capacity of anthropologists to make their definitions count for those whom they categorize has generally been modest, although their indirect influence should not be underestimated.

The three social orders – the *individual*, the *interactional* and the *institutional* – they can be distinguished only for the purposes of understanding better the human world. They are thoroughly intertwined in each other; occupying the same space and each made up of embodied, socialized, individuals. The unitary sense of self lies behind self-image. Self-images meld with public images in the complex negotiation of shared meanings, understandings and practices that constitutes group identification. Group identification and categorization combine in situationally specific relations of resistance or reinforcement to produce the social reality in historical time and space of institutionalized ethnic collectivities. I could, of course, as easily have approached these interrelationships from the other end, beginning with the relationship between groups and categories. The traffic on this street flows in both directions. Making this point re-emphasizes the internal–external simultaneity of processes of ethnic identification: individually, interactionally and institutionally. None has precedence, whether conceptually, historically or developmentally. Nor can any of them be imagined in the absence of the others.

Contexts of ethnic categorization

Identity is produced and reproduced during interaction, and interaction is always situated in context. I will now look at some of the specific contexts and processes of social categorization. These – and I wish I had thought of this metaphor myself – are what Cornell and Hartmann (1998: 153–94) call the 'construction sites' of ethnicity. Although the emphasis will be upon *ethnic* categorization, the overall picture is generalizable to other social identifications (Jenkins 2000a). This section will begin to draw out the implications of my arguments for a research agenda concerned with ethnicity and ethnic identity. It will also relocate the theoretical discussions so far, into the everyday contexts of social life in which we do our research.

The basic shape of the empirical agenda is presented schematically in Figure 5.1. It is not intended to be exhaustively comprehensive; it is simply an attempt to sketch in some flesh that can be hung on the bones of my argument. To keep the discussion manageable, two simplifying assumptions are implicit in the discussion that follows: first, that ethnic categorization is likely to be more often pejorative, negative or stigmatizing than not, and second, that there are no contemporary social settings in which the formal–informal distinction does not have some relevance.

The contrast between the formal and the informal in Figure 5.1 should not be seen as a sharp distinction. It is, rather, a continuum of emphasis. The degree to which *primary socialization*, for example, is the private domestic responsibility of the child's immediate caretakers – unsupervised by state or local community – and the degree to which it is formally organized and regulated by the state or municipality, is a matter of enormous variability. So too is the relationship between primary socialization and subsequent formal education. Similarly, *routine public interaction*, although typically informal, can also, in specific circumstances, be formalized (as in the case of inter-'racial' public encounters in the South Africa of apartheid). At the other end of the spectrum, *administrative allocation* and *organized politics*, for example, are shot through with informality in every aspect of their organization and practice. If for no other reason, this is because informality is not conceptualized as a residual category, as whatever is left in the absence of formality, or once the formal dimensions of a situation have been identified. Formality and informality are specific kinds of social relation that have developed, historically, hand in glove: 'The formal is simultaneously an absence and a presence within the informal, and vice versa' (Harding and Jenkins 1989: 137). Each depends upon and takes part of its meaning from the other.

The importance of *primary socialization* in the social construction of identity has already been alluded to, and will be mentioned again. Suffice it to draw attention briefly to a number of points here. First, there is no necessity that ethnicity will feature explicitly in primary socialization; much depends here upon local circumstances and histories. If it does, however, ethnicity may take its place alongside the primary identities of humanness, gender and selfhood (Jenkins 2008: Chapters 6 and 7): they are deeply rooted in first encounters and in the egocentric axiomatic constitution of the human world that is the embodied individual point of view, and resist easy transformation. Finally, primary socialization is an exchange of communication between infant and others, but in the first instance, and for quite a time thereafter,

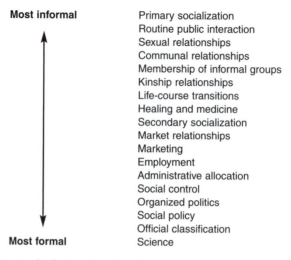

Most informal

Primary socialization
Routine public interaction
Sexual relationships
Communal relationships
Membership of informal groups
Kinship relationships
Life-course transitions
Healing and medicine
Secondary socialization
Market relationships
Marketing
Employment
Administrative allocation
Social control
Organized politics
Social policy
Official classification

Most formal   Science

Figure 5.1   Contexts of ethnic categorization

it is an exchange in which information *in* dominates: if we know who we are, it is because, a long time ago, beyond the reach of conscious recall, other people told us (Dunn 1988; Kaye 1982; Richards 1974). Very early socialization is the realm *par excellence* of categorization, setting a template for our receptivity to being categorized in later life. The taken-for-grantedness of selfhood that is thereby fostered may also, and only apparently paradoxically, be the *sine qua non* for the rapidly developing post-infancy social agency to which the recent sociology of childhood has sensitized us (James *et al.*, 1998).

Routine public interaction is the face-to-face interaction that occurs, much of it outside ongoing social relationships, within the gaze of others. Informal ethnic categorization organizes 'relations in public' in a number of ways. First, there are the verbal and non-verbal cues which are used to allocate unknown others to an ethnic category. In some cases, these cues are a dimension of group identity, explicit signals of ethnic identity: language, clothing, bodily adornment, etc. Others, however, such as many aspects of non-verbal behaviour, are likely to be involuntary or unconscious (and here we see again the importance of habit and the body again, *pace* Bourdieu). Items of behaviour are appropriated by others as criteria of ethnic categorization, without those who 'own' them participating in this identification (or even, perhaps, being aware of it). Aspects of physical appearance – whether 'real' or imaginary and typically crystallized in ethnic stereotypes – are also a staple of anonymous public categorization.

Other forms of routine public behaviour are instrumental in the construction and mobilization of ethnic categories. Particular mention should be made of humour, verbal abuse and violence (all of which are, of course, also important in the context of enduring relationships and in the private sphere). With respect to humour, the case of the 'ethnic joke' is well known (C. Davies 1990). Anthropological analyses of joking suggest that ethnic joking is likely to characterize situations where social restraints inhibit the overt expression of inter-ethnic hostility (Douglas 1975:

90–114). Ethnic jokes – and here one may perhaps legitimately stretch the concept of the joke to include performances such as the Brer Rabbit tales of the American South, or the Anansi stories of the Caribbean – are a potent site of passive resistance to domination. They are also equally effective in the categorization of ethnic subordinates. Jokes facilitate categorization where it may not be socially acceptable or explicitly possible; there's no such thing as *just* a joke, and ethnic jokes are no exception.

Inter-ethnic verbal abuse and violence do not, perhaps, require too much discussion here, except to suggest that humour, insult and violence shade into each other and are intimately connected (Allen 1990). Verbal abuse and violence, in particular, are concerned with the beating of ethnic boundaries through the enforcement of definitions of what the ethnic 'Other' *is* or must *do*. Power is at the heart of the matter. However, for a variety of reasons, authoritative social control – legitimate according to local specifications – has provided political and legal anthropology with the bulk of its subject matter. Violence and its threat have, in the process, been somewhat underestimated as routine mechanisms of control and strategies for achieving goals. Violence to others, up to and including killing, may – in addition to all of its other dimensions – be the ultimate form of categorization. I will return to this in Chapter 7.

Power and control are also central to *sexual relationships*, which straddle the divide between the public and the private. The sensitivity of inter-ethnic sexual relationships has been documented in a wide variety of settings (e.g. Dollard 1957: 134–87; Okely 1983: 154–6; Pryce 1979: 80–94). It may be expressed in notions of group 'possession' of women and must, in part therefore, be considered as an aspect of patriarchy as well as ethnicity. In terms of ethnicity, what is typically at issue is the definition of which men may or may not have access to which women. The resolution of the issue is typically asymmetrical, in reflection of the power relationships between the groups in question, and between men and women. Access to another group's women may loom large in the ethnic identity of a dominant group, with lack of (male) control in this respect being a defining feature of subordinate categorization. When systematized racism enters the picture, a general prohibition of 'miscegenation' may – officially or legally, anyway – deny the men of a dominant group access to ethnically subordinate women.

Communal relationships, the more or less tightly knit networks that evolve over time in residentially shared localities, provide many opportunities for ethnic categorization. Most obviously, communities are often ethnically relatively homogeneous. Gossip may serve to mark the boundaries between one ethnic community and another and is one of the most effective ways of policing inter-ethnic sex and friendship relationships. All kinds of social interaction across communal boundaries are – following Barth and Anthony Cohen – important in boundary maintenance (hence the need for policing at times of changing boundaries). Local peer groups are particularly efficient at socializing their members into group identity, and dramatizing the articulation of ethnic categorization with respect to other ethnicities.

Membership of informal groups may be a dimension of everyday communal life. However, there are informal social groups which are not grounded in local communality but serve nonetheless as efficient contexts of ethnic exclusion and, through their tacit – or not so tacit – criteria of membership, of categorization. Mundane examples are to be found in ethnic peer groups within schools and in work organizations. There is also a spectrum of more formally constituted organizations – from the Ku Klux Klan to B'nai B'rith to immigrants' mutual aid associations – whose membership is ethnically specified and which pursue ethnically defined goals.

Kinship relationships – whether consanguineal or affinal – are subject to a degree of public regulation. In many societies this regulation is formally embodied in law. There are few examples, however, of the formal categorization of permissible marriage partners in strictly ethnic terms, and where they can be found, as I have already observed, they typically involve organized racism in one form or another (laws prohibiting 'miscegenation' have been current in this century, *inter alia*, in some states of the American Union, Germany and, most recently, South Africa). The informal regulation of inter-ethnic sexual relations in the communal arena remains the most potent force maintaining ethnic exclusivity in marriage. Categorization generates a situation in which the operation of a courtship and marriage market, structured by individually internalized ethnic categories which are expressed consciously as preferences and unconsciously as encounters, will tend to reproduce the ethnic status quo without recourse to explicit regulation.

Kinship relationships may, of course, be intimately bound up with *life-course transitions* (Hockey and James 2003). Among the key social junctures are: the acceptance/recognition of the new infant, puberty, the transition to adulthood, parenthood, significant stages of mid-life, withdrawal from economic activity, transition to the category of the aged, and death. The formality or informality with which these transitions are handled are locally variable, but two things which seem common almost to the point of universality are that these transitions of identity/status are typically symbolized in rituals of passage, whether religious or secular, and that categorization, manifest in recognition or consecration by others, whether ritual specialists or audience, is fundamental. They are never unilateral or inevitable. They are also potent markers and statements of ethnic identification (e.g. Pleck 2000: 141–249)

A number of key social categorizations – the quick and the dead, the well and the sick, the curable and the incurable, the safe and the contagious, the sane and the mad, physician and patient – and their application to, in the main, individuals, are the stock in trade of *healing and medicine.* This social field may also contribute to life-course transitions. In all societies diagnosis and intervention, where deemed appropriate, attract at least a degree of specialization. However, even in modern industrial societies, where this specialization is most extensive and formal, informality and uncertified lore remain significant. Authority does not always derive from formal socialization into professional medicine, and informal ethnic healing traditions persist. The authority and power of institutionalized bio-medicine is not to be underestimated; nor is the degree to which ethnic categorizations, whether implicit or explicit, contribute to diagnosis, treatment and the distribution of health resources (e.g. Helman 2007; Nazroo 2001)

Secondary socialization may also contribute to life-course transitions, particularly before the assumption of social adulthood, but other identifications are involved too. In most contemporary societies, formal socialization is established in institutions of education and training and their systems of categorization (assessment and examination, leading to diplomas and accreditation). The occupational division of labour is critically dependent on secondary socialization, and the degree to which these systems categorize and stratify individuals and populations according to ethnicity should not be underestimated. However, one should not neglect informal secondary socialization within the family, communal life, peer groups and the workplace, particularly with respect to the impact of categorizations such as ethnicity and 'race'.

Another field of social life that is hierarchically structured in terms of power and formally regulated to a limited extent is the domain of *market relationships*. Governed, on the face of things, by economic principles that emphazise the pursuit of either profit or relatively equitable exchange (notions of equity and acceptable profit being contextually defined), business and trading are nonetheless structured by ethnic categorization. This is so with respect to who can trade with whom, who can trade in what, and the price that different categories of people must pay for similar commodities or services. Ethnically organized market relationships can be found in contexts as diverse as the housing markets of Britain and the United States (Banton 1983: 336–65), the trading networks of northern Norway (Eidheim 1969) and the exchange relationships of 'primitive' New Guinea and northern Australia (Sahlins 1972: 277–314).

The job of *marketing* specialists is the systematic identification of consumer categories, and these may be ethnically constituted (Costa and Bamossy 1995). These categories are designed to allow for the efficient promotion of goods and services via targeted advertisements, and the development of new products for specific markets (i.e. categories of consumer). It is now a sociological commonplace that consumption and identification are intimately related, although the emphasis has typically been on self- and group identification (Bourdieu 1984; Mackay 1997), even when shopping is seen as largely other- rather than self-oriented (Miller 1998). However, the categorizations of marketing are significant too. They may, for example, encourage the *de facto* exclusion of certain social categories from access to, *or desire for*, high-status goods (which, of course, is exactly the point: how else is the imagined value of status to be maintained?).

Lamont and Molnár (2001) open up further our understanding of the relationship between marketing and ethnic categorization. As moneyed consumers, African-Americans have historically been disadvantaged and stereotyped negatively. Whether because of alienation or in resistance, many have responded by adopting distinctive strategies of self-identificatory display and conspicuous consumption – exemplified recently in the hip-hop B-Boy and B-Girl styles – which may have reinforced those stereotypes. Working within this context, black marketing specialists are now self-consciously attempting to foster new and positive categorizations of African-American consumers, in their own eyes and in the eyes of the 'mainstream'. Instead of appropriating and recasting the stereotypes, an attempt is being made to intervene directly in the process of categorization.

Employment is a particular kind of market relationship, characteristic of modern, industrialized societies. It may be informal or formal, but, for increasing swathes of the world's population, entry into the labour market represents – apart, perhaps, from limited eligibility for membership of a welfare system – their only possible relation to the means of production and, hence, their only source of livelihood. In ethnically heterogeneous labour markets – which are the rule rather than the exception – ethnic categorization is a powerful criterion governing the allocation of job-seekers to jobs by those who are authorized to make recruitment decisions.

This is encouraged and reinforced inasmuch as recruitment to the positions of supervision and management which involve hiring and firing is, of course, also likely to be ethnically biased. In addition, the cumulative effect of ethnic categorization in housing markets and in access to education serves further to limit, systematically and disadvantageously, the labour-market options of particular groups.

A key moment during employment recruitment is the interview, no matter how perfunctory it may be. Although formalized diagnostic testing is becoming increasingly influential in initial screening (Hanson 1993), interviewing and committee decision-making are central to processes of *administrative allocation* (Batley 1981). These formal and informal practices serve to allocate resources and penalties within and from public- and private-sector formal organizations. In addition to employment, these rewards and penalties include public housing (Flett 1979), welfare benefits (Howe 1985) and social work interventions of one kind or another (Hillyard and Percy-Smith 1988: 170–203; Liddiard and Hutson 1991; Spencer 2001). Processes of interviewing and bureaucratized collective decision-making are important sources, alongside formal rules and certificated expertise or knowledge, of the institutional rationality which legitimizes the powers of delegated discretion exercised by officers in deciding individual cases. They are also the site of the creation of a distinctively modern and subordinated generic social category, that of the bureaucratic *client* (Collmann and Handelman 1981; Järvinen and Mik-Meyer 2003).

It is the discretionary nature of these gatekeeping encounters, within a permissive bureaucratic framework, which allows ethnic categorization its inevitable entry into the process – whether explicitly or implicitly (Erickson 1976; Grillo 1985; Karn 1983) – along with other ascriptive and stigmatizing categorizations (Lipsky 1980; Prottas 1979; Scott 1970). Administrative allocation processes have an increasing reach within modern states. Their significance in the social construction of patterns of disadvantage and of the everyday experience of being a member of a stigmatized social category, whether ethnic or not, should not be underestimated. Administrative allocation is a privileged context for the transformation of the nominal into the virtual (a distinction which was briefly introduced in Chapter 4). Ethnic categorization in this context is likely to *count* in the lives of the categorized. It is authorized, officially legitimate categorization, from which consequences flow.

Intimately related to administrative allocation – and, where it is bureaucratized, dependent on it – institutionalized *social control* is among the most important contexts of categorization. Although all the social fields mentioned so far include elements of social control, specialized institutions of control such as the police, courts and other tribunals, prisons and private-sector security industries have some autonomy, if only for analytical purposes. Formal legal authority is likely to be supplemented by widespread discretion and informal practices. Categorization is significant in two mutually reinforcing respects. First, the law is never blind, anywhere. Some categories of people – and *which* categories is, in context, neither arbitrary nor random – are more likely to fall foul of it, other things being equal, than others. We know that ethnic categorization is consequential in this respect, in many different jurisdictions. Second, the social control field is itself productive of the – very consequential – categorization of both individuals and collectivities, and once again ethnicity is relevant in this respect: moral panics about the criminality of this or that ethnic group are well documented (see Hall *et al.* 1978 and Thompson 1998: 57–71, on black street crime in Britain).

Social control is the core business of the state. *Organized politics* is the source of the statutes and regulations that underwrite the legitimacy of state and other bureaucracies. In states with histories of ethnic conflict, this conflict will be mirrored in the political system. In these situations, political parties and politicians may foster ethnic categorization through public rhetoric, legislative and administrative acts and the distribution of resources via networks of clientage. Official categorization of this kind, can also, however, involve the *denial* of the existence of historically constituted ethnic groups, as in the Nazi state's refusal to acknowledge Sorbian identity in Lusatia (Burleigh and Wippermann 1991: 130–5).

Even in societies without an explicitly ethnically structured polity, similar trends may be observed, as and when the calculus of politics favours them. Rhetoric is in these cases perhaps more significant than legislation or administrative act. As moral entrepreneurs, politicians, in conjunction with newspaper proprietors, journalists and commentators, public officials and spokespersons for interest groups, may participate in the development and promotion of moral panics about ethnically constructed issues, such as immigration, black street crime (as referred to above) or 'black youth' as a general problematic category (Solomos 1988). People in these positions are influential in the public constitution of a 'problem', in its identification with particular ethnic categories (or, rather, their identification with it), and eventually in the framing of legislative and administrative responses. Less subtly, politics has historically provided the platform for the expression and mobilization of overt ethnic chauvinism; moral panics about ethnic 'problems' shade into the incitement of inter-ethnic conflict and violence.

Looking at unintended consequences, *social policy* responses to perceived social problems may also contribute to the politics of ethnic categorization. The attempt to target resources and intervention at a section of the population which is perceived to have particularly urgent or specialized 'needs' may serve either to call into existence a new social category or strengthen an existing categorization. This classification may emphasize the worthiness to receive resources of the category in question, as in the case of 'the elderly'. It may, however, identify members of the category in question as socially deficient or lacking in some fashion, and serve to label them further as 'undeserving' or 'troublesome', as in the construction and mobilization of the category of undeserving 'asylum seekers' – as opposed to deserving 'refugees' – in recent British political discourse (Sales 2002). It seems particularly likely that welfare, social inclusion and equal opportunity initiatives, and other redistributive policies, will have these effects.

Policy is intimately bound up with *official classification*, a definitive practice of the modern state (Dorling and Simpson 1999). An increasingly conventional understanding of the elaborate and pervasive schemes for classifying populations that characterize bureaucratic government is that they mark a historical shift in state approaches to social control, from the public exercise of power over the body to the private disciplining of the mind (Foucault 1979). However accurate this may in some senses be, it is worth reminding ourselves that, as in Nazi Germany, the classification of persons may be a precursor to attacks on the body. The conjunction of power and knowledge that is embodied in legitimate social categorization has many facets. Suffice it to mention two here: the first, in principle at least, benign, the second emphatically not.

The first is that indispensable adjunct to the planning processes of modern government, the census of population (Cohn 1988: 224–54; Kertzer and Arel 2002; Sundar 2000). In order to gather meaningful data, population categories must first be defined. Among these are ethnic (or 'racial') categories (Lee 1993). Thus they become established in official discourses, discourses which are powerfully constitutive of social reality through public rhetoric, the formulation of policy, the targeting of resources and social control measures. The census categories may be used to collect and construct other statistics – on crime, unemployment, health – which also feed into policy formulation and implementation. These official categorizations are not *necessarily* directly reappropriated as self- or group identifications. History, context, and, not least, the *content* and the *consequences* of the categorization, all matter. For example, the diverse membership of the 'Asian-American' category, a product of the US Census and the classificatory needs of affirmative action, have yet to be welded into anything other than a contingent, instrumental, categorical collectivity. A 'pan-ethnic' group identification remains elusive (LeEspiritu 1992). In Britain, the category 'black', favoured by some ethnic minority activists as a response to a common experience of racism, is in tension with a range of cultural and class differentiations which continue to render it a highly contested identification (Modood 1992). However, because these ethnic categories – or, indeed, the collection of the information at all – may, for a variety of reasons, be contested by the sections of the population to whom they are applied (see also Blum 2002), and the state may use them to justify consequential policy in areas such as immigration control, internal policing and collective resource allocation (Anderson and Fienberg 2000; Bhat *et al.* 1988), even census categories cannot be said to be completely irrelevant to group identifications. Their contestation and consequences may contribute, directly and indirectly, to self- and group identification.

The second point is that census and other statistics are collective and reasonably anonymous; they do not directly categorize named *individuals* (although they may feed into administrative allocation). Indeed, not many states categorize their individual citizens in this fashion. Minor examples of such an approach include the compulsory categorization and recording, for purposes of affirmative action monitoring, of the ethnic identity of employees in many US Federal, state and private-sector organizations, or the identification of 'nationality' – denoting Republic of origin – on the pre-1989 USSR internal passport. Other states, however, most notably Nazi Germany and the Republic of South Africa, having defined citizenship in terms of 'race' – a crucial escalatory move in ethnic categorization – have gone on, necessarily, to develop far-reaching systems of 'racial' categorization, governing every aspect of life (and death). The role of 'expert' knowledge in the construction of those systems and their bureaucratized administration is a grim reminder of the repressive possibilities inherent in administrative allocation (Bauman 1989; Burleigh and Wippermann 1991; Müller-Hill 1988).

This lamentable history brings me, finally, to *science*. A telling presence in many of the contexts of social categorization discussed so far, it differs from healing and medicine, for example, in at least two respects that are relevant here. It is by definition (or at least in terms of its own narratives) a *wholly* formalized – and rational or disinterested – ensemble of discourses and practices, and it is in principle concerned more with general categories than individuals.

In fact, science as applied to humans is one of the most pervasive and significant contexts of collective social categorization, at one historical period or another generating and elaborating the following powerful collective identifications: 'race'; normality, subnormality and abnormality; disability; social class; deviance; a range of mental illnesses and syndromes; a range of physical illnesses and syndromes; sexual orientation; and so on (Hacking 1990; Jenkins 1998a, 1998b). All of these become consequential – and typically far from disinterested – when turned into testable criteria of individual categorization and/or intervention (de Swaan 1990; Hanson 1993). Ethnic and 'racial' categorizations continue to figure in scientific practice, and controversies, in fields such as epidemiology (e.g. Kaplan and Bennett 2003; Kaufman and Cooper 2001).

There are many other contexts of ethnic – and indeed other – categorization to which research attention should be directed: friendship relations, education, and religion are among the possibilities. Some of the contexts I have discussed are themselves so broad – administrative allocation, for example – that they could usefully be disaggregated for the purposes of empirical research. A number of points should be remembered in any consideration of the research issues raised by this section:

- First, although my own research background may have encouraged me to draw upon illustrative material from complex, urbanized societies (and disproportionately from Europe and North America), this schematization of 'contexts of ethnic categorization' is intended to have the widest possible application. Even so, it is true that practices such as *administrative allocation*, *social policy*, *official classification* and *science* are deeply implicated in modernity. However, since modernity is now at least the medium-range context of all human life, no matter how isolated or apparently 'traditional', and states and their institutions of administration and classification are historically very long established in many parts of the world, this may not place too many constraints on the general applicability of the scheme.
- Second, categorization is unavoidable in our efforts to know and understand the human world, and in all social identification. Thus, although it may be defensible to assume, as I have done here, that ethnic categorization is disproportionately likely to be negative in its consequences (and possibly intent), there is no necessary equation between stigmatization or oppression and categorization in general. Categorization can be neutral, and it can be positive and valorizing (Jenkins 2008: Chapter 8).
- Third, the different social contexts of categorization should not be understood as separate or hierarchical 'levels'. They overlap systematically in complex and interesting ways: routine public interaction, for example, takes place within a number of the other social contexts mentioned. A similar point could be made about informal social groups, which exist within (and contribute towards the organization of) many different contexts. And so on. One important research task is to problematize and examine this mutual reinforcement.
- Fourth, the mutual reinforcement of categorization in overlapping social contexts – what once might have been called over-determination – contributes to the consequential power and resilience of particular categorizations. Categorizations such as ethnicity or 'race', which are often significant in many

social settings, may thus harden up into identifications that are robust and resistant to change (cf. Ruane and Todd 2004). This is of great importance in attempting to understand the obstinacy of racism, for example, and, as discussed in Chapter 4, the fierce persistence of ethnic attachments in some settings, even when they might not appear, to the outside eye, to be in the 'best' economic or political interests of those who identify with them.

- Finally, the dialectical implication in each other of internal and external definition, group identification and categorization, should not be forgotten. Although the discussion in this section has largely been about categorization, the social contexts identified are also significant in processes of internal definition. Given the interpenetration of the two, how could it be otherwise?

Categorization and power

Categorization contributes to group identity in various ways. There is, for example, something which might be referred to as 'internalization': the categorized group is exposed to the terms in which another group defines it and assimilates that categorization, in whole or in part, into its own identity. Put baldly, however, the suggestion seems to beg more questions than it answers: *why* should the external definition be internalized, for example, and *how* does it happen? At least five possible scenarios suggest themselves.

In the first, the external categorization might be more or less the same as an aspect of existing group identity, in which case they will simply reinforce each other. It seems altogether plausible, in fact, that some degree of external reinforcement or validation is crucial to the successful maintenance of internal (group) definitions. Similarly, categorization may be less likely to 'stick' where it is markedly at odds with existing boundaries and identifications.

Second, there is the incremental cultural change that is likely to be a product of any long-standing but relatively harmonious inter-ethnic contact. The ethnic boundary is osmotic, and not just in terms of personnel: languages and cultures may interact too, and in the process identities are likely to be affected. We, for example, may gradually and imperceptibly come to define ourselves somewhat differently in the light of how they appear to define us, and how they treat us (and, equally likely, vice versa).

In the third place, the external category is produced by Others who possess, in the eyes of the original group, the legitimate authority to categorize them, because of their superior ritual status, knowledge, or whatever. Such a situation implies greater social than cultural differentiation – if a distinction posed in these terms is admissible (Jenkins 2002a: 39–62) – inasmuch as legitimate authority necessarily requires at least a minimal degree of shared participation in values or cosmology.

Fourth is a simpler case, or at least a cruder one: external categorization is imposed by the use of physical force or its threat, i.e. the exercise of power. The experience of violation may become integral to group identification. The categorized, without the physical capacity to resist the carrying of identity cards, the wearing of armbands, or whatever more subtle devices of identification and stigmatization might be deployed, may, in time, come to see themselves in the language and categories of the oppressor. They are certainly likely to behave in an appropriate manner.

Finally, there are the oppressed who resist, who reject imposed boundaries and/or their categorical content(s). However, the very act of defying categorization, of striving for autonomous self-identification, is, of course, an effect of being categorized in the first place. The rejected external definition *is* internalized but, paradoxically, as the focus of denial.

In these five possibilities, a distinction between power and legitimate authority is apparent. However, the contribution of categorization to group identity depends upon more than 'internalization'. The capacity of one group of people to effectively define or constitute the conditions of existence experienced by Others is enormously important in the internal–external dialectic of collective identification (something similar, at the individual level, was discussed above, in the context of labelling). Categorization is consequential, and it is in the consequences that it may be most effective. This calls up the distinction I have proposed between the *virtual* and *nominal* dimensions of ethnic identification, and emphasizes the virtual.

To revisit an example given earlier, the categorization in particular ways of the Mapuche by the Spanish and white Chileans must be expected to have influenced the behaviour of the Chileans towards the Mapuche: 'native policy' as Stuchlik puts it. The Chileans, like the Spanish before them, because of their eventual monopolization of violence in the local context and their consequent control of resources, were – and, indeed, still are – in a position to make their categorization of the Mapuche count disproportionately in the social construction of Mapuche life. And the internal–external dialectic can be seen at work: resistance to the Spanish was, for example, an important factor creating internal group identification in the shape of military alliances, and generating, between the sixteenth and nineteenth centuries, a wider collectivity of 'the Mapuche' out of networks of small, mutually related kin groups (Stuchlik 1976: 15). In many senses, therefore, what it means to be a 'Mapuche' is in part a consequence of what the Spanish or the Chileans have *made* it mean.

The effective categorization of a group of people by a more powerful Other is not, therefore, 'just' a matter of classification (if, indeed, there is any such thing). It is necessarily an intervention in that group's world that will, to an extent and in ways that are a function of the specifics of the situation, alter that world and the experience of living in it. Just as the Chileans have the capacity to constitute, in part, the experience of 'being a Mapuche', so, for example, employment recruiters in Britain – who are still typically white – contribute to the social constitution of the collective experience of growing up as a member of a black ethnic minority.

To return to Barth – and Weber – here one sees the unintended consequences of action at work. It is partly in the cumulative mutual reinforcement of these unintended consequences that the patterns of history, both in the present and as a framework of constraint and possibility for future generations, are produced. Since 'culture' is a matter of everyday life and its exigencies, the power of others to constitute the experience of daily living is a further important contribution of categorization to group identity. It is also powerful support for the view of ethnic identification – as everyday practice and historical process – that I have developed here.

One of my starting points is that ethnicity should be conceptualized within a theoretical framework that allows for its integration into the topic of 'identity' in general. In its turn, however, identity must be constructed as a proper subject for theorization in a manner that allows the inclusion of individual and collective identities within a unified analytical framework (Jenkins 2008). Even the most private of identities is not imaginable as anything other than the product of a socialized consciousness and a social situation. Even the most collective of identities must, in some sense, exist in the awareness of individual actors.

Viewed in the abstract, identity – whether ethnic or otherwise – can be understood as two interacting but independent entailments: a name (the *nominal*) and an experience (the *virtual*). The latter is, in a sense, what the name *means*; this is primarily a matter of its *consequences* for those who bear it, and can change while the nominal identity remains the same (and vice versa). The nominal and the virtual unite in the ongoing production and reproduction of identity and its boundaries. The nominal–virtual distinction recognizes that ethnic identities – and, indeed, all identities – are *practical accomplishments* rather than *static forms*. They are immanently, although not necessarily, variable. As a social form – in the constitution of a historically enduring ethnic group, for example – ethnicity is always potentially variable, nominally and virtually.

In the practical accomplishment of identity, two mutually interdependent but theoretically distinct processes are at work: *internal definition* and *external definition*. These operate differently in the individual, interactional and institutional orders. Analyses of ethnicity – particularly within social anthropology – have, however, emphasized internal definition and *group identification* at the expense of external definition and *social categorization*. This is more than just a matter of empirical neglect. It is actually a lopsided understanding. Identification is always the practical product of the interaction of ongoing processes of internal *and* external definition. One cannot be understood in isolation from the other.

A concern with external definition and categorization demands, finally, that analyses of ethnicity should focus on *power* as well as on *authority*, and on the manner in which different modes of domination are implicated in the social construction of ethnic and other identities. This is not an original observation. But if we do not do this, the result is likely to be a model of ethnicity that is as trivial as it is one-sided. Unless we can construct an understanding of ethnicity that addresses *all* of ethnicity's facets and manifestations – from the celebratory communality of belonging to the final awful moment of genocide – we will have failed not only ourselves, but also the people about whom we write.

6 Ideologies of Identification

In Chapter 4 I suggested that ethnicity is a ubiquitous mode of social identification, and that homologous phenomena such as racism and nationalism can be understood as historically specific allotropes or versions of the wider principle of ethnic affiliation and classification. This chapter will explore these arguments in greater detail and will critically examine some current conceptualizations of ethnicity, racism and nationalism, and the relationships between them.

'Race' is typically differentiated from ethnicity in terms of a contrast between physical and cultural differences (Banton 1988: 1–15). Whether explicit or implicit, and however formulated, this basic model underlies most social science discussions of the topic: 'racial' differentiation is something – the contentious issue is *what* – to do with physical differences between people. However, the 'physical differences' with which we are concerned in matters of 'race' are only differences that *make* a difference because they are culturally or socially signified as such (Wade 1993, 2002). There is, therefore, nothing 'objective' about 'race'; hence the need felt by many of us to continue to hedge the word around with scare quotes.

Although it is possible to define these concepts in the above general manner, the *relationship* between 'race' and ethnicity is something about which there is little consensus and a good deal of touchiness. There may not even always be agreement that the distinction is, in itself, valid or important. In previous chapters I referred to Sandra Wallman's argument (1986: 229) that phenotype or physical appearance – and this is what is generally meant by 'race' – is no more than 'one element in the repertoire of [ethnic] boundary markers'. A perspective similar to Wallman's in many respects, although arrived at from a very different direction – 'a multiculturalist context that seeks to redress racial disadvantage by providing for ethnic difference' – is offered by Floya Anthias, who argues 'that "race" categories belong to the more encompassing category of ethnic collectivity' (1992: 421). 'Race', she suggests, is simply one of the ways in which ethnic boundaries are constructed.

There is much to be said for arguments that recognize a systematic relationship between ethnicity and 'race'; indeed, this book must be counted among them. However, the versions offered by Wallman or Anthias are unconvincing, for several reasons which I have discussed elsewhere. First, while 'ethnic' social relations are not *necessarily* hierarchical, exploitative and conflictual, 'race relations' would certainly appear to be. Although ethnic boundaries often involve relations of power, and social categorization is inherent to the internal–external dialectic of ethnic identification, hierarchical difference is not *definitive* of ethnic relations. In other words, it is possible to imagine – and, in fact, to document empirically – ethnic inter-group relations in which the groups involved neither look *up to* nor *down on* each other. Second, leaving power to one side and simply focusing on process, 'race', unlike ethnicity, seems to be much *more* a matter of social categorization than of group identification (although still a matter of both). Third, while ethnic identity is, of course, part of a structured or coherent body of knowledge about the human world – as an aspect of culture, how could it be otherwise? – 'racial' categorization often appears to be both more explicit and more elaborated in its justification. Finally, and to repeat this chapter's point of departure, regardless of whether the comparative perspective is historical or cross-cultural, ethnicity seems to be a ubiquitous social phenomenon; those situations which we describe as 'race relations' are not.

The last two points – the role of explicit justificatory knowledge, and the greater or lesser ubiquity of each – raise slippery questions about the respective ontological statuses of ethnicity and 'race', questions which lurk unacknowledged within many discussions of the problem. These are questions that are begged by the physical–cultural distinction. Furthermore, operating with a contrast between 'the physical' and 'the cultural' risks sneaking into our discussions through the back door other, even more troublesome, conceptual oppositions, such as 'objective' versus 'subjective', or 'material' versus 'ideal'. This may result in confusion, at best, and conflict about the nature of the topic under discussion, at worst.

In order to begin the work of clarification, I want to suggest that ethnic identification, although it is every bit (and only) a social and cultural construction, should be conceptualized as a basic or first-order dimension of human experience. There are three, rather different, aspects to this claim. The most general concerns the ubiquity of ethnic attachments. If we define ethnicity very broadly – as collective identification that is socially constructed with reference to putative 'cultural' similarity and difference – then it seems uncontroversial to suggest that this has probably been around for as long as cultured humans have lived in social groups. This is, however, a point of view that requires considerable care in its articulation:

> Classifying the most diverse historical forms of social identity as 'ethnic' creates the scientifically questionable but politically useful impression that all ethnicities are basically the same and that ethnic identity is a natural trait of persons and social groups … This is not an argument which bears up to historical scrutiny. Rather, it is a nominalist operation intended to provide scholarly legitimation for ethnonationalist ideologies. (Lentz 1995: 305)

This warning is important, timely, and well taken. There *is* a danger, in adopting too general a definition of ethnicity, of neutering the concept, while at the same time according it dubious extra-social potency. But to say that ethnicity seems to be one of the 'givens' of culture and human social life should *not* be misconstrued as saying that it is 'natural', other than in the sense that culture is a 'natural' propensity of humans, which, in turn, is to say little beyond problematizing the value of the culture-nature distinction (Jenkins 2002a: 111–38). To illustrate the point by analogy, the basic realities of sociality (Carrithers 1992) and the close caretaking of infants and children are ubiquitous in human experience. This doesn't mean – although it can easily be construed thus – that there are universal, and normative, patterns or forms of either.

In the same way, to argue that collective identifications and attachments based on perceived cultural differentiation appear to be historically ubiquitous is *not* to justify ethnic or nationalist excesses, along the lines of 'they – or we – can do no other'. Such an argument *is* vulnerable to politicized misrepresentation: a good example of how this can happen is the way in which Geertz's original argument about 'primordial attachments' has been academically caricatured, as discussed in Chapter 4. But while the danger of rewriting history by definitional fiat – and lending support to arguments that are not only repugnant but certainly untrue – is omnipresent, and demands that we exercise vigilance, it is not inevitable. Ethnic attachments are not necessarily malign; what matters is that we should try to understand the circumstances in which they become so.

And there is another, arguably worse, danger: of overlooking the consistency over time of the principles of collective identification and affiliation with which we are concerned and thus, in the process, misunderstanding them. Ernest Gellner – whose hostility towards nationalism can scarcely be in doubt, and who knew what its costs were – recognized this in his discussion of the loyalty that people feel for the groups to which they belong and the fact that they identify with them:

> If one calls this factor, generically, 'patriotism', then ... some measure of such patriotism is indeed a perennial part of human life ... nationalism is a very distinct species of patriotism. (1983: 138)

If we do not acknowledge a very general, ideal-typical model of something that we can call 'ethnicity' – which, witness Barth's 'the social organization of culture difference', for example, will necessarily be imprecise – how are we in principle to distinguish ethnic attachments from kinship, neighbourhood or organizational attachments, for example, and how, correspondingly, can we compare different 'ethnic' situations?

The second aspect of the claim that ethnicity should be understood as a basic dimension of social life alludes to taken-for-grantedness and embeddedness. Ask the question: what is it that constructs ethnic identification? At least part of the answer has got to be *culture*. While Hughes and Barth are absolutely correct to insist that cultural traits don't constitute ethnic difference, Handelman (1977) and, more recently, Cornell and Hartmann (Cornell 1996; Cornell and Hartmann 1998: 173–84) are equally correct to remind us that the 'cultural stuff' is not irrelevant either, a point of view that is also strongly implied by the 'ethnicity as cognition' arguments of Brubaker (2004: 64–87; Brubaker *et al.* 2004) and Levine (1999). And *our* culture – language, non-verbals, dress, food, the structure of space, etc. – as we encounter it and live it during socialization and subsequently, is *for us* simply something that *is*. When identity is problematized during interaction across the boundary, we have to make explicit – to ourselves as much as to Others – that which we have hitherto known without *knowing about*. This is what Bourdieu (1990: 53–97) calls *habitus*, the embodied and unreflexive everyday practical mastery of culture: unsystematic, the empire of habit, neither conscious nor unconscious. Nothing could be more basic and nothing more inextricably implicated in ethnicity (Bentley 1987).

In the third place, however, a great deal turns upon local histories, circumstances and situations. This, again, is to return to an earlier thread of my argument: ethnic attachments do not have the same salience and force everywhere, or for everyone. Experience, if nothing else, insists that this is the case. For many people(s), ethnicity is a background factor, part of the cultural furniture of everyday life, and consequently little attended to. But for many others ethnicity is an integral and dynamic aspect of self-conscious selfhood and everyday discourse, rooted in early socialization and produced and reproduced in the ongoing concerns of the here-and-now. Ethnicity may have an individual psycho-social *reality*, which bestows upon it a particular immediacy and compelling urgency (and the word *may* is the most important word in this sentence). This capacity for ethnic identity to *really* matter – *when* it matters – is what Geertz was suggesting in his characterization of ethnicity as a primordial attachment. Geertz is talking about what people *feel*, as is Walker Connor in describing the 'ethnonational bond' as 'beyond reason' (1993). Similarly, John Rex has argued that ethnicity differs in this sense from group membership based on interpersonal obligation, cultural rules or shared interests (1991: 10–12). Ethnic identity may be imagined, but it is emphatically not imaginary; locally that imagining may be very powerful.

As I have argued in Chapter 4 and elsewhere, taking seriously the notion that ethnicity may be a primary – rather than a 'primordial' – social identity doesn't mean abandoning the social constructionist understanding of ethnicity, or naturalizing it in the manner of evolutionary psychology or sociobiology (van den Berghe 1981, 1986). It does allow us, however, to appreciate one of the important differences between 'race' and ethnic identity. If ethnic identity is basic to the human condition, in the sense towards which I am feeling my way here, 'race' is not. And if ethnicity is arguably a basic, universal facet of the human cultural repertoire, ideas about 'race' are not. 'Racial' categories are second-order cultural creations or notions; they are abstractions, explicit bodies of knowledge that are very much more the children of specific historical circumstances, typically territorial expansion and attempted imperial or colonial domination. 'Racial' categorization has had a shorter and more patchy history than ethnic identity.

Furthermore, and again in contrast to ethnicity, because of its genesis in systematic domination, and the specifically 'physical' referents which endow it with putative immutability, 'race' may be an aspect of identity which children acquire in strikingly different patterns of acceptance or rejection, depending upon whether they belong to 'racially' stigmatized categories or not (Milner 1975: 35–100; Troyna and Hatcher 1992: 19–23). Lest this last point be misunderstood as entailing some kind of deterministic inevitability – and remembering that 'race' is every bit as socially constructed as ethnicity – the internalization of a negative self-image or the rejection of 'racial' stigmatization also depends on the contributions which schooling, familial socialization and the politics of resistance can make to the production and promotion of countervailing positive images and experiences (Stone 1981: 44–89). The point in this context is that routine primary socialization, in the context of ethnically marked shared 'culture', generally provides, as a matter of course and almost incidentally, an implicit repertoire of positivity – embodied in language, religion, kinship institutions, etc. – on which to draw, if appropriate, in order to resist subordination and denigration. The same is not necessarily true about 'race'.

None of this, of course, is to deny the possible significance that aspects of physical appearance (phenotype) can possess as ethnic boundary markers. However, phenotype and 'race' should not, as in the quotation below, be conflated:

> when 'race' is used in everyday discourse, it is usually to refer to or to signify the
> existence of phenotypical variation, that is, variations in skin colour, hair type,

bone structure and so on … What exists is not 'race' but phenotypical variation: 'race' is a word used to describe or refer to such variation. (Miles 1982: 20)

The relationship between 'race' and phenotype cannot possibly be this neat. For example, visible phenotypical differences – such as hair colour, perhaps – may be invoked in ethnic identification without ideas about 'race' also being invoked. On the other hand, putative 'racial' differentiation may be categorically asserted on the basis of physical differences that are either invisible to the unassisted naked eye – cranial indices are an obvious example here – or utterly imaginary. Finally – and Miles seems, paradoxically, to recognize this himself when he says that one does not exist but the other does – phenotype and 'race' are different orders of thing: phenotype is the material product of the interaction of genetic endowment (genotype) and environment; 'race' is a cultural fiction.

Other authors can appear to be just as confused. Thus Wade, criticizing 'the seemingly unexceptional approach' of Banton and Rex, argues that their work,

poses it [i.e. phenotype] as an obvious objective biological fact when in fact it is a highly socially constructed one. For it is not just *any* phenotypical variation that has become racialised (in any of the changing definitions of race), but a specific set of variations that have become salient in long-term colonial encounters. (Wade 1993: 21)

Phenotype cannot, on the one hand, be 'highly socially constructed' and, on the other, the range of physiological variations – as implied by 'not just *any* phenotypical variation' – out of which specific sets are historically selected for attention. Wade has subsequently tried to clarify this issue, but he still leaves us with a tension between the socially constructed 'phenotype that is taken to underlie race' and phenotype as 'all aspects of appearance – actually it includes even more than that' (Wade 2002: 4). At best, one appears to be more socially constructed than the other. Perhaps the real message here is that the concept of the 'phenotype', given its biological origins and meaning, does not have anything useful to offer the social science of 'race'.

While I might not want to go all the way with Banton in arguing that 'there is no distinctive class of social relations to be identified as racial relations' (1986: 49), his viewpoint resonates with that which I am suggesting here. To express that point of view in another way, ethnicity and 'race' are different kinds of concept, they do not actually constitute a true pair. To oppose the one to the other does not, therefore, seem to make much sense. The most that can be said is that, at certain times and in certain places, culturally specific notions of 'race' – or, more correctly, of 'racial' differentiation – feature, sometimes very powerfully, in the repertoire of ethnic boundary-maintaining devices; for a recent study of the racialization of contemporary Welsh identity, for example, see the work of Scourfield *et al.* (2006; Scourfield and Davies 2005). To anticipate my argument below, and in general agreement with Robert Miles (1989), it is racialization and racism – or, to anticipate myself even further, racism*s* – to which we should be attending, rather than 'race'.

Does it matter that we should agree on the nature of the difference between 'race' and ethnicity? Perhaps not, but it is certainly more than a 'quibble', and it is important to attempt to be clear about the matter. The issue has probably been responsible for even more confusion, and generated greater imbalances between heat and light, than the tussle between primordialists and situationalists. Consider, for example, the problem into which Anthias finds herself led when she argues that:

> racisms do not rely only on 'race' categorisation, but use the ethnic category more generally as their essential building block. The historical manifestations of racism, however, are linked to a diversity of economic and political projects and do not, therefore, emanate exclusively from ethnic processes ... A group does not have to be depicted as a 'race' ... to be subjected to racist practices or effects. My view is that all those exclusionary practices that are formulated on the basis of the categorisation of individuals into groups, whereby ethnic or 'racial' origin are criteria of access or selection, are endemically racist. (1992: 422, 433)

Her basic project, to take the relationship between 'race' and ethnicity seriously without reifying either concept, is worthwhile, but words are here in danger of becoming too empty of meaning to have any continuing usefulness. However, this quotation does remind us of the importance of social categorization in matters of ethnic and 'racial' identity, and it is to this that I now turn (with apologies for a small amount of inescapable repetition).

Group identification and social categorization (again...)

Barth's argument that ethnicity is transactional, and may be situational or changeable, does not necessarily – although it might seem to (Rex 1986: 26) – conflict with a view of ethnicity as a basic or first-order social identity, rooted in the fertile earth of early socialization. Just as ethnic identity may be more or less negotiable in some situations than in others, so specific ethnic identities, depending upon history and ongoing events, may be 'weaker' or 'stronger'. Sometimes ethnicity may take its place alongside the primary identities of humanness, gender and individual selfhood (Jenkins 2008: Chapters 6 and 7); in other local contexts it will matter less. To argue that ethnic identity is a basic or first-order dimension of the cultural experience of being human is not to deny either the likelihood of variation in its affective urgency and immediacy, or the possibility of its manipulation and negotiation.

As argued in detail in the previous chapter, the transactions during which ethnicity is produced and reproduced have two complementary characters. First, there is *internal definition*: actors, whether as individuals or in groups, define their own identity. Although conceptualized as internal, these processes are necessarily interactional because, even in the case of the introspection of the solitary individual, they are predicated upon the assumption of an audience, even if only 'at some point', and – otherwise we could not talk about ethnicity – derive their meanings from a socially constructed cultural repertoire. Second, there is *external definition*. This is the definition of the identity of other people: it may be as simple and straightforward as the validation of the others' internal definition(s) of themselves, and as complex and conflictual as the attempt by one actor or set of actors to impose an identity on another.

External definition cannot, even in theory, be a solitary act. For one thing, more than just an audience is involved: the others here are *object(s)*, and a meaningful

acting *upon* their lives is implied. For another, the capacity to impose one's definition of the situation upon other people implies that one possesses sufficient power
or authority to do so. We can only talk about power in the context of social relations;
similarly, authority, by definition, can only be said to exist in its legitimation by others (Smith 1960: 15–33). Relations of power and authority provide one connection
between ethnic identification, on the one hand, and social class and gender, on the
other. In that they are important principles of hierarchical social differentiation in
most social contexts, gender and access to economic resources are likely to permit
or obstruct the ability of one actor or set of actors to effectively categorize others.

The distinction between internal and external processes of identification is largely
in the eye of the analytical beholder. In everyday life internal and external definition
are routinely and chronically implicated in each other, in a dialectic of identification.
Categorizing 'them' is part of defining 'us'; our identification of 'us' is entailed in and
by a history of relationships with significant others (Hagendoorn 1993). To recognize
this is, of course, to return to Barth's original argument, and to 'shift the focus of
investigation from internal constitution and history of separate groups to ethnic
boundaries and boundary maintenance' (Barth 1969a: 10).

In terms of collectivities, a group is internally defined and a category externally
defined. In their everyday social interaction people systematically classify themselves and others. They distinguish, in doing so, between identities that are self-
generated and those that are other-imposed. An example of the difference between
social groups and social categories might be the transition from *Gemeinschaft* (the
mechanical solidarity of community) to *Gesellschaft* (associational organic solidarity) identified by Tonniës and Durkheim. This historical shift can be understood in
two different ways, depending upon one's perspective on modernity and progress.
From one point of view, it is a change from a society in which the primary loci of
identification lay in ascribed, *categorical* identities of various kinds, to one in which
relatively free association on the basis of elective self-identification has assumed
greater importance. From the other, we see a move away from the local intimacies
of the communal *group*, to the anonymity of a mass society in which relationships
between people are mediated by market relationships and self-interest.

So, while social groups define themselves, their name(s), their nature(s) and their
boundary(ies), social categories are named, characterized and delineated by others.
However, the plausibility of both interpretations of the transition from
Gemeinschaft to *Gesellschaft* outlined above, suggests – once again, *pace* Barth –
that social collectivities are actually shaped, to greater or lesser degrees, by a combination of group identification and social categorization. Each is simultaneously
implicated in the other; social identity is produced and reproduced in the dialectic of internal *and* external definition. Whether, in any particular case, one talks
about a group or a category will depend upon an assessment of the *(im)balance*
which has been struck between internal and external processes in any local case.

Ethnicity and 'race'

To return to the subtlety and awkwardness of the relationship between ethnicity
and 'race', the distinction between groups and categories may be able to illuminate

the problem further. Banton, for example, has argued that, 'Membership in an ethnic group is usually voluntary; membership in a racial group is not' (1983: 10). Ethnicity is thus about inclusion (*us*), while 'race' is about exclusion (*them*): group identification as opposed to social categorization.

This is a plausible way of looking at things, which makes sense of much of the difference between 'race' and ethnicity. However, at least two qualifications of Banton's argument are necessary. First, I have argued that processes of group identification and categorization are routinely and reciprocally implicated in each other. It may be possible to *characterize* this situation or that as one or the other, but it can never be more than a matter of *emphasis*. Defining 'them' in terms of 'race' may be an important dimension of our definition of 'us' (which will, accordingly, carry some 'racial' charge). Some groups may, therefore, identify themselves – 'us' – in positive 'racial' terms. Among the most obvious recent historical examples of this are the *Herrenvolk* ideology in Nazi Germany and its close cousin in Nationalist South Africa, but something similar also seems to characterize some strands of contemporary Israeli Jewish identity, for example, or 'black nationalism' in the United States and elsewhere. As the latter cases suggest, group identification in terms of 'race' may represent the historical negation of a powerful negative 'racial' categorization, by reworking it as a positively valorized identity.

The second difficulty with Banton's formula is that many models of 'them' are hostile ethnic categorizations that do not appear to involve the ascription of 'racial' differentiation in any clear-cut sense. Here, however, it may be important to remember that, particularly in Europe and the United States, 'racial' rhetoric has been publicly disreputable since the Second World War. The 'ethnic cleansing' of the 1990s would probably have been described differently in 1940. Which, of course, is another reminder that 'racial' classifications are no less culturally signified and socially constructed than ethnic identities: 'race', in particular, is very much a product of the ebb and flow of history (Banton 1998; Burleigh and Wippermann 1991; Dikötter 1992, 1997; Fenton 1999; Ringer 1983; Wade 1993, 2002).

At this point, there is a further definitional question to be asked: what do we mean when we talk about racism? It is important to acknowledge that there is no consensus about the word's suitability, or even about its acceptability for the purposes of academic discourse. Even though I cannot agree with Banton in suggesting that 'It is possible to discuss the sociology of race relations without using the word "racism"' (1988: 28), he is correct in counselling caution about our use of the word (1983: 1–3). He argues, first, that the word's various political connotations and its epithetical status are apt to promote and conceal vague and unsystematic thinking. Second, he suggests that the use of one totalizing word overlooks what may be significant differences between different places and times: different phenomena may become lumped together under one, crude, rubric.

Banton's first point is well taken, although he does not suggest that the problem he identifies is inevitable. His second reservation, however, is even more substantial. To rephrase his objection, the concept of racism reifies what may be a set of historically specific, if perhaps broadly similar, ideologies under the umbrella of a concept that, supposedly, is capable of consistent and rigorous definition and, consequently, application in all circumstances:

> Once people slip into the assumption that racism or capitalism or communism exist in the sense that, say, influenza exists, then they are led into one trap after

another. One such error is to overlook differences between historical periods. (Banton 1983: 3)

This is partly right and partly wrong. It is right inasmuch as differences between times and places are significant and should not be overlooked. It is wrong inasmuch as the attempt to define a general ideal-typical model of racism does not necessarily depend upon the kind of crude positivism which the remark about influenza lampoons; it is, in fact, a necessary prerequisite for the successful comparative study of racism*s*. But how should such an ideal type be formulated?

There are – and, indeed, what else would one expect? – almost as many definitions of racism as there are people writing about it (for good surveys, see Back and Solomos 2000, Bulmer and Solomos 1999). At the risk of oversimplifying the matter, it is possible to identify a number of options (or, perhaps more accurately, issues):

- *either* (1) racism is a set of organized beliefs about 'racial' categories and their inferiority or superiority, which people consciously hold and can, to some degree, articulate; *or* (2) racism exists in institutional arrangements and practices which have systematically detrimental outcomes or consequences for 'racial' categories, rather than in consciously held beliefs, attitudes or values;
- and *either* (3) racism involves categorization on the basis of purported biological differences; *or* (4) racism involves categorization on the basis of any set of criteria which will allow difference to be asserted.

Choosing between these options and their possible combinations is not straightforward. It may be possible to concede that they all have their uses. The one point about which I feel confident enough to be definite concerns options (1) and (2), above (cf. Jenkins 1986a: 5–6). The *intention* to discriminate against or otherwise disadvantage 'racially' categorized others need not actually be present for racism to be identified (and not only because intentions are, ultimately, unknowable). A *consciousness* of 'racial' categorization – explicit classificatory and evaluative knowledge – and the differential *treatment* of those who are categorized thus, are surely, however, prerequisites of racism. The epistemological and other problems that are raised immediately by option (2) are enormous. To suggest that racism is not, somehow, at least a part of what people know and can talk about is to locate it *where* in the human world? If racism is not cognitive and discursive, it is difficult – and thoroughly unrewarding – to imagine what its ontological status might be.

My argument is that racism(s) and categories of 'racial' classification and differentiation are most usefully conceptualized as historically specific allotropes of the general, ubiquitous, social phenomenon of ethnicity. They arise in the context of situations in which one ethnic group dominates, or attempts to dominate, another and, in the process, categorizes them in terms of notional immutable differences, often couched in terms of inherent inferiority and construed as rooted in different biological natures. The recognition that, as in the 'new racism' identified by Martin Barker (1981), the rhetoric of *inferiority* may in specific circumstances be downplayed or abandoned, in favour of apparently less malign notions of *difference*, is important (see also Baumann 1996; Brah 1996; Gilroy 1987). It is socially constructed images of *immutable difference* – and neither word is more important than the other here – which are at the heart of the matter.

The usefulness of 'racial' categorization for the legitimation of colonial or imperial conquest and domination probably cannot be overemphasized. There are, however, other kinds of ethnic legitimation. One such is nationalism (Calhoun 1997; Day and Thompson 2004; McCrone 1998). Defined as a political philosophy, insisting that the combined rights to exclusive occupation of territory and freedom from alien rule are embodied in the existence of a distinctive national community of culture and, usually, language, it is understood by many commentators as a historically specific phenomenon, with its roots in the bourgeois revolutions of modern Europe (Anderson 1983; Gellner 1983; Hobsbawm 1990). Nationalism in this sense is about hegemony; the object of legitimation is, at least in part, the *internal* hierarchy of industrial society (i.e. class). An imagined community of national similarity and inclusion – based on cultural homogeneity – is created and invoked to justify or camouflage the exclusion by a new dominant bourgeoisie of another new class of urban, industrial workers.

To say the least, this seems a little too straightforward. Anthony Smith is surely correct to insist (1986, 1994) that nationalism also has deeper historical roots, in ethnic communality. A useful distinction might perhaps be drawn here between *nationalism* and *national identity* (Smith 1991). It is in the urgency and immediacy of national identity, Gellner's 'patriotism', that one source of the power of nationalism to mobilize populations lies. The call to arms on behalf of 'blood and belonging' that nationalism is, *in some circumstances*, able to issue should not be underestimated (Bauman 1992; Ignatieff 1994). Nationalism has stoked the fires of national identity in the many conflicts that have resulted from post-colonial attempts at nation-building in the third world, and in those which, during the 1990s, seriously threatened – and may yet threaten again – attempts to construct a viable geo-political framework for post-communist eastern Europe. It is currently doing the same thing in the Middle East. What's more, the apparently comfortable fit between nationalism's 'constructed primordiality' and modern state-building – or, to put this another way, between ethnicity and citizenship – helps us to understand nationalism's obstinate potency in the modern world, despite the many confident declarations of its decline or imminent demise (e.g. Gellner 1983: 121; Hobsbawm 1990: 164–83).

Ideologies of identification

National identity and nationalism involve, almost by definition, group identification and social categorization, inclusion and exclusion. Whatever they may be, they are perhaps most usefully regarded, therefore – and in much the same way as 'race' and racism – as a historically specific manifestation of ethnicity. However, racism and nationalism have something else, which is both elusive and obvious, in common. They are both -*isms*: relatively coherent, if not necessarily explicitly organized or consistent, understandings of the world, which are integral aspects of specific social identities and which serve to identify individuals and groups and to locate them in the human world.

In a word, racism and nationalism are both *ideologies*. They are bodies of knowledge – a word that in this context denotes neither validity nor reliability – which

Basis of identification	Ideology
Kinship	Familism
Co-residence	Communalism
Co-residence	Localism
Co-residence	Regionalism
Ethnicity	Ethnicism
Ethnicity/Nationality	Nationalism
Ethnicity/'Race'	Racism

Figure 6.1 Identification and ideology

make claims about the way the world *is* and, crucially, about the way it *ought* to be. This knowledge is mobilized in the definition of criteria of group membership and principles of exclusion. It specifies the rights and duties that attach to membership, and the forms of treatment that it is appropriate to extend to non-members. These are bodies of *political* knowledge, oriented towards the systematic constitution of the world in particular ways and the advancement of sectional interests.

The question arises of the relationship between ethnicity, including 'race' and national identity, and other forms of identification, with their attendant ideologies. A partial list of these – excluding, for reasons of limitations on space, class, gender, humanity, and doubtless others – is presented schematically in Figure 6.1. There is a hierarchical overlap between different bases of identification and their attendant ideologies. For example, kinship, because of the coincidence of descent and residence in many societies, may be associated with localism. Similarly, co-residence may generate both localism and regionalism; ethnicity may be bound up with regionalism, ethnicism *and* nationalism. Nationality, in its turn, may in some circumstances be as likely to find its ideological expression in racism as in nationalism.

As discussed in Chapter 4 and illustrated in Figure 4.1, the taxonomic logic of ethnic identity is basically hierarchical. One metaphor for illustrating this is the Russian doll set: inside each doll nestles a smaller doll. Imagine each succeeding doll dressed in different national, ethnic and local costumes, as the focus of identification becomes more and more particularized. However, it can never really be anything like this simple: as was also discussed in Chapter 4, ethnicity overlaps with a hierarchy of other sources of identification, each with its own possibilities for inclusion and exclusion. How these relate to each other must in the first place be a matter for empirical exploration rather than theoretical specification.

Most of the ideologies of identification listed in Figure 6.1 will be familiar in one form or another, in that they have accepted usages in the social science literature. The one exception to this is, interestingly enough, 'ethnicism'. In part, this reflects the fact that we use 'ethnicity' to refer to both a source or 'kind' of social identification *and* its attendant ideology. It may also, however, be the case that when faced with an ethnic ideology – an ethnicism – our response is to identify it as either nationalism or racism. Hence the coining of hybrid terms such as 'ethnic nationalism' (Smith 1991: 79–84) when, really, it is hard to imagine a nationalism that is not, in some sense, 'ethnic'. Similar conceptual redundancy is suggested by the notion of 'ethno-regionalism' (Hechter and Levi 1979).

A specific example of the kind of confusion produced by the absence of an ideological model of ethnicity is, perhaps, the argument about whether the Northern Ireland conflict is a 'race relations' situation (McKernan 1982; Moore 1972; Nelson 1975) or a case of racism (Brewer 1992; Clayton 1996: 50–83; Miles 1996). The most obvious problem here is the ethnic ideology of Protestant loyalism. Loyalism is not *obviously* nationalist: that particular high ground has been claimed by its opponents, and for that reason, if no other, loyalists are, it seems, reluctant to identify themselves thus. Much depends here upon our definition of nationalism – Finlayson, for example, has argued (1996) that Northern Irish Protestant ideology is a nationalist discourse – and our preparedness to overlook local definitions of the situation. Even allowing for those considerations, loyalism cannot, by default, simply be removed to the other obviously available category, i.e. racism (which is not to deny that Ulster loyalists may *also* be racist). Ethnicity is so often celebrated as a positively 'good thing' – by obvious and explicit contrast with the evils of racism (there is more ambivalence about nationalism) – that there may be some reluctance to acknowledge its ideological and conflictual possibilities, which are, as a consequence, easily interpretable as reflections of either racism or nationalism.

A reconsideration of the relationships between ethnicism, nationalism and racism is overdue. If we conclude that 'ethnicism' does not hold much water as a working concept – perhaps because of its over-generality or lack of specificity – then the continued utility of the attendant concept of 'ethnicity' must perhaps also be regarded as problematic. More likely, however, is a solution to the problem that will encourage us to draw finer distinctions between ideologies of identification than we do at present. Such an exercise will also necessarily involve the drawing of empirically grounded analytical distinctions between, for example, various ethnicism*s*, nationalism*s* and racism*s* (Balibar 1991). As matters stand at present, our concepts may, in some cases – and racism *as a generic term* is the most obvious example here, since the word is constructed as much for purposes political as analytical – be too crude or monolithic to be of more than limited value, particularly for comparative analysis and research.

One last characteristic of ideology is also important. Ideology tells us how the world is, and how it ought to be. Let us concentrate on the last part of that definition. In part, it tells us how *we* ought to be. In this sense, our ideologies may be burdensome to us. This is, indeed, how many people experience nationalism, or ethnicism: as a constant social pressure, a collective impetus towards a degree of belonging or conformity with which they do not feel comfortable. And there is also, of course, the matter of how *they* ought to be. In this, the inherent categorizing and imperial potentialities of ideology reveal themselves most clearly. Ideology and categorization are perhaps something more than merely logically related.

In this chapter I have been working towards clarification, rather than aiming for definitive conclusions. Some areas of conceptual confusion have been identified and a beginning made on their disentanglement. I have suggested the usefulness to our thinking about ethnicity and 'race' of three theoretical moves.

The first is to reconcile the situationalist view of ethnicity, inspired by Barth, with the emphasis on primordialism, and the power of belief, suggested by Geertz. This analytical move prepares the ground for a possibly imprecise but nonetheless plausible distinction between ethnicity and 'race' in terms of historical ubiquity and affective immediacy. By this token, ethnicity and 'race' do not, strictly speaking, appear to be the same order of social phenomena, in much the same way, perhaps, that diamond or graphite are not the same 'thing' as carbon.

The second move is to differentiate between internal processes of group identification and external processes of social categorization. Each is chronically and inextricably implicated in the other in the production and reproduction of identity. Although ethnic identity and 'race' both involve internal identification and external categorization, the emphasis in each may fall on a different moment of the dialectic of identification.

The final move is to differentiate between social identities and their attendant ideologies of identification. This encourages the acknowledgement of a neglected area of concern: ethnic ideologies that are neither racist nor nationalist in their primary orientation. It also allows the adoption of a comparative and historical perspective – upon racisms rather than racism, nationalisms rather than nationalism, and ethnicisms rather than ethnicism – without sacrificing the small amount of general ideal-typical theoretical continuity that such comparisons demand.

Explorations

The chapters that follow are not, in any deliberate sense, intended to exemplify the arguments that I have developed in the first section of the book. If nothing else, this is true because they present arguments in their own right. They are certainly no less argumentative or theoretical than Chapters 1–6. Chronologically, their original writing took place alongside – in and out of – the others, and they belong to the same flow of work. In contrast to those earlier chapters, they explore their arguments through engagement with the historical and ethnographic detail of actual places and settings. This creates a different feel – it is another way of writing altogether – and a different style. The two sections – arguments and explorations – are complementary strategies for exploring the same issues.

The exploration of material about Northern Ireland, Wales and Denmark follows the evolution of my research interests over the last thirty years. That evolution has, if I am being perfectly honest, been shaped at least as much by serendipity and biography as by a long-term intellectual project. My interest in these places does have a bearing on one of my general arguments – that ethnicity is not to be restricted to 'them' or to the exotic Other – but this is not *why* I find them so interesting. It might be more accurate to suggest that my personal interest in Northern Ireland, Wales and Denmark is responsible for my appreciation of the everyday, non-Otherness of ethnicity and the issues that it raises. Similarly, my interest in why and how ethnicity *matters* to people has emerged out of my experiences in these places, as, too, have the comparative explorations of nationalism in Chapters 9 and 10.

Northern Ireland is not the easiest place in the world about which to write. The politics of writing – of naming, of identification, of categorization – are sensitive. In particular, I know that my consistent use of the geo-political expression 'Northern Ireland' – rather than its alternatives, such as 'the six counties', 'the north of Ireland', 'Ulster', or whatever – will annoy some readers. This form of naming has, however, the merits of reflecting much everyday practice in the place itself, of being in accord with present international usage (which includes Dublin), and of indicating clearly the formal nature of the political beast about which I am talking.

Finally, one last difference between making theoretical arguments and exploring evidence is worth mentioning. More than any other kind of writing, exploration is provisional; the account always remains open. These chapters were written – and subsequently revised for the second edition – in this spirit. It is also how I would like them to be read.

7 Majority Ethnicity

Ethnicity is not a peculiar attribute of minorities, nor is it restricted to exotic Others. This chapter looks at a politically dominant and self-conscious ethnic *majority* – Northern Irish Protestants and, particularly, the Northern Irish Protestant élite – and how, during a long history of conflict, they have mobilized and manipulated ethnicity and exploited ethnic communality to their advantage. During the modern history of Ireland, Protestants have been a numerical minority within the island's population, so this may appear to be an odd understanding of the situation.[1] There are, however, three senses in which Ulster Protestants should be seen as a majority. First, they are, and have been since the territory's creation, a majority within the six counties of Northern Ireland. Second, for most of the history of 'English' or 'British' Ireland Protestants were a political majority, in the sense that they unambiguously held power. Third, for most of the time since the seventeenth century they have been allied with – and, at least in some senses, part of – a dominant, metropolitan Anglo-Saxon majority within the British Isles (Hechter 1975).

In looking at the mobilization and manipulation of ethnicity, I am drawing on that strand of the anthropological model which emphasizes that ethnicity is a social *resource*, to be drawn upon or exploited in varying contexts. However, inasmuch as most anthropological studies of ethnicity in 'Western' societies have looked at minority situations, they have tended to underplay the salience of other factors, such as class in particular and the social construction of power relationships in general. At best, factors such as these, where they are acknowledged, are typically treated as external 'structure', impinging on on the people studied as more-or-less distant constraints on their lives (Davis 1975; Grillo 1980). Inasmuch as sociology has, for various reasons, moved away somewhat from class analysis during the last two decades, and anthropology has concentrated ever more firmly on 'culture', this blind spot has probably got worse. To understand Northern Ireland, where state and economy were constructed by and in the social relationships between a dominant ethnic group and a subordinated ethnic group, and between the local majority and an external metropolitan power, a less abstract understanding of state and economy is necessary.

Another central focus of the anthropology of ethnicity has been its concern with the maintenance of *boundaries* between ethnic groups. This research orientation has led to many insights, not the least of which being that ethnicity is essentially relative, its nature shifting with the contexts of its mobilization. And this chapter will maintain that perspective: ethnicity is a function of inter-group relations; in the absence of such relations and their concomitant group boundaries ethnicity is unthinkable. But most of my attention here is elsewhere: on the mobilization of ethnicity as a resource by a dominant élite, in their strategies for the internal control of their own class-stratified ethnic group. Thus the focus of attention is to some extent shifted from *inter*-group to *intra*-group relationships.

In terms of the themes I am exploring in this book, this chapter is concerned with power relations, and with the interweaving of ethnicity with other social identifications, in this case, class. Together with the discussions of religion in Chapter 8 and state formation in Chapter 9, my approach is in broad harmony, even if not always detailed agreement, with the historical model proposed by Ruane and Todd (1996), in which five 'dimensions of difference' – *religion* (Catholic/Protestant), *ethnicity* (Gaelic Irish/Old English/English/Scottish), *colonialism* (native/settler), *civility* (barbarous/civilized) and *politics* (Irish-nationalist/British-unionist) – have, since the first English conquest of parts of Ireland, unfolded, interacted and played out over different time-scales and during different periods. These ways of looking at the situation offer a nuanced framework within which to begin to understand the complexities of Northern Ireland.

The foundations of modern Ulster ethnicity: the Plantation

For our purposes, the history of the Northern Irish Protestant community may be traced back to the Ulster Plantation of the first decades of the seventeenth century. Although there had been some earlier colonization of the counties of Antrim and Down by Scottish settlers, the Plantation marks the beginning of a long history that leads to the present – for they cannot *yet* be said to be over – 'troubles'. Here are 'the colonial roots of antagonism' (O'Leary and McGarry 1996: 54–106). It was nothing less than an attempt at the wholesale de- and re-population of the north of Ireland. The established inhabitants – Gaelic in language and culture, Catholic in religion, and resistant to rule from London, or, indeed, Dublin – were to be replaced by 'planting' Anglophone, Protestant, loyal settlers in their stead.

Originally envisaged as an essentially military adventure, to secure the hitherto rebellious earldoms of Tyrconnel and Tyrone for the English crown, the scheme acquired a commercial orientation very early on. Following an agreement between the crown and the corporation of the City of London, the latter set up a joint-stock enterprise:

> to plant the country of Coleraine, and to rebuild and fortify its two main towns, Coleraine and Derry. In return, they were to receive extensive privileges, including the patronage of all churches within their territory, the fisheries of the Foyle and the Bann, and a long lease of the customs at a nominal rent. (Beckett 1966: 46)

The links of commerce thereby established between the province and the mainland set the pattern for much of Ulster's subsequent history. However, the relative geographical isolation caused by the Irish Sea, and the differences from the rest of Ireland which I shall discuss below, were also to set a pattern for the north-eastern counties. The history of the Protestants of the province since the Plantation is a curious mixture of insularity and backwardness contrasted with varying degrees of incorporation into the political, cultural and economic mainstreams of Britain.

Throughout the rest of Ulster, the Plantation took on a similar character to that described above, either directly initiated by the government in London or encouraged by them at one remove through 'undertakers' or agencies such as the London Company. In Antrim and Down, however, following the government-approved dismemberment of Con O'Neill's Clandeboye estates, the Plantation became more a matter for private adventurers. Here, in particular, the Plantation acquired a distinctly Scottish character, in contrast to the strong English influences at work further west.

As a result of this colonization there developed a series of marked differences between Ulster and the rest of the island. There one saw the development of an essentially rural and agricultural society, based on commercially oriented tenant farmers, with an intensive subsistence peasantry on the western margins. In the north-east there eventually developed, by contrast, an urban and industrial society, based in the first place on smallholdings leased from the undertakers by the colonist yeomanry and small tenantry, many of whom had a background in the textile industry then emerging on the other side of the Irish Sea (Crotty 1966; Cullen 1969; Gibbon 1975: 9–12).

One of the original aims of the Plantation, and in this its military origins reveal themselves, was the physical removal of most of the native Irish population from the best areas in the north. In this aim the Plantation failed, however, and this for at least two reasons. First, many of the colonists, in particular those holding large estates, were happy to find (Catholic Irish) tenants available on the spot and took advantage of their continued presence. Second, the Irish who were to be moved frequently resisted, as is witnessed by the planter's need for fortified houses or 'bawns'. The 'final solution' to the Ulster problem was not to work as well in practice as its architects in London had expected.

Nonetheless, although many or most of the former inhabitants remained, things had changed dramatically for them, and changed for the worse. Within twenty years, at the beginning of the seventeenth century, all of their customary rights to land and property vanished; in effect, they became aliens in their own country. A few, a very few, either retained their status or were granted new lands, but they constituted a tiny minority:

> The great mass of Ulster Irish remained on their former lands, but degraded to the status of tenants-at-will. As they became increasingly impoverished, economic pressure tended to drive them out of the more fertile and into the worst lands, where their descendants are still to be found. (Moody 1974: 5)

In 1641 the fruits of this policy towards the native Irish ripened into rebellion. Led by Sir Phelim O'Neill, and spurred on by fear of a Puritan-dominated House of Commons at Westminster, the Ulster Catholics rose up in revolt. Eight years later Oliver Cromwell arrived in Dublin and by 1652 the rebellion was over. The Irish were punished severely, by confiscation of most of their remaining land and by deportation. The result of the 1641 rebellion was the consolidation of the original aims of the Plantation and the commercial domination of Ireland by the settlers, particularly in the north-east and the towns.

The end of the century saw further violence, most notably the siege of Derry in 1689 and William's defeat of the Jacobite army at the battle of the Boyne in 1690.

The Treaty of Limerick in 1691 and the flight of the 'Wild Geese' to France signalled the final collapse of the Stuart cause. For Irish Catholics the major results of the Williamite wars were the Penal Laws of the early eighteenth century, which, although they were subsequently gradually relaxed, remained in force until Catholic emancipation was granted in 1829. In addition to the already severe restrictions on Irish trade, Catholics were excluded by the Penal Laws from the army, barred from politics at both local and national levels, and deprived of access to education. Protestant estates could not be sold to Catholics, Catholics were not allowed to lease land for more than thirty-one years and the inheritance laws encouraged the minute subdivision of Catholic-owned land. Nonconformist Protestants, those who refused to recognize the authority of the established Church, also suffered to an extent, but in the north they were somewhat protected by the 'Ulster Custom', informal local land-tenure arrangements which meant that tenants could sell their interest in a property and could not be evicted so long as they paid their rent.

The history of seventeenth- and early eighteenth-century Ulster has two important features for this discussion. In the first place, two contrasting ethnicities were established: native Catholic Irish, on the one hand, and Ulster Protestant settlers, on the other. The latter category was subdivided or segmented into the mainly Presbyterian Scots of the east of the province and the mainly Church of Ireland (i.e. Anglican) population of English descent of the western counties, although the nineteenth century did see a significant migration into Belfast of members of the Church of Ireland.[2] Although this communal and confessional distinction within the Protestant population remains important today, the ethnic cleavage has historically been – and remains – that between the native Irish and the settlers, with religion providing the main explicit boundary-maintaining mechanism. A shared Protestant ethnic identity emerged as differences between Anglicans and dissenters, English and Scots, were subsumed in the face of their more significant differences with and from the Catholic Irish.

One way to understand the salience of religion is as a consequence of the gradual decline of distinctive Gaelic Irish culture in the north. Taking such a view, religion eventually became all that was left as a cultural marker of difference between the populations. While this interpretation may have some merit, it is probably only applicable to very recent times, with the 'cultural convergence' produced by modernization, consumerism and the penetration of external cultural influences. A more plausible explanation – because, in fact, northern Gaelic Irish culture survived better than one might have expected: in north Antrim, the Sperrins and south Armagh until the early twentieth century – is that religion became such a key constituent of the boundary because within the north of Ireland Protestants consistently *categorized* their ethnic Other thus, institutionally and interactionally. From the time of the Penal Laws onwards, religion *was* the nominal boundary, synonymous with political disloyalty, on the one hand, and fecklessness and unworthiness on the other. This is recognized today, for example, in the local Northern Irish characterization of ethnic chauvinism as *sectarianism*.

The second point to note is that ethnicity in Ulster has been grounded in *consequences* – particularly economic consequences – since the earliest days of the Plantation. Catholics were first of all alienated from the land and eventually, via the Penal Laws, debarred from professional or political careers, further isolating them from the possibility of entrepreneurial economic activity. Thus the foundations of Protestant capital accumulation were laid during the seventeenth and eighteenth centuries, built on the effective exclusion of Catholics from professional life, commerce and agricultural prosperity.

The consolidation of ethnic domination: the industrial revolution

The Protestant colonists came from areas of England and Scotland that had existing traditions of capitalist commodity farming and domestic textile industry. The potential for industrial development which this implied was given a further boost in 1698 by the arrival at Lisburn, Co. Antrim, of Louis Crommelin and his fellow Huguenots, refugees from religious persecution in Catholic France. Their sudden appearance is at least partly explained by the fact that Huguenots had been among William's best troops in the campaigns of ten years earlier. The significance of their immigration rests mainly in the fact that they brought to Ulster the craft of weaving damask, a very fine, patterned linen fabric; plain linen cloth was already a well established manufacture in the province by the time of their arrival. Following the abolition by the British government, in 1696, of the tax on plain linens from Ireland,

> many English dealers began to buy Ulster cloth because it was cheaper than the Dutch and German linens. Since it continued to sell very well more weavers throughout Ulster began to weave for the London market and the industry spread to places as far apart as Strabane, Antrim and Monaghan before 1710. (Crawford 1972: 1)

Thus there were several reasons for the success of the textile industry in Ulster. First, there was the knowledge and skill of the settlers, both the original planters and the later Huguenot refugees. The importance of their craftsmanship, combined with some experience of small-scale capitalist production cannot be overestimated.

Second, the economically privileged position of the Protestant settlers, particularly their secure land tenure system, mentioned earlier, encouraged the harnessing of this entrepreneurial potential. It supported modest capital accumulation, encouraging farmer-manufacturers to expand by either employing weavers or 'putting out' extra work (Gill 1925). Finally, and perhaps of determinate importance, because – for political reasons which are obvious – their case had the ear of the London government, Ulster Protestants were in a position to petition for, and achieve, important economic concessions such as the withdrawal of the tax on plain linens in 1696:

> The prosperity of the linen industry in Ulster was due to English demand for Irish linens ... and to its duty-free entry into the English market. (Crawford and Trainor 1973: 33)

On these foundations, the technical know-how of the settlers, their secure relationship with the land and their links with the mainland – based on what was, in the local context, a bond of shared politicized ethnicity – the Ulster textile industry was developed.

It was this industry, originally domestic in its nature, that provided the necessary base from which industrial development gradually took off in north-east Ireland. The trend in the rest of the country, with some important exceptions in urban centres such as Dublin and Cork, was increasingly towards large-scale agriculture, with the emphasis being on cattle. Until the famine years of the 1840s the western margins and the less fertile upland areas continued to be characterized by the smallholdings of the native Irish peasantry.

Once linen manufacture had been firmly established it became less reliant on the land tenure customs of Ulster and evolved into an independent industry in its own right. This had important consequences for the industrial and social future of the province:

> the linen industry affected the character of Ulster society … It not only gave employment to manual workers; it produced a substantial middle class of bleachers and drapers, many of whom acquired considerable wealth … It also promoted urban development, for the towns were the natural centres for marketing the cloth woven by rural weavers; and at least in some areas, there was a tendency for weavers to concentrate in the vicinity of these market towns. (Beckett 1973: xii–xiii)

Thus in the wake of capitalist industrialization – albeit on a modest scale at this time – we have the concomitant development and elaboration of class stratification within the Protestant ethnic community. Manufacturing, far from being a reflection of prosperity rooted in the land, was rapidly becoming a source of capital accumulation in itself.

Further economic stimulation came as a result of the agitation by the Volunteers for free trade and other reforms. In 1779 many of the remaining restrictions on the Irish export trade were lifted and in 1782, following a political meeting in Dungannon, Co. Tyrone, the Dublin parliament was largely emancipated from control by Westminster. In the years immediately following, the Dublin government of Grattan's parliament did much to stimulate grain production, brewing, woollen manufacture and the cotton industry. The north-east counties had a head start on the rest of Ireland and benefited disproportionately from these reforms.

The new parliament failed, however, to grasp the nettle of Catholic emancipation, a cause that attracted some sympathy at this time from Nonconformists. The organizational expression of this sympathy was Wolfe Tone's Society of United Irishmen, founded in Belfast in 1791. Once again, however, as so many times before and since, self-interest and ethnicity successfully undermined the movement's radical ideals. In County Armagh, an area dominated by the textile industry and distinguished by an approximate demographic balance between Catholics and Protestants, a violent encounter occurred in 1795 which led to the formation of an Orange Society, which spread quickly in the countryside. With it came an increase in violent attacks on Catholic weavers, many of whom fled. There is considerable evidence of sympathy and support for the society among landlords and the magistracy; when a yeomanry was established to counter the United Irishmen's 1798 rebellion, the Orange Society provided many of its members. The Protestants may have been increasingly stratified along class lines; nonetheless, ethnicity remained the major axis of political mobilization (Haddick-Flynn 1999; Kelly 2000; Senior 1966).

By the beginning of the nineteenth century Belfast had come to rival Dublin in importance as a mercantile and financial centre. In terms of manufacturing the north-east had established a predominance that was to last a long time. The expansion of the textile industry, new technological developments and the boom in cotton production stimulated by the Napoleonic Wars all combined to encourage systematic mechanization, both in yarn spinning and weaving. By the 1830s factory production was rapidly becoming commonplace, with linen manufacturing eventually reasserting itself as the market for cotton became increasingly competitive again in the conditions of peacetime.

The mechanization of the labour process in textiles led to the development of a local engineering industry, based in the first instance on the market for machinery and repair services among the local mill owners. This development was heavily dependent on the mainland, particularly for specialist expertise. However, despite the influx of entrepreneurs possessing such expertise, the enterprises set up during this period were local companies that were not accountable to external sources of control:

> Few of the early engineering works in the north of Ireland were established by local men; Joe Rider, John Hind, Stephen Cotton, George Horner and E.J. Harland came from England, James Combe and James Mackie from Scotland. From the middle of the nineteenth century, however, local men trained in the original works began to set up business for themselves or to take over the management of existing firms when founders retired or got into financial difficulties ... It seems clear that the early entrepreneurs were attracted to the north of Ireland, not by the local market for small metal goods, but by the opportunity to exploit new techniques, such as iron founding, the making of steam engines and textile machinery, and the provision of a machinery repair service ... the region was kept in touch with progress in industrial organisation in Britain not only by the political union of the two countries but also by periodic infusions of new blood from the British engineering industry. (Coe 1969: 193, 194, 196)

Business or other economic links with the mainland were not all one way, however. In addition to the inward flow of technology and entrepreneurial personnel, there was also a flow of investment capital, in particular – though not exclusively – a flow of local capital *out*, for investment in England and Scotland. Due to the restricted scale and scope of the local economy, the local economic élite's links with their fellow businessmen 'across the water' – sometimes the close links of family or marriage – provided a useful avenue for diversification and investment (ibid.: 190–2). From the middle of the nineteenth century onwards, Ulster rapidly became incorporated into the burgeoning industrial economy of the rest of the kingdom.

The increasing importance of large-scale manufacture, which required easy access to the sea for the import of the necessary raw materials and the export of its finished products, resulted in Belfast becoming the centre of industrial and commercial activity. The situation developed for three reasons. First, there was the city's centrality within the predominantly Protestant area east of the River Bann;

second, its ease of communication, via the natural corridor of the valley of the River Lagan, with the smaller textile towns of the rest of the province; and third, its position as the major deep-water port on the north-eastern seaboard, providing ready access to the markets of the Empire and the rest of the world. The establishment of steamship services to Glasgow and Liverpool in the 1820s further strengthened Belfast's position. In 1800 the city had been smaller than either Limerick or Waterford; by 1891 Belfast had overtaken Dublin in both size and commercial importance.

Naturally enough, the industrial development of the Belfast area drew in many immigrants from the rest of the province. Although it was already happening before the Famine, rural distress in the 1840s and the subsequent flight from the land accelerated this population movement. Many of the new city-dwellers were Catholics from the southern and western districts of Ulster, attracted to Belfast by the availability of employment. They tended to take unskilled jobs in textile production or as navvies, building the new town. Skilled work, particularly in engineering, remained the preserve of the Protestant working man; industry and commerce were controlled by the local Protestant bourgeoisie – either local or newly arrived – and hiring practices reflected the traditionally sanctioned hierarchy of Catholic and Protestant (cf. Reid 1980). Relations between an employer and his workforce were often paternalistic and a firm recognition of the relationship between employment and ethnicity structured the emergent labour market in the city, although this did not prevent the emergence, from the 1870s, of labourism and trade union organization (Patterson 1980). Historians of this period leave us in little doubt as to the systematic manipulation of ethnicity by the local élite, both in furtherance of their political ends – the maintenance of Protestant supremacy and the link with Britain – and, more indirectly perhaps, but no less definitely, their economic goals. The link between the political and the economic was clearly recognized by both workers and employers and formed the basis of the Unionist class alliance.

With the increasing importance of shipbuilding and marine engineering from mid-century onwards, the industrial structure that was to characterize the local economy until the 1970s began to emerge. The development of the shipyards reflected the presence of a deep-water harbour, the large numbers of skilled men, such as boilermakers, in the local engineering industry (although many more were brought in from Clydeside), and the enthusiasm of the Harbour Commissioners in developing the Queen's Island site. As the nineteenth century drew to its close, the Belfast region became incorporated more and more into the wider United Kingdom economy, particularly that region of it which includes the other major Irish Sea ports, Glasgow and Liverpool. Employers and men participated in national and regional industrial negotiations and disputes, and the commercial life of the city drew ever closer to Britain, much local capital continuing to be invested on the mainland (Coe 1969: 191; Lyons 1973: 270–86). By 1900 the economy was provincial no longer.

This account of the industrialization of Northern Ireland allows us to examine some of the links between ethnicity and economic activity. During this period the linked processes of urbanization, industrialization and mechanization served to reinforce the economic and political dominance of the local Protestant bourgeoisie.

Their economic position was made more secure, and their sphere of activities expanded, through the importation of technological resources from the mainland. Access to external investment markets when the local opportunities for capital accumulation became too limited further consolidated their economic base. These strategies were facilitated by their links of shared ethnicity – religious, political, and in terms of origins – with the English and Scottish bourgeoisie, who were a source of technologically innovative entrepreneurs and provided opportunities for Ulster Protestant businessmen to invest money in their enterprises. The economic and political interests of the local businessman – and the two are inextricably linked – were also well served by the stratification of the working class along ethnic lines. Class issues were never forgotten in local politics – the distinction between skilled and unskilled Protestant workers, although much undermined by restructuring, remains important today – but the increasing orchestration of ethnic solidarity by the Orange Order as the nineteenth century wore on ensured that, particularly following the Home Rule crisis of 1886, sectarian issues dominated the political arena. The important connection between ethnicity and access to work would probably have seen to that if nothing else did, and this tendency was reinforced by the pre-eminence of élitist craft unions among organized labour.

Sectarian ethnicity was not the only factor, of course. It must not be forgotten that, from the point of view of Northern Protestants, the underdevelopment of the rest of Ireland was a powerful (if with hindsight somewhat self-fulfilling) argument against Home Rule. A genuine and understandable fear of losing a relatively prosperous lifestyle informed politics and industrial relations. The outcome of these fears for the Ulster employer, occasional disputes notwithstanding, was the continuing control of his workforce and a high degree of industrial harmony. This was a subtle and ongoing process of negotiation and accommodation:

> Ulster Unionism emerged as the product neither of a conspiracy of landed notables and industrialists to 'dupe the people' nor from the spontaneous convergence of a set of forces without prior political relations. (Gibbon 1975: 145)

Systematic connections between ethnicity, economic activity and politics in Ulster were established during the two centuries following the Plantation. These connections were, and are, neither accidental nor determined by socio-economic structure. They can only really be understood as the consequences of the pursuit – not always consistent – of rational political and economic goals by the government in London and the Ulster Protestant establishment. They became, finally, systematically organized with the rise to importance of the Protestant industrial and commercial élite of Belfast in the second half of the nineteenth century. Their roots, however, lay much earlier.

Organized labour and the manipulation of ethnicity

So the foundations of a hierarchical ethnic division of labour were laid in the military subjugation of the Ulster Irish and the subsequent Plantation. This division of labour was further consolidated as the industrial revolution progressed in north-eastern Ireland. I shall conclude with some discussion of the subsequent development of the capitalist economy in Ulster, in particular during the life of the Northern Ireland state, between 1921 and the prorogation of the Stormont parliament in 1972.

Before the First World War, there had been some class-based political organization and industrial action, most notably Jim Larkin's organization of unskilled labour, both Protestant and Catholic, in Belfast in 1907 (Gray 1985). Industrial unrest rose to new heights, however, in the wake of the war, as it did throughout the United Kingdom:

> Industrial militancy was growing among Belfast workers. There had been a massive engineering strike at the beginning of 1919 which had brought Belfast industry to a halt for four weeks. Ominously for the Unionists the leader of the largely Protestant strikers had been a Catholic, Charles McKay. The workers' new class consciousness seemed to carry through to the local elections in January 1920, for twelve Labour councillors were elected to Belfast Corporation, one of them topping the poll in the Protestant stronghold of Shankill. (Farrell 1976: 27)

It might have been expected that, in the appalling social conditions of working-class areas of Belfast at the time, the labour movement would have taken seed and flourished. However, this was also a period of intense sectarian conflict, stemming from the pre-war Ulster Volunteer Force crisis and the Civil War in the rest of the island. The troubles of this period, combined with the blatant playing of the 'Orange Card' by local employers and, later, by the new Stormont government, played a substantial part in undermining inter-ethnic or cross-sectarian socialist activism. Listen, for example, to Sir Edward Carson, MP and Unionist leader, speaking at Finaghy in July 1920:

> these men who come forward posing as the friends of labour care no more about labour than does the man in the moon. Their real object ... is that they mislead and bring about disunity *amongst our own people*; and in the end, before we know where we are, we may find ourselves in the same bondage and slavery as is the rest of Ireland in the South and West. (Farrell 1976: 28; My emphasis)

During this period the identification of an equivalence between socialism and Irish nationalism, with respect to their perceived interests, was first formulated by Protestants; opposition to the latter generating rejection of the former. The Northern Ireland Labour Party struggled on under this electoral handicap until its eventual demise in the early 1980s.

The upshot of this during the years following the First World War was the wholesale expulsion of Catholic workers from many areas of Belfast industry, most notably the shipyards, a state of affairs further encouraged by the fact that differences in skill levels between Catholics (a majority of whom were unskilled) and Protestants (a high proportion of whom were skilled) led, in some respects, to the reproduction of the ethnic division of labour among the trade unions. There was no General Strike in Belfast in 1926, and the unique events towards the end of 1932, when Catholic and Protestant workers marched together in Belfast to protest at their unemployment and destitution, were put down by the Royal Ulster Constabulary armed with rifles and armoured cars. But even though poverty dire

beyond modern imagining was a fact of everyday life for urban working-class
Protestants and Catholics, and in rural areas, throughout the 1930s (Bardon 1992:
529–34), sectarian ethnicity never ceased to matter:

> The extent of co-operation between the poor of both religions during the outdoor-
> relief riots of 1932 has been exaggerated and romanticized, and there is no evidence
> that intercommunal tensions were eased for more than a few days. (*ibid.*: 539)

Sectarian violence returned in 1934 and, with a vengeance, in 1935. Although it
was significant, it is possible to overemphasize the role in these disturbances of the
local Protestant establishment's manipulation of ethnicity:

> That politicians' sectarianism influenced public opinion is undeniable. However,
> that it alone was the cause of the riots is too far-fetched a conclusion. The strength
> of popular, everyday sectarianism cannot be underestimated. (Munck and Rolston
> 1987: 59)

To take the most measured view, 'while neither Craig [Viscount Craigavon, the
Unionist Prime Minister] and his colleagues had created these divisions, they did
little to assuage them' (Bardon 1992: 467). Nor, although in 1935 it was directly
asked to by the Nationalist Party, did a Westminster government which had much
in common with Northern Ireland Unionists – in terms of party politics, view of
the world, and social networks and background – choose to intervene.

After the Second World War, the Unionist government, newly incorporated, with
some reluctance, into the British Labour Party's welfare state, resolved to revitalize
the Ulster economy, which was suffering now from the over-concentration on textiles and heavy engineering of its formative phases. The main development strategy
was the attraction of outside companies to the province by means of generous capital subsidies. Most of the new enterprises set up were sited in Protestant areas east
of the River Bann and most of the new jobs correspondingly went to Protestants. This
was particularly the case in engineering, which required skilled men. Furthermore,
the new capitalism accepted quite readily the practices of the old. The toleration of
local practices was a small price to pay for good industrial relations:

> A good many new businesses conformed without protest to the practices of old cap-
> ital. In 1965, when new industry provided about 60,000 of 190,000 manufacturing
> jobs, the first Development Plan complained that only 10 per cent of new vacancies
> were being filled through labour exchanges. Evidently Orangeism was becoming
> absorbed into the new workplaces. (Bew *et al.* 1979: 189)

The relatively unproblematic nature of industrial relations in the Province at this
time is well illustrated by a government survey, the Quigley Report (Department of
Manpower Services 1974). Although there has been considerable controversy
about this,[3] the basis of that industrial harmony seems to have been taken-for-
granted, axiomatic discrimination in employment against Catholics. The outcome
for the employer was the lowest unit labour costs in western Europe (Department
of Manpower Services 1979: 20–1).

Thus organized labour was effectively split along ethnic lines, the Protestant
section bought off by the Unionist government and the local business élite, and

inhibited from large-scale working-class identification and political action by its own industrial background and sectarian ethnicity. The arrival of the new multi-national enterprises served only to strengthen this state of affairs, inasmuch as it suited their best interests – the maintenance of a relatively quiescent workforce and easy access to subsidies – not to resist it.

The management of this mobilization of ethnicity can only be understood if one appreciates the interpenetration of the political, legal and business spheres in Northern Ireland prior to the imposition of direct rule from Westminster in 1972. Between 1921 and 1972 the Northern Ireland state was the institutional embodiment of this interpenetration; perhaps the main integrating organization holding the system together was the Orange Institution (Bew *et al.* 1979; Buckland 1980; Harbinson 1973):

> The [Northern Irish] Prime Minister said in 1932: 'Ours is a Protestant Government and I am an Orangeman'… In the House of Commons the Prime Minister said: 'I am very proud indeed to be Grand Master of the Orange Institution of the Loyal County of Down. I have filled that office for many years and I prize that far more than I do being Prime Minister. I have always said I am an Orangeman first and a member of this Parliament afterwards. (Mansergh 1936: 240–1)

Unless it is appreciated how closely overlapping were ethnic attachment, economic interest and political power in Northern Ireland, and how they came together in the Orange Order and the Unionist Party, the working of the informal network of political patronage, one of the linchpins in the maintenance of ethnic domination, cannot properly be understood (although it is interesting to note the similar predominance in politics in the Republic of Ireland of informal patronage networks: Bax 1976; Sacks 1976). The small scale of the local political and economic arena, and its relative autonomy prior to 1972, are vital to any explanation of the workings of this system of ethnic closure. The taken-for-granted coming together of the everyday workings of government, commerce and agriculture, in the hands of a small network of like-minded members of the same ethnic community, allowed influence to operate and manipulation to occur without too much need for conspiracy.

Since the suspension of Stormont in 1972 and the downgrading of the powers of elected local authorities in Northern Ireland in 1973, Northern Ireland has changed, and more than a little. In the first instance, it seems likely that incorporation into the British state – direct rule – did little in the immediate short term to undermine the informal apparatus of Protestant control (O'Dowd *et al.* 1980). However, over the last twenty-five years or so, a number of factors have gradually transformed the situation: the local political dominance of Westminster, in the shape of the Northern Ireland Office, the development of a 'new' post-Unionist Northern Ireland Civil Service, the collapse of traditional Protestant skilled working-class employment, the impact on local employment practices of fair employment legislation and European and North American influence, the emergence of a local business élite which is dependent upon local consumers rather than labour and has reoriented itself away from an explicit emphasis on ethnic communality, the increasingly fractious disunity of Unionism, and the entry of Republicans into local and provincial government, such as it presently is. Whether or not discrimination against Catholics diminished in the decades after the imposition of direct rule has been the topic of considerable academic debate (Compton 1991; Cormack and Osborne 1991; O'Leary and McGarry 1996: 260–7; Osborne and Shuttleworth 2004; Smith and Chambers 1991). That issue aside for the moment, one arguable outcome of these changes has been a 'crisis of identity' for Protestants (Bruce 1994; Buckley 1989; McKay 2000). Among other things,[4] this crisis reflects the loss by the local Protestant establishment of their central, controlling role in the management of the Province, the changed economic circumstances of the Protestant working-class, *vis-à-vis* Catholics, and the reluctance – or perhaps inability – of either to acknowledge their role, and culpability, in the violence of the last four decades.

But there is more to the Protestants' problem than this. One of my arguments in this chapter is that, historically, Ulster Protestant ethnicity has developed along two principal relational axes, involving complex interactions of similarity and difference: internally, with respect to Catholics, and externally with respect to the rest of Britain. Neither of these is unambiguously a relationship of similarity or difference, and each is implicated in the other. Put over-simply, Northern Irish Protestants have two significant Others; and each is, in different ways depending on the situational context – and to some extent only – us as well as *them*. While this can be as confusing for Ulster Prods as for anyone else, ambiguity *per se* is not the source of their present difficulty with respect to their sense of themselves, their sense of who they are.

The problem in this respect lies in the undermining, or perhaps more accurately the transformation, of the British axis. The *categorizers* (of Catholics) now find themselves the *categorized* (by the British, and by the rest of the world). Those who have put Others in their place for centuries are experiencing what it means to be put in their place. Those who have long looked down on Others, now find themselves looked down on *as* the Other. Those who have, historically, constructed part of their identity out of and in the link with Britain – and an imagined footing of equality – must now face the hierarchy inherent in that relationship, and their subordinate position within it. Long implicit, it is now out in the open. The Protestant place in the imagined community of the United Kingdom looks increasingly marginal, if not altogether insecure. In the face of the distancing which began with Harold Wilson's televised accusation of 'spongeing' in 1974, after the Ulster Workers' strike, a relation of kinship or alliance with 'across the water' can no longer easily be taken for granted – or even sustained – as one of the boundaries of Protestant ethnicity. And the alternative in that direction, independence, remains – in the absence of any renegotiation of relationships across the *other* boundary, with Northern Irish Catholics – largely unthinkable. The Anglo-Irish Agreement of 1985, the subsequent prominence of the London–Dublin relationship in the wake of the paramilitary cease-fires, the 1998 Belfast Agreement – the Good Friday Agreement – to which these led, the subsequent 'peace process', and the gradual emergence of a new, even if tentative, local political settlement, have, for many Protestants, done nothing except dramatize the difficulty in which they find themselves. Although it is important to recognize the potential political flexibility for which this situation allows, in terms of emergent new Protestant self-identifications (Mitchell 2003), in McKay's words (2000), Northern Protestants have, indeed, become 'an unsettled people'.

Culture and economic advantage?

Protestant ethnicity in Ulster was initially established and subsequently manipulated within the fields of military conquest and economics. The economic differences between Catholics and Protestants in Northern Ireland to which I have drawn attention remain significant (the research evidence which this paragraph and the next summarize can be found in Osborne and Shuttleworth 2004). Census and other official survey data indicate that, as a result, no doubt, of a complex of factors – including fair employment legislation and policy initiatives, a changing political climate, and a general economic upturn – there have, however, been some significant changes: the overall relative employment position of Catholics has improved, although they remain under-represented in the senior Civil Service and the security sector, while Protestants are now, relatively speaking, under-represented in the education and health sectors. Despite *some* narrowing of *some* gaps, however, and some mobility in middle-class occupations, Catholics remain more likely to be unemployed than Protestants, more likely to be employed in the service sector than in manufacturing, and are over-represented in semi- or unskilled manual occupations. This ethnically skewed occupational distribution is likely to ameliorate only slowly, according to projections of future occupational and educational change.

Whatever its complex causes, the persistence of ethnic economic disadvantage probably does not have much to do with different levels of cultural capital, as indicated – admittedly imperfectly – by formal educational achievement (Osborne 2004). While, in the past, Protestants consistently did 'better', educationally speaking, it is likely that, at least in part, this was a reflection of the different social class profiles of the two groups. However, the educational trend has changed, as have social mobility and the social class profiles, although some apparent bias of Catholic pupils – although this may be better expressed as Catholic schools – against vocational maths- and science-based subject combinations continues.

Historically, these patterns are probably best understood as a *result* of a long history of ethnic exclusion and closure, rather than one of its *causes*, and, as such, are relatively slow to change under changed circumstances. Similarly, with respect to attitudes to work, recent research has discovered negligible differences between the two ethnic groups. There would, therefore, appear to be no ready-to-hand 'cultural' explanation for the differences in employment patterns between Protestants and Catholics.

The Protestant folk view of the situation was, for a long time, relatively straightforward: economic advantage was their just reward for hard work, thrift, and hardheadedness in business. During the late 1960s, when the Civil Rights Movement began to make a political issue out of it, many, if not most, Protestants denied the existence of discrimination in employment against Catholics (Ruane and Todd 1996: 155). Research into local ethnic stereotypes carried out in the early 1970s discovered that 'industrious' was a major theme in Protestant self-descriptions (O'Donnell 1977). In this case, as in every case, group identification goes hand in glove with the categorization of Others. Here is a young Protestant man, himself unemployed, talking to the author in the late 1970s (Jenkins 1982: 31), threading some further themes into the categorization:

you go down to the dole in Corporation Street and you'll see them in their thousands. I went down there one day and nearly never came back. That's another thing, they're nearly always on the brue [registered as unemployed] ... claiming for everything, and doing the double [working illegally while on benefit]. Although maybe I shouldn't say that because there's a lot of Prods doing the double too. But I reckon there's hell of a lot more Catholics on the dole, claiming for everything off the Government.

Nor was it only a matter of working-class stereotypes. Thomas Wilson, an Ulster Protestant and an economist, eloquently exemplified this:

> As for business life, Presbyterians and Jews are probably endowed with more business acumen than Irish Catholics ... For generations they were the underdogs, the despised 'croppies', the adherents of a persecuted religion, who were kept out of public life by the Protestant conquerors. They were made to feel inferior, and to make matters worse they often were inferior, if only in those personal qualities that make for success in competitive economic life. (Wilson 1955: 208–9)

Three decades later, Wilson appeared to have moderated his views, emphasizing (1989: 108) the importance of local *perceptions* that Protestants possessed a distinctive and superior work ethic. One could turn this round to say – which is, to be fair, a plausible reading of the 1955 quotation – that what mattered was the *categorization* of Catholics as idle, unreliable, shiftless, lacking in enterprise.

The notion that Protestantism – *qua* doctrine – encouraged economic enterprise in Ulster found its way into other academic analyses (e.g. Baker 1973: 803), which was not surprising in view of the debate about Max Weber's argument linking the 'Puritan asceticism' of the Reformation with the development of capitalism. Whatever the merits of the Protestant Ethic thesis, however, there is a firm case for resisting the notion that Protestant economic supremacy in Northern Ireland had anything to do with the cultural norms – whether doctrinal or otherwise – of Protestantism. The economic advantages enjoyed by Ulster Protestants must be traced back to the Plantation and the systematic dispossession of the indigenous Irish population. This act of initial domination, creating as it did two ethnicities in conflict – one advantaged, one disadvantaged – was consolidated during the industrial revolution, institutionalized during the fifty-one years of semi-autonomous Unionist government, and has yet to be completely undermined. Historically and more recently, the opportunity structure for Catholics – itself the result of Protestant political domination – and the intimate relationship between Unionism and the local business élite are sufficient explanations for the continuing ethnic division of labour in Northern Ireland.

As I pointed out above, that ethnic division of labour is changing, even if it is moving slowly towards approximate meritocracy. With it, local perceptions and attitudes may also be moving. Not least, new factors to be taken into account are Catholic and Protestant perceptions of the changing economic realities. In this respect, the attitudinal data – which must be approached with the sensible reserve that one should always extend to survey findings of this kind – can be summarized thus:

> The fact that Catholics perceive an improvement in their position and that Protestants are somewhat ambivalent about this points to the success of the [fair

employment] legislation. The data suggest, however, that there is potentially a fly
in the ointment. Although the evidence is fairly weak, trends indicate that
Protestants are increasingly likely to perceive discrimination in the area of employment. Taken together with evidence suggesting that employment is now more of an
equality concern for Protestants than it is for Catholics, and the fact that a substantial minority of Protestants (38 per cent) believe that legislation protects Catholics
at the expense of Protestants, this is an area that raises some cause for concern.
(Hughes 2004: 182)

One interpretation of these findings is that, for many Protestants, their categorizations of Catholics have changed little from the historically established stereotypes
that I described earlier. From their point of view, any improvement in the situation
of Catholics is more likely to reflect unfair special treatment than merit and fair
achievement (see, for example, McKay 2000: 153).

This account of Ulster Protestant ethnicity and intra-group relations has at least
one major weakness. The need to keep to a manageable length has encouraged a
tighter argument than I would have wished. Consequently, the ins and outs of history have been smoothed over, if not ironed out altogether. Protestant workers were
not, for example, as easily or comprehensively 'bought off' as I may at times seem
to have suggested: witness the gulf between 'respectable' Unionism and paramilitary loyalism. That split also highlights another oversight: important differences
between the urban middle class and rural Protestants would find a place in a more
detailed discussion.

The mobilization of ethnicity as a resource in the pursuit of political dominance
and capital accumulation may, if the Ulster situation is any guide, take many forms.
In particular, during the period of industrialization and urbanization, that strand of
Protestant ethnicity which of necessity 'faced outward' encouraged and facilitated –
and was produced and reproduced by – the links with Britain through which
technology was imported, capital exported for investment elsewhere, and political
support mobilized. From the late nineteenth century, ethnic ties were increasingly –
and, apparently, at least to some degree self-consciously – part of the local Protestant
bourgeoisie's strategy for dealing with the threat of organized labour. The 'management' of the class-stratified Protestant community was achieved in a number of
complementary fashions, the two most important being the control of recruitment
into employment – in a labour market which always had more job-seekers than
jobs – and the creation of political unity, a class alliance against the external threat
of Catholic nationalism. Protestant commercial and industrial supremacy in Ulster
has been built on these foundations.

Intra-group relations are not the whole story, of course: what about the boundary
between Protestants and Catholics? The internal relations of the Protestant community have contributed, in no small way, to the categorization of Catholics. However,
this isn't just a matter of *nominal* identification; the *virtualities* of categorization
are also significant. Hence my emphasis on economic activity in this chapter. For
centuries, Ulster Protestants were disproportionately able to constitute what it
meant – beginning with the most everyday matters of subsistence – to be Catholic.
The specifics of that experience may have changed and shifted as circumstances
shifted and changed, and there were doubtless local and individual exceptions and
ameliorations, but the essential fact remained. Northern Catholic identity was to a

significant degree – and for long enough for it to acquire a certain consistency, the solidity of history expressed in Barth's notion of the *universe of discourse* – a social construct emerging out of categorization (by Protestants) and out of the economic and other consequences of that categorization. The balance began to change in the 1960s, as external factors and developments within the Catholic community began to encourage a more vocal and successful assertion of Catholic group identification than had hitherto been possible. It has changed even more since, as Protestants have gradually seen their power to categorize – and to govern – slipping away.

The economic sphere is, however, only one aspect of categorization and its consequences. As suggested in Chapter 5, violence – particularly killing – can be understood as the ultimate act of categorization.[5] Nominally, it forecloses on the possibility of a response or a redefinition; virtually, in terms of consequences, it is equally absolute. It really is 'putting them in their place' (and, as the republican hunger strike of the early 1980s demonstrated, it can work both ways: death can make the ultimate *claim* to identity and, in the process, brand the persecutor with the mark of Cain). Although there is no space to explore the matter in detail, the differences in the nature of Catholic and Protestant paramilitary violence can be interpreted within this framework. Summarized rather baldly, and taking intra-community violence out of the picture, while Protestant paramilitaries mainly focused their attacks on Catholic civilians, Catholic paramilitaries largely took the security forces to be their primary target (O'Leary and McGarry 1996: 34–40). As the Protestant power to categorize and define Catholics – a power upon which so much Protestant group identification has historically depended – dwindled in other respects, violence was one means of 'putting them in their place' that they were able to retain.

Events in Drumcree, on the outskirts of Portadown, Co. Armagh, since July 1995, when the 'traditional' claim of local Orangemen to process down the Garvaghy Road, through a Catholic neighbourhood, was pressed home despite residents' opposition, illustrate that there are other ways of putting people in their place. Subsequent years saw escalating protests and counter-protests in Drumcree and Portadown, and when, in 1998, the parade was re-routed by order of the new Parades Commission – itself established as a result of the Drumcree situation – the violence worsened. Since 1996, whether directly or indirectly related to the Drumcree confrontations, lives have been lost in Portadown and elsewhere, and the damage to the 'peace process' – because the matter is not regarded as settled yet, despite a more peaceful parade in 2007 at Drumcree – should not be underestimated (Bryan 2000a, 2000b; Fawcett 2000: 95–9; McKay 2000: 119–86).

In Northern Ireland, violence and territory are, as they have ever been, intimately linked (Murtagh 2003; Shirlow and Murtagh 2006). The local institutionalization of relatively low-level violence – and in Northern Ireland these things are always relative – at significant territorial boundaries, and attempts, in response, to develop 'interface management' strategies, have been among the defining features of the post-1998 'peace process' (Byrne 2005; Jarman 2003; Shirlow and Murtagh 2006: 81–100). Historically, the annual cycle of parades during 'the marching season' was, as it still is, about the institutionalized dramatisation of territorial interfaces, by Catholics and Protestants alike (Bryan 2000a; Fraser 2000; Jarman 1997), and in recent years massive displays of partisan flags have added a dimension of semi-permanence to this process (Bryan 2005). However, given the long-standing ethnic constitution of state, power and place in Northern Ireland, this 'beating of the bounds' has never been an even-handed tit-for-tat. It is even less so in the present climate. The tenacity with which the 'loyal orders' have pursued the 'right to march' at Drumcree, and not only at Drumcree, makes most sense when it is realized, despite vocal protestations to this effect, that it is not the recognition of Orange 'cultural traditions' that is at stake. What *is* at stake is the continued capacity of some Protestants, at least, to put Catholics in their place, in this case by denying that they *have* an autonomous place, free from incursion. When all else fails, struggles over identity and power remain, and Ulster loyalists may continue to seek ways to translate their imaginings of domination into reality.

8   The 'Cultural Stuff'

In a well-known passage in the 'Introduction' to *Ethnic Groups and Boundaries*, Barth argued that the focus for the investigation of ethnicity should be 'the ethnic *boundary* that defines the group, not the cultural stuff that it encloses' (1969a: 15). By 'cultural stuff', he means language, religion, customs and laws, tradition, material culture, cuisine, etc. In arguing this he stood, as outlined in Chapter 1, in a direct line of descent from Max Weber. And it remains an argument that must remain at the centre of our thinking. In insisting that there is no simple equation between the seamless tapestry of cultural *variation* that is the human world and the discontinuities of ethnic *differentiation*, it prevents us from mistaking the morphological enumeration of cultural traits for the analysis of ethnicity. It also reminds us that where or how any particular ethnic boundary is drawn is arbitrary, rather than self-evident or inevitable.

However, this might also suggest that the 'cultural stuff' out of which that differentiation is arbitrarily produced and reproduced is somehow irrelevant, which surely cannot be true. For example, a situation in which the As and the Bs are distinguished, *inter alia*, by languages that are mutually intelligible for most everyday purposes – as with Danish and Norwegian – would seem to differ greatly from one in which the languages involved are, as with English and Welsh, utterly different. Similarly, relations between groups of rival Christians are likely to be different – although not necessarily *better* – than between a Christian and Muslim group.

Handelman made a generally similar point three decades ago (1977: 190), suggesting – and using 'category' and 'group' interchangeably – that the 'categorical corporate holdings of culture', far from being irrelevant, specify 'a corporate history in time and space'. They tell a story about 'why the category is substantial and legitimate', providing group members with 'the elements of a "social biography" which connects "culture" and behavior, and the past to the present'. If nothing else, Handelman argued, this aspect of the 'cultural stuff' is important for distinguishing ethnicity from other kinds of identification. Anthony Cohen's discussion (1985) of the 'symbolic construction of community' appears to imply something of the same. Similarly, in attempting to understand the complexities of why ethnic attachments are more or less contingent and flexible, Cornell and Hartmann (Cornell 1996; Cornell and Hartmann 1998: 173–84) have argued for a partial shift of analytic attention, back to what goes on *within* the boundary, to what co-members share as much as what differentiates them from Others; to the *content* of ethnicity, which includes the 'cultural stuff'.

Recently, a number of discussions of nationalism have focused on what appear to be cognate issues, the changeable meaning and content – both collectively and for individuals – of national identifications (Brubaker 1996; Reicher and Hopkins

2001; Todd 2005; Todd *et al.* 2006). Brubaker *et al.*, for example, drawing on my distinction between nominal and virtual aspects of identification (see Chapter 4), contrast the nominal and the experiential modalities of 'being Hungarian' or 'being Romanian' in Cluj, and the complex interplay of everyday contingencies, collective categorical content – 'cultural stuff' – and individual decision-making (2006: 207–38). Individuals can be described in the same way, by themselves and by others, yet do their 'identity', and experience their 'being', in very different ways

In this chapter I want to look at some of the 'cultural stuff' of ethnicity in Northern Ireland. In particular, I am going to discuss the contribution made by the cultural *content* of ethnicity – specifically religion – to the nature of relations at and across the *boundary* between the groups involved. The nominal content of ethnicity in Northern Ireland is indeed religious; the opposition between Catholic and Protestant is its root classification. As argued in the previous chapter, the historical and everyday *virtualities* of this, its consequences, can be traced in the economic field and, although this was not explored in detail, with respect to violence. But how does religion contribute to the situation apart from being a convenient marker of ethnic difference?

That the Northern Irish 'troubles' are about religion remains an important facet of the image of the situation that is held by the British public and many external observers. This image allows violence to be explained away as an irrational anachronism, and the Northern Irish people to be dismissed as 'backwoodsmen' or 'ignorant peasants' who have yet to discover the modern era, let alone the twenty-first century. It has, probably inadvertently, been reinforced by analyses with titles such as *Holy War in Belfast* (Boyd 1969) and 'Religious War in Northern Ireland' (Easthope 1976). A strong version of the thesis that the 'troubles' in Northern Ireland are, indeed, a conflict of religion has been defended vigorously by John Fulton (1991); more moderate versions have been put forward by John Hickey (1984), Maurice Irvine (1991) and Claire Mitchell (2006). The centrality of Protestant theology to the Northern Irish conflict figures prominently in the work of Steve Bruce (1986, 1994) and Brewer and Higgins (1998, 1999; Higgins and Brewer 2003). In this chapter I will explore in what senses, if indeed any, it is correct to understand the Northern Ireland problem as a religious conflict.

Varieties of religious conflict

Before looking at the local detail of Northern Ireland, it may be useful to consider some general characteristics of situations of religious conflict, and how they relate to ethnicity. I am not, for example, concerned with the existence of doctrinal, ceremonial or cosmological differences between religions or sects. In the sense in which the word is used here, it is not religions as ideological systems that are in conflict, but their members. The very existence of different religions, sects, or communities of worship presupposes that there will be differences of opinion – which may be fundamental and total – between them, as bodies of belief, with respect to their corporate world-views, religious and moral doctrines and ritual practices. They can, therefore, legitimately be said to be always 'in conflict' – in a weak sense – with respect to these issues.

The existence of conflicts of this kind doesn't *necessarily* lead to actual conflict-ual struggles – whether violent or non-violent – between individuals or groups who identify themselves as devotees of the doctrines concerned. It is with religious con-flict in this latter, strong sense of the word that I am here concerned. What is it about a situation of conflict and struggle that distinguishes it as religious? We may begin by saying that such a situation is religious if a significant number of the par-ties to the conflict define it as being primarily about religion or religion-related matters. It is possible to tentatively identify five ideal-typical conflict situations that may be characterized as conflicts of religion in this strong sense.

The first may be described as a *missionary* conflict: members of one religious group seek to expand outside their own territory and proselytize non-members. This may involve force in the proselytizing or in the local response to it. Examples can be found ready to hand in both Christian and Islamic history. Some of the eth-nocide reported from Amazonia in recent years appears, on the face of things, to fall into this category. However, it is also true to say, as this example illustrates, that in many such situations missionary zeal goes easily hand in hand with baser eco-nomic motives; it isn't easy to disentangle one from the other. In other words, mis-sionary religion may also be an ideology of identification, no less useful for the legitimation and justification of dirty work, where appropriate, than, for example, racism or nationalism.

In the second place, there is the *holy war*: a dispute over territory or posses-sions that are regarded by at least one of the parties to the conflict as sacred or otherwise symbolically significant. Examples of this are once again all too easy to find: one only has to point to the long-standing disputes over the Holy Places of Palestine between Christians, Muslims and (more recently) Jews. In practice, of course, as in the case of *jihad* – a word with which the modern world has recently had to become reacquainted – the distinction between missionary con-flict and holy war may be more difficult to discern than is apparent from these bald definitions.

Third, a situation in which two or more religious groups occupy the same terri-torial and social space, and the dominant group penalizes the religious practices of the subordinated group(s), may be described as *religious persecution*. Familiar examples of this kind of conflict are the Inquisition of medieval Europe or, if one accepts the characterization of Soviet state socialism as a secular religion (Lane 1981), the persecution of religious minorities in the former Soviet Union. Similarly, one can point to many colonial situations in which a missionary conflict became, with the consolidation of conquest, religious persecution. Conflicts of this kind frequently also involve other, broader, cultural issues, such as the right to use an indigenous language.

Fourth, *religious competition*, is characterized by two or more religious groupings – although most usually two – coexisting within the same space and struggling for dominance. Since there is a tendency for one or other of the parties to achieve that aim, such situations are often short-lived, in historical terms. An imperfect example of this kind of situation, because it was also bound up with secular politics, may be found in the Catholic–Protestant conflicts in the Netherlands in the sixteenth and seventeenth centuries (Goudsblom 1967: 17–19). The resolution of a situation of religious competition may often result in religious persecution in the period that follows.

Finally, there is a particular kind of situation of conflict that is about *religious politics*; that is to say, struggles for power and influence within religious institutions or groups. Religious organizations are probably no more and no less vulnerable to conflicts of this kind than their secular counterparts. Schisms within modern Sikhism between the Akali Dal and the Nihang Buddha Dal factions – a conflict which was successfully manipulated to its own advantage in the Punjab in the 1980s by the Indian Congress Party – is an example of religious politics, as is the conflict between Shia and Sunni Muslims in the contemporary Middle East. These examples highlight the possibilities that exist for religious politics to become implicated in secular politics, and vice versa.

How to distinguish between one type of situation and another in the real, as opposed to the ideal-typical, world is not so straightforward. More than one of these types of conflict can be present at the same point in space and time, as in the example of the early modern Netherlands, where it is possible to discern elements of a missionary conflict alongside religious competition. Similarly, a situation of one type may change rapidly into a situation more closely resembling another. In addition, as has already been mentioned, issues other than the religious may be implicated in religious conflicts. These distinctions and definitions are, therefore, nothing more than a potentially useful set of categories against which to set the description and analysis of particular situations.

An obvious question at this point is how does religion interact with other sources of identification – such as class consciousness, economic interest, party solidarity, or nationalism – which can make important contributions to the genesis and continuation of conflict? This question was at the foreground of attempts to understand the ethnic conflicts that spilled blood all over the former Yugoslavia during the early 1990s. More generally, does it make sense to delineate a domain of the 'religious' that is distinct from these other factors? These questions are more easily asked than answered. However, it may prove possible to shed some light on the issues by returning to ethnicity, which can be either a *source* of conflict, or the cultural or ideological *idiom* in which conflict is pursued. Ethnicity is also, of course, a source of social *solidarity*. Difference and similarity, again.

With respect to group identity, ethnicity is about the differences and similarities that are recognized as significant by their members. But which differences provide local models of ethnic identification with their content? Among others, the following are obvious possibilities: language, territorial occupation, religion, and a shared history (particularly, perhaps, a history of conflict with other ethnic groups). The important point to note in this context is that religion may be – I might even want to put this more strongly: is *likely* to be – an important dimension of ethnic identity. This, of necessity almost, poses the further question: when are religious conflicts actually ethnic conflicts, and vice versa?

Framed thus, the question permits no straightforward or clear-cut answer. However, some headway may be made by returning to the earlier definition of religious conflict: in this sense, a conflict is 'religious' if it is defined as such by a significant proportion of the parties to it. Without wishing to evoke disputes about false knowledge or ideology that have long since passed their sell-by date, the further question can, of course, be asked: what if the participants in a conflict only *think* it's about religious issues? What if it's *really* about ethnicity (or nationalism, or class struggle, or whatever)? Short of declaring, by epistemological fiat, that *our* analytical models of social reality are intrinsically more trustworthy than *their* folk models – in effect that the social scientist, like mother, knows best – there is no easy resolution of this difficulty. On the one hand, socially competent actors are reasonably knowledgeable about the meaning and consequences of their own practices and the practices of others. On the other, however, in a situation in which the actors disagree about what's going on, the social scientist is arguably in a position to make at least *some* more sense of the situation than the immediate participants (Bauman 1990: 12–15; Jenkins 2002a: 27–31). All one can do is to examine the specificities of each case and attempt to judge accordingly.

Religious differences and conflict in Northern Ireland

Since the late 1960s, Northern Ireland has been the arena for a bitter and violently contested three-cornered conflict, involving the two major segments of its population and the British state. Despite the current, post-1998 'peace process' and a welcome dramatic decline in violence it is too early to be confident that the conflict is over. These 'troubles' are the latest in a history of such conflicts in the island of Ireland taken as a whole; their genesis and subsequent development must be understood in the context of that history, some of which has been outlined in the previous chapter. In what sense, therefore, can the present 'troubles' be thought of as a religious conflict?

If for no other reason, the Northern Irish conflict has a religious aspect because the two local protagonist groups identify themselves nominally as Catholics and Protestants. These are not, however, the only labels with which each community categorizes the other, or identifies themselves. Depending on the context, 'British', 'Ulsterman', 'unionist', 'loyalist' or 'Orangeman', for example, may equate with Protestant, and 'Irish', 'fenian', 'taig', 'republican' or 'nationalist', with Catholic (O'Donnell 1977: 139–45). These bear witness that, in Northern Ireland, group identity is complex rather than simple, multiplex rather than single-stranded. In this case, it would appear to draw upon political, religious and ethnic-cultural themes as the source of its significance.

Nor is religion *just* a label. It is important to acknowledge that, taken solely at face value, Catholic and Protestant are, for many Northern Irish people, considerably more than nominal identifications. In an increasingly secular – although not actually disenchanted – north-western Europe, Northern Ireland (with the rest of Ireland) stands out in terms of belief and practical devotion. Survey evidence is clear that, with respect to both camps:

> People in Northern Ireland are not only far more likely than people in Britain to belong to a religious organisation, they are also more likely to attend church ... In the ordinary senses of the word, the people of Northern Ireland are considerably more 'religious' than those of Britain. The churches in Northern Ireland are more conservative or orthodox in their theology than their British counterparts. (Bruce and Alderdice 1993: 6, 19)

Being a Protestant or being a Catholic makes an important everyday, and at least an every-seventh-day, difference to the Northern Irish. Religion has its own intrinsic virtualities; it is not just nominal, it is much more than a label (although this isn't true for everyone: the survey evidence that Bruce and Alderdice summarize suggests that about a third of the population attend church 'rarely'). With respect to the meanings that frame identification and everyday life in Northern Ireland, while there is no doubt that the secular impulse is stronger today than ever, it would be unwise to neglect the significance of religious beliefs and observances (Mitchell 2006: 22–8). Although the labels Catholic and Protestant in Northern Ireland are indexical of many other differences, they also refer to authentic religiosity.

Apart from the names by which the opposing groups are identified, and identify themselves, in what other senses can religious differences *per se* be said to be part of the Northern Irish conflict? In the first place, doctrinal and theological differences between Catholicism and Protestantism are intimately bound up with the gulf that separates the two traditions with respect to the necessity and nature of mediation between God and humankind. In Northern Ireland this finds particularly frequent expression, for example, in Protestant anti-papist fulminations and accusations of idolatry and authoritarianism. These, however, are conflicts in the weak sense of the word, and are not of major interest *in this context*: the same doctrinal differences exist between the two religious communities elsewhere without civil strife occurring. With respect to religious differences of this kind, dissent between the various Protestant denominations and sects is also important. An extreme – and, in the local context, highly visible – example of this kind of disagreement is the hostility expressed by groups such as the Reverend Ian Paisley's Free Presbyterian Church towards the Ecumenical Movement and its local Protestant supporters. Once again, however, virulent Protestant denominationalism of this sort is not peculiar to Northern Ireland, nor is it – even in Northern Ireland – inevitably productive of violent conflict.

So what about the contribution of religion to conflict – in the strong sense – in Northern Ireland? One of the most apparent, and perhaps the most widely commented-on, religious dimensions of the situation lies in the field of education. Regardless of modest growth since the 1980s in the number of integrated schools, there are effectively two major education systems in Northern Ireland, as there have been since the 1920s: one Protestant (controlled schools) and one Catholic (maintained schools), each insulated in all major respects from the other (Akenson, 1973; Gallagher 2003: 61–3). The clergy are highly influential in both systems; indirectly in the Protestant, directly in the Catholic. Apart from the interactional segregation that this situation reinforces, there remain, despite a common curriculum since the late 1980s, differences between the two systems with respect to the teaching of Irish history, sport, religious education (obviously) and maths and science (Gallagher 2003: 65; Osborne 2004: 78–80).

However, it is no easy matter to assess the contribution made to the conflict in Northern Ireland by religiously segregated education. Although on the level of common sense one might expect it to have had some effect, Murray has argued that segregated education simply reflects the prejudice and social segregation of Northern Irish society in general and that the specific influence of education on the local situation has been 'grossly exaggerated' (Murray 1983: 149). Be that as it may – and Murray's argument is persuasive – there can be little doubt that segregated schooling serves to reproduce, even if it does not create, the boundaries between the two ethnic groups. This is particularly important with respect to infant and primary schools, the institutional social worlds within which a good deal of formal and informal primary socialization takes place, in ethnic terms and from ethnic points of view.

At which point it is pertinent to ask about integrated schools. These began to appear in the 1980s, initially as local initiatives of concerned parents; by 2000–1, 4 per cent of school pupils were in integrated schooling (Gallagher 2003: 62). If for no other reason, the small number of young people involved makes it difficult to say much about the impact of integrated education on the conflict. Although psychological research suggests that the experience of integrated education encourages greater inter-group tolerance (McGlynn *et al.* 2004) and there is no shortage of generally encouraging commentary by educationalists (e.g. Smith 2001), the politics of integrated education have, so far, proved to be anything but straightforward (Morgan and Fraser 1999). Perhaps the wisest conclusion, for the moment, is that the jury remains out.

Religion also appears to contribute to conflict in Northern Ireland if we look at the regulation of sexual relations and marriage (which, mediated through friendship networks and courtship, is also related to education). One striking aspect of this problem concerns marriage between Catholic and Protestant (Lee 1981). In the wake of the papal *Ne Temere* decree of 1908, and the McCann case of 1911, intermarriage was firmly discouraged by the Catholic hierarchy, and, even though there was some relaxation of the official Catholic position in 1970, considerable pains may still be taken, both inside and outside the family, to ensure that the children of a 'mixed marriage' are brought up as Catholics. This is an issue on which the Roman Catholic Church in Ireland appeared in the 1990s to adopt a firmer line than in other countries. Given the sensitive demography of Northern Ireland, the Church's policy in this respect is widely interpreted by Protestants – although this interpretation ignores the fact that the Church actively and publicly discourages intermarriage – as a stratagem designed eventually to tip the electoral balance in favour of the reunification of Ireland.

Nor does pressure against the mixed marriage come from only one side. Although there may not be the same kind of institutionalized barriers to intermarriage on the part of the Protestant churches, many Protestant clergy and lay-members also strongly disapprove of religious exogamy, possibly because, as a result of the local view of Roman Catholic policy discussed above, the traffic is largely seen to be one-way. Indeed, survey evidence suggests that, for precisely this reason, Protestant lay-people are actually more disapproving of mixed marriages than their Catholic counterparts (Boal *et al.* 1997: 159–60; Gallagher and Dunn 1991: 12; Mitchell 2006: 62). The consequences are informal, although frequently effective, measures to discourage such unions (McFarlane, 1979).

However, ethnic closure – especially in the face of the emotions – can never, thank goodness, be absolute. Of the 61 per cent of respondents who reported the religious composition of their own marriage to the 1991 Northern Ireland Social Attitudes Survey, 9 per cent were in a Catholic–Protestant 'mixed marriage', which may underestimate the global percentage of inter-ethnic unions (Bruce and Alderdice 1993: 14); broadly comparable results have been produced by recent data from the Northern Ireland Life and Times surveys (Mitchell 2006: 61; Niens *et al.* 2003: 130).

A third sense in which religion, or religious issues, can be said to influence the Northern Irish conflict is with respect to the position of the Roman Catholic Church in the Republic of Ireland. As the 1978 Northern Ireland Attitude Survey found, 'a principal reason for unionist antipathy towards a united Ireland is the position of the Catholic Church in the Republic' (Moxon-Browne 1983: 39). The relationship between church and state in the Republic is a complex matter (Clarke 1984; Inglis 1998; O'Reilly 1992; Whyte 1980). The issue is not whether Catholicism in the Republic does in fact exercise an overweening, or even a significant, influence upon state policy and legislation. Indeed, the fact that contraception has been legalized in the Republic – in the face of a campaign of stiff opposition from the Church – suggests that this influence may be on the wane, and other indications of this trend could be suggested (Hug 1999; Inglis 1998). The problem is, rather, that many Protestants in Northern Ireland persist in the belief that the Roman Catholic Church has considerable – or even total – sinister power in the Republic (Heskin 1980: 28–30; Mitchell 2006: 122). They fear for their civil and religious liberties accordingly.

Matters are not always clear-cut in these respects, however. For example, abortion – illegal in the Republic, and so strictly limited as to be, for most practical purposes, illegal in the north – is not an issue of major controversy between Catholics and Protestants in Northern Ireland (Porter 1996: 288–9). Much Northern Irish Protestant opinion opposes abortion *in principle*, if with less collective consistency and in smaller numbers than their Catholic fellow travellers on this issue (Cairns 1992: 157). It is no less interesting, however, that a study of Catholic and Protestant churchgoers suggests that, when it comes to abortion *in practice*, in real world situations, there is also considerable convergence with respect to the circumstances in which abortion might be acceptable (Boal *et al.* 1997: 150–2). Allowing for that, Ian Paisley has publicly expressed his horror of abortion and roundly condemned the practice on the basis of scripture, and members of his church – including his daughter – have shared public anti-abortion platforms with members of the Roman Catholic hierarchy. He, and many other Protestants, would support moves to restrict even further the minimal local availability of abortion, or prohibit it altogether as against the laws of God and nature. The security of their conviction being what it is, however, such a position is not seen as either an unwarranted religious intrusion into the business of the secular state, or a restriction on the freedoms of the individual citizen. At issue for many religiously enthusiastic Protestants, rather than the maintenance of some general constitutional separation between church and state, is opposition to any extension of the power or influence – as they perceive it – of the *Roman Catholic* Church.

So far, I have been discussing aspects of religion that may create social distance between Catholics and Protestants, or increase Protestant fears about the consequences of the reunification of Ireland, but probably contribute only indirectly to violence between Catholics and Protestants. Religion is in this sense:

> a basis for segregating the population into two communities, largely ignorant of each other and susceptible therefore to prejudice and stereotyping. (Whyte 1990: 51)

Religion may, however, provide more immediate, and in their contribution to the 'troubles', more consequential factors. With respect to the informal regulation of routine public interaction, for example, religion-related items are an integral feature of the set of culturally specified markers by means of which actors 'tell the difference' or allocate ethnic identities to significant others (Burton 1978: 37–67; Gambetta and Hamill 2005; Jenkins 1982: 30–1; Lanclos 2003: 124–48). Without this repertoire of locally significant differences certain kinds of violence – the random assassination campaign of the early 1970s, for example (Dillon and Lehane 1973) – would be more difficult to pursue with any certainty of outcome. Among other things, the following signs or symbols are differences-which-make-a-difference for this purpose: religious or quasi-religious medallions or badges, knowledge of appropriate ritual forms – such as, for example, the Hail Mary – school attended, and Christian name, many Catholics bearing the names of saints. These are not the only, or even necessarily the most important, ethnic markers; they are merely the obvious *religious* markers, and they are significant. 'Telling the difference' is an everyday cultural competence; here is the same Protestant young man who was quoted in the previous chapter:

> They wear crosses, fellas and all. A lot of our girls wear crosses but rarely the fellas. And they wear these white badges, here [*points to lapel*], the old men, I don't know what they are, it's like a flame in it. Priests wear them as well. I was told what they were one time … You can always tell by their names, Patrick and Seamus and Josephine. Nine times out of ten if it was Patrick he'd be Catholic … They're very strict about their religion. That wee girl I was going with, we were talking about religion and I asked would she change and that was as far as I got. (Jenkins 1982: 30–1)

More generally, the bare fact that the two political communities are of opposing religious persuasions is of considerable moment in providing each group with an everyday identity, recognized by themselves and by their opponents, which is to some extent capable of transcending and subsuming the internal differences of ideology, class, doctrine and political strategy, which perpetually threaten their fragile solidarity (Mitchell 2006). In the case of the nationalist community this unity is given institutional form and cohesion by the Catholic Church itself. For the theologically less unified unionist community, such a service may be performed, as Rosemary Harris has suggested (1972: 156), by the Orange Order. While this institutional significance can be overplayed – many Catholic churchmen have been ambivalent in their relation to the physical-force tradition of republicanism, and Orangeism doesn't command a majority of Protestants as members, outside its limited rural strongholds – the point has some validity. There is, however, no symmetry across the boundary; the situation encourages Protestants to categorize Catholics as a monolithic ethnic bloc (see also Mitchell 2006: 82–3):

> the two communities are not mirror images of each other. The Protestant community is more fragmented than the Catholic. It is divided by denomination – a phenomenon which has no counterpart on the Catholic side. It is divided by theological preference: while among Catholics there are differences of emphasis between conservatives and progressives, there is nothing so sharp as the fundamentalist/liberal division in Protestantism … The Protestant community is more deeply divided by class than the Catholic community … We have here one reason for Protestant suspicions of the Catholic community. (Whyte 1990: 49, 50)

The centrality to religion of symbolism also contributes in an important and particular fashion to its role in the unification or collectivization of diversity. Anthony

Cohen has argued convincingly (1985) that communal identities are, in his words, 'symbolically constructed': symbols can be shared without necessarily meaning the same thing to community members. This allows considerable diversity to shelter, and to knit together, behind a symbolic mask of collective religious identity. The supporter of physical-force republicanism and the pacifist can, for example, both be devout and practising Catholics and identify with each other in the practice of their faith. Furthermore, since the Catholic Church is less fragmented, and Catholicism much more elaborately symbolized in terms of ritual and belief, it has a greater potential than the Protestant Churches to function – very visibly – as a 'communal umbrella' (Mitchell 2006: 72–81). Hence further impetus to the categorization of Catholicism as monolithic. To return to the theoretical point of departure, this is a further indication of the importance of content – the 'cultural stuff' – to relationships across ethnic boundaries.

The other sense in which religion is directly implicated in the conflict is perhaps more straightforward. Religion often concerns itself with issues that are apparently political, and politics may equally be self-consciously religious. An example of this elision of the two domains of discourse may be found ready to hand in the Orange Order's Twelfth of July processions (Bryan 2000a; Cecil 1993; Larsen 1982). An important feature of these events, the purpose of which is the commemoration of King William's victory over King James at the Battle of the Boyne in 1690, is the meeting at 'the field' at the end of the march; among other things, this is an opportunity for speechifying by local Unionist politicians and Protestant clergymen. A recurrent theme of such speeches is the need for vigilance in defence of the Protestant heritage of the Reformation, and the importance of the Orange Order and the Northern Ireland state to that defence. Similarly, a well-worn theme at the Reverend Ian Paisley's religious meetings, although he was an active Member of the European Parliament between 1979 and 2004, is denunciation of the European Union as a papist plot, foreseen, what is more, by the Book of Revelation in the New Testament. Returning to Handelman's point about 'social biographies', for Catholics as well as Protestants, religion and religious readings of history contribute in no small manner to the weaving of oppositional mythical charters that legitimate the present impasse (Irvine 1991: 172–212). Religion contributes in a similarly mythic way to the construction of the future, as a historicist teleology of collective destiny.

More generally, there is a long – and particularly Protestant – tradition of political clerics: many loyalist politicians have been ministers of religion, and clergymen have often found it useful to draw on political rhetoric as part of their evangelizing. By the same token, politicians are also capable of leavening their public message with religion. An apposite – if somewhat extreme – example from the early 1980s concerned Mr George Seabrook, a Northern Ireland Assemblyman, Belfast City Councillor and sometime member of Paisley's Democratic Unionist Party (DUP), who was charged, in July 1984, with using threatening or abusive language likely to cause a breach of the peace. His offence was to suggest, at a meeting of Belfast Education and Library Board, that the City Council should buy an incinerator to burn Catholics, whom he described as 'Fenian scum'. A self-confessed bigot, the specifically religious dimension of Mr Seabrook's remarks is betrayed by his suggestion that Catholic priests be burned, and his later statement that he would only apologize 'the day after the Pope marries'.[1]

It is tempting to dismiss this kind of venom as the extremism of a lunatic fringe. Before so doing, however, it must be pointed out that in response to Mr Seabrook's public utterances the DUP stopped short, in the first instance, of disowning him completely, being content to suspend him pending an apology. Such an apology not being forthcoming, his membership of the party eventually lapsed at the end of 1984, to the evident relief of his erstwhile leaders. Rhetoric of this sort is representative of a particular strain of Protestant political discourse, in which are mingled Old Testament savagery, born-again fundamentalist piety, old-fashioned Empire Loyalism, and virulent ethnic chauvinism (Brewer and Higgins 1998; Bruce 1986; Higgins and Brewer 2003). To appropriate a local epithet, this is a tradition of 'bitter' Protestant politics. As such, it is the emotional and political bedrock upon which rests the phenomenon of Paisleyism:

> Although not all his political supporters would subscribe to his doctrinal view, there seems no doubt that Paisley's own brand of Protestantism provides an ideology that bears the same relation to the DUP's political tactics as Marxism does to a Communist party in Eastern Europe. The ideology serves to legitimize political actions, it serves as a unifying force, but it is flexible enough to be adapted to alternative policies in the pursuit of broadly similar goals. (Moxon-Browne 1983: 96)

In emphasizing this particular manifestation of the Protestant churches politically militant, one should not, of course, forget that an important body of Protestant opinion is politically moderate. It was, for example, Protestant clergymen who organized and participated in the Feakle talks with representatives of the Provisional Republican movement in December 1974; this is a strand of dialogue which has continued, on and off, up to the present, contributing to the negotiations which led to the original cease-fires of 1994. However, it is probably true to say that this sort of centrist moderation is not representative of the majority of Northern Irish Protestants.

The relationship of the Catholic Church to politics is different again. Having no major role to play in the Northern Ireland state – apart from its importance in the sphere of education – it has tended to abstain from public or 'official' politics. Occasionally individual priests may involve themselves in local-level political issues or even more rarely, as in the case of Father Denis Faul, for example, in issues such as civil liberties, and senior members of the hierarchy do, from time to time, issue statements about specific incidents. This, however, is the sum of *public* political activity on the part of the Catholic Church. In recent decades, individual Catholic churchmen have also played an ecumenical part in the informal and out-of-the-public-eye network of cross-community discussions that are, in a manner perhaps as yet not fully appreciated, part of the current 'peace process'.

The Catholic Church's relationship to republican politics, whether parliamentary or paramilitary, is ambiguous and equivocal. On the one hand, there is a necessary – and genuine – historical affinity with the goals and ideals of republicanism, broadly construed. On the other hand, the inherent conservatism of the Church prevents it from supporting either the violence that characterized the campaign of the Provisional IRA, or the socialism of marginal groups such as the Workers' Party. The hierarchy's dilemma in this respect is, effectively, the same as that of successive Dublin governments: how should the Church support the Irish republican ideal in Northern Ireland without being seen either to condone political violence or to encourage the radical politics that it regards as anathema? The contradictions and uncertainties which characterize local-level relationships between the Roman Catholic Church and militant republicanism – contradictions which came to a public head during the Republican hunger strike protest at the Maze prison in 1980–1 – are well documented in ethnographic accounts of working-class Catholic neighbour-hoods in Belfast (Burton 1978; Sluka 1989).

Thus there are at least four distinct strands of connection between religion and conflict in Northern Ireland. First, in terms of the signification of everyday cultural difference, religion is probably the most important factor. Much else – nearly every-thing else – is shared: language, popular culture, consumerism, cooking, kind of housing – the list would have to be a long one. There *are* other cultural differences, reflecting both the recent reinvention of Gaelic tradition, north and south of the border, and the overt symbolization of politics in public spaces by both Catholics and Protestants (Bryan 2005; Bryson and McCartney 1994; Buckley 1998; Loftus 1994; Rolston 1991, 1992, 1995, 2003), but religion – and all that goes with it – is perhaps the one that most touches most people. It makes a significant contribution to the ongoing social construction of the cultural content of the two different and mutually antagonistic ethnicities without which we would not be talking about this particular conflict.

Second – and this is so intimately related to the first point that the distinction may seem nit-picking – religious differences, as they are organized formally in the churches and in education, and less formally in families and social networks, structure the spatial and interactional patterns of much everyday social life in Northern Ireland. Formal and informal institutional factors, taken together with the authenticity of religiosity for many Northern Irish people, certainly don't make har-monious inter-ethnic relations 'on the ground' easier.

Third, some of the specific social doctrines and theological tenets of the Roman Catholic Church, combined with the history of the political relationship between the Church and the Republic of Ireland state, contribute to a view of Irish politics, widely held by Protestants in Northern Ireland, which, even given the present social and sexual liberalization of the Republic, links the reunification of Ireland to authoritarian Catholicism and diminished civil and religious liberties.

Fourth, within the Protestant community one finds a characteristic blend of politicized religion and sanctified theological politics, which combines fundamen-talism, anti-Catholicism, ethnic chauvinism and anti-republicanism into a power-ful, although not necessarily coherent, sectarian ideology that has as its focus the maintenance of Protestant control and 'cultural traditions' in the six counties of Northern Ireland.

As a counterbalance, it should be remembered that some, perhaps many, mem-bers of the various religious traditions in the Province see a role for religion, and religious values, in helping to resolve the conflict. Unfortunately, as yet their efforts still appear to be more than outweighed by countervailing factors of one sort or another. It must also be emphasized that although Northern Ireland has very high rates of church attendance, nominal membership of a religious grouping does-n't *necessarily* entail obedience to the dictates of faith or the pronunciations of the clergy. The pragmatics of birth control among Catholic women in the north is as good an example of this as one might require. It is *not* correct to depict Northern

Irish people as 'priest-ridden', and this may be a particularly inaccurate representation of those who are most directly involved in violent politics. Impressionistic evidence suggests that such people are often among the least devout of their co-religionists. Finally, to add further complexity to the picture I am painting here, it is worth quoting some of the conclusions of a study of Catholic and Protestant churchgoers in Belfast:

> There are good grounds ... for querying the stereotypical perceptions of Catholics and Protestants as discrete monolithic groups. Indeed ... a remarkable degree of convergence exists in their characteristics and convictions ... Overall, Belfast's churchgoers are conservative, committed to traditional doctrinal stances, and ardent in devotional practice, even if Protestants are more Bible-centred and con-versionist, while Catholics could be described as a community of faith. In spite of that, there is a sameness in their ethical codes, especially in respect of sexual matters ... (Boal *et al.* 1997: 168–9)

'Sameness' does not mean 'the same': this research also suggests that Catholics are less sabbatarian and disciplinarian than Protestants, for example, and younger Protestant churchgoers more theologically conservative than their more liberal Catholic counterparts. There is, however, sufficient *similarity* between the Catholics and Protestants in this study to inspire some critical scepticism, at least, about the utter totality of religious difference – let alone conflict – in Northern Ireland.

So, no claim is being made here that the Northern Irish conflict is actually *about* religion, or that religion is the *cause* of the conflict. It would be very difficult to support convincingly such an interpretation of the situation, either currently or historically. Although a minority of participants may see it in these terms – and there can be little doubt that a particular strand of local Protestantism sees itself as still engaged in the business of defending, or even extending, the frontiers of the Reformation – the majority of Northern Irish people emphatically do not appear to see the 'troubles' as being *primarily* concerned with religion *per se* (Moxon-Browne 1983; Rose 1971).

But, if it isn't actually *about* religion, what is it about? The most important 'non-religious' dimensions of the Northern Ireland conflict are, in fact, well known. There is no need here to repeat the detailed discussion of them in the original paper from which this chapter is derived (Jenkins 1986b). To summarize, the major issues that fomented 'the troubles', each of which is a reflection of the other, are membership of the United Kingdom and the reunification of Ireland. This is pri-marily a constitutional and nationalist conflict.

Intimately related to the major problems of national identity and government, however, other factors have made important contributions to the persistence and virulence of the present 'troubles' in Northern Ireland: religious differences, the economic and social disadvantage of Catholics, the relative privilege experienced by Protestants, the dire economic deprivation of the Province as a whole during a long period up to the 1990s, the policies and practices of the British and Irish states in a variety of respects, and – not be neglected – a long tradition of violent politi-cal action (this will be discussed in the next chapter). The significance of these fac-tors cannot be understood, however, without reference to the 'national question', the context within which they have arisen and from which they acquire their local meanings and force.

Ethnicity, politics and religion

To return to this chapter's original point of departure, it should be apparent that I have been making the case that the Northern Irish conflict is not a 'religious conflict', in the strong definition that was proposed there. Although religion has a place – and indeed an important one – in the repertoire of conflict in Northern Ireland, the majority of participants see the conflict as primarily about politics and nationalism, not religion. There is no reason to disagree with them. Thus the central *nominal* content of local ethnicity – confessional difference – has to be set alongside a range of other things if we are adequately to understand the situation. Catholic and Protestant are ethnic identities that derive only part of their content from religion.

This is not to say that the 'cultural stuff' of religion, *qua* religion, is irrelevant. Any such conclusion would be against the spirit and the letter of my argument. Bearing in mind the five categories of religious conflict proposed in the opening section, one can identify religious persecution during certain periods of Northern Ireland's history, and point to elements of religious competition and religious politics (particularly within, and between, the denominations of Protestantism) in the current situation. These are all present as sub-themes of the overarching conflict over national allegiances: religious issues and motifs provide actors with a vocabulary and institutional arena through the medium of which that conflict may be waged. On the other hand, the reality and undoubted force of confessional differences add fuel to the bonfires of nationalism and patriotism (and, of course, vice versa). It is possible to conclude, therefore, without any sense of contradiction, that although the Northern Ireland conflict is not *about* religion, it is, in fact, at every level bound up with religious differences. It is an ethnic conflict with a religious dimension.

In saying this, I am disagreeing with an earlier argument of my own, that religion in Northern Ireland is 'mainly a convenient boundary marker' (Jenkins 1984: 260). I am also disagreeing with McAllister's argument (1982) that religious commitment – measured by ritual behaviour, devotion or self-definition, and belief in the supernatural – has had little influence on the conflict. Inasmuch as McAllister was testing the hypothesis that 'the Northern Ireland conflict *centres* on religious values and behaviour' (ibid.: 343, my emphasis), he was, of course, only concerned with the strong model of religious conflict, discussed earlier. To suggest that religion is something more – and actually a good deal more – than a boundary marker dramatizing the ethno-national political differences between unionists and nationalists is an understanding of the situation that fits, in some respects, with the arguments of Buckley and Kenny (1995) and Ruane and Todd (1996: 307–9). It also resonates with much of Mitchell's analysis of the relationship between identity, politics and religion in Northern Ireland:

> religiously informed ideas have been used to make sense of, and cope with, political and structural conditions. The content of Protestant and Catholic religious traditions have been applied, in varying degrees, to a context of conflict. In such a way, the insecurity of Protestant settlement was imbued with religious notions of siege and contractual loyalty. Many Catholics gave meaning to social and economic consequences of invasion through religious ideas of suffering and victimhood. The role of the Catholic Church was enhanced by experiences of struggle as a faith community,

as it built alternative social structures to British and Protestant power, and provided resources for identification ... In this context, Protestant fears of going under politically as a community were infused with religious ideas of freedom and individualism versus a seemingly authoritarian Catholicism. So, we see a two-way relationship between religious content and political structure. (Mitchell 2006: 139)

Mitchell and I may disagree about where the balance is struck in that two-way relationship, about which side of the situation is more significant, but this is merely a matter of emphasis. There is more to agree about than not.

The situation in Northern Ireland is likely to have implications for our general understanding of conflicts that appear to have something to do with religion. This is a timely issue, and increasingly urgent. An obvious point is that religious affiliation is not, in any sense, an 'uncontaminated' social identification in its own right, somehow isolated from or 'above' other categories or identities. To adopt such a view would be to fly in the face of the intuitions of decades of social anthropological comparative research, and there is nothing in the contemporary Northern Irish situation to justify it. It is likely – if not inevitable – that religion will overlap and interact with other principles of affiliation and identification, particularly ethnicity, locality, nationality, class and economic interest. It is therefore to be expected that a 'pure' religious conflict, untainted by any other considerations or issues, will be, to say the least, rare. This isn't to suggest that conflicts which are *primarily* about religion, and which hence fall within the scope of the definition of religious conflict proposed earlier, will not occur, but simply to insist that conflicts that are *only* about religion – or indeed only about *anything* – are unlikely. It is equally unlikely that conflicts will be solely ethnic, or solely class-based, for example, although these may well be their dominant themes.

Bearing in mind the polysemic and multiplex character of conflicts 'in the real world', and recognizing that group identity, the basis of recruitment for social conflict, is multi-dimensional, it seems sensible to identify a weaker form of religious conflict than that which I have hitherto used as a benchmark. In other words, one can apply the five ideal types of religious conflict outlined earlier to the religious dimensions of a conflict that does not appear, in itself, to be primarily about religion: It is thus necessary to differentiate *religious conflicts* from *conflicts with a religious dimension*, in which religion is a sub-theme, an elaboration on the main issue underlying the conflict.

The conflict in Northern Ireland is primarily *about* nationalism and the politics of ethnic domination. However, inasmuch as religious affiliation is effectively coterminous with ethnicity in this instance, the situation may accurately be described as a conflict with a religious dimension. The various struggles in the six counties are contributed to and coloured by religious themes, confessional differences providing the protagonists with an important medium through which to interpret and further their respective causes and a fundamental basis for group identification and social categorization. It would be a very different situation indeed without this repertoire of differentiation, historical contextualization, justification and teleological imagination. It might certainly be less intractable. On the other hand, the troubled question of national allegiance is an important factor in the exacerbation of existing – and specifically religious – disputes between Catholics and Protestants.

To return, in closing, to the 'cultural stuff', the basic conclusion is that boundaries, and the interactions across them, are intimately and indissolubly bound up with the cultural contents of ethnicity. Although he has not developed it in detail, this is a conclusion towards which Barth himself has eventually been led. During a retrospect on *Ethnic Groups and Boundaries,* he acknowledged that:

> the issue of cultural content *versus* boundary, as it was formulated, unintentionally served to mislead. Yes, it is a question of analyzing boundary processes, not of enumerating the sum of content, as in an old-fashioned trait list. But ... central and culturally valued institutions and activities in an ethnic group may be deeply involved in its boundary maintenance. (Barth 1994: 17, 18)

On a related tack, Cornell and Hartmann's argument (Cornell 1996; Cornell and Hartmann 1998: 85–9) is worth consideration: that patterns of ethnic persistence and change – the variable potency of ethnic attachments – depend upon the relativities of 'internal bases of ethnic attachment', namely shared interests, shared institutions and shared culture. In this view, shared institutions and shared culture, rather than interests in common, are the most significant factors promoting group stability and the persistence of ethnic attachments. Interests are, by definition, more likely to be a function of situation and circumstance, and hence more vulnerable to change, reinterpretation and manipulation. Although this argument has its problems – the extent to which interests arise out of shared culture and institutions, and are hence not easily separable out as an 'independent variable', is perhaps the most obvious (Jenkins 2006b: 394) – it encourages two further thoughts about Northern Ireland.

The first of these is that in religion the institutions and the 'cultural stuff' come together in a most consequential manner. In Northern Ireland, taking into account the segregation of schools and of locality and residence, alongside the authenticity for many locals of their religiosity and the segregation of much everyday life, they come together with a vengeance. In Cornell and Hartmann's terms, the stage is set for ethnic identifications that are deep-seated and obstinately resistant to change. Which, it is hard to deny, is a reasonable characterization of Northern Ireland. Being a Catholic or a Protestant *really means something* to most Catholics and Protestants – although the range and variation in what it means to individuals might, following Cohen's argument (1985) about the 'symbolic construction of community', be moot – and ethnicity is, historically if nothing else, an intransigent basis of local group identification and social categorization. In my terms, as discussed in Chapter 5, the ethnically organized conjunction of the institutional and the cultural during the earliest years of socialization (in school, residential space, church) establishes the potential for ethnic identity to be entered into as a *primary identity.*

And, to go beyond Cornell and Hartmann's argument, there may be something specific about the 'cultural stuff' in this case anyway. Religion is distinctive in its particular ritual and symbolic content. It is arguably the case (Jenkins 2008: Chapter 14) that the ritual symbolization of identity – in *rites de passage,* but in many other ritual observances, too – is an effective way to make collective identities matter to individuals, affectively and cognitively. Through participation in ritual, people may come to identify themselves in a manner, and with a degree of commitment and enthusiasm, that amounts to something altogether greater than the sum of its parts. This is likely to be another religious factor contributing to the strength of ethnic attachments in Northern Ireland.

The second, much more tentative, thought is about the implications of all this for the current 'peace process' and the future likelihood of a working political settlement in the six counties of Northern Ireland. Local 'interests' – collective desires for an end to violence, an acceptable solution to the national question, and an equalization of economic disadvantage, which have become more apparent recently – may to some extent be hostages to the ongoing potential of institutions and culture to generate continued ethnic difference, distance and enmity. Despite the establishment of a power-sharing administration, led by Ian Paisley's Democratic Unionist Party in partnership with Sinn Féin, in May 2007, optimism remains an awkward and uncomfortable position. Just because the 'cultural stuff' is imagined doesn't mean that is imaginary. Far from it. And that the 'troubles' have not been *about* religion cannot be taken to mean that religious differences are insignificant.

9 Violence, Language and Politics

In this chapter I want to revisit, from a different direction, the different contexts of identification and analysis first discussed in Chapter 4. Ethnicity is one of the most significant of identities with respect to the relationship between localities and their regional or national arenas and institutions. In the contemporary world, one of the most important ideological manifestations of ethnicity is nationalism, conventionally defined as the expression and organization of political claims to territory *and* self-determination. I am going to focus on the question of how to understand the differences between nationalism in two regions – Northern Ireland and Wales, one a 'Province', the other a 'Principality' – of the same nation-state, the United Kingdom. In doing so, I will also take another oblique look at one of the themes raised in the previous couple of chapters, the matter of the 'cultural stuff', in this case language rather than religion.

Northern Ireland and Wales

The two territories have many things in common. Culturally, they are part of the 'Celtic fringe' of the United Kingdom. Each is small enough to be a locality and big enough to be a region, and each has a relatively low population density. They have mixed urban-industrial and rural-agricultural economies, although the industrial area of south Wales is larger and more populous than the equivalent greater Belfast area of Northern Ireland. Each has recently experienced a shift of its industrial profile, in favour of the service sector. Where Northern Ireland was for many years significantly more economically disadvantaged than Wales, their unemployment rates are now approximately the same, with Northern Ireland actually having lower unemployment on some measures.

The most obvious difference between them is that, although Wales is part of the British mainland, sharing a land border with England, Northern Ireland is separated from the bigger island by sea, sharing a land border with the Republic of Ireland. This is not simply a geographical difference: it symbolizes a significant political reality. Even allowing for recent limited legislative devolution, Wales forms a political unity with England. England and Wales remains a single jurisdiction with respect to law and the administration of the justice system, and constitutes, with Scotland, the (relatively) ancient kingdom of Great Britain. Northern Ireland, however, as a consequence of the political settlement of the 'Irish problem' in 1921, lies outside this structure; with Great Britain, it constitutes the United Kingdom of Great Britain and Northern Ireland, which is the state arena that deals with foreign, defence and macro-economic policies.

Compared to Wales, Northern Ireland's constitutional position is more ambiguous in at least two respects. First, although successive British governments have reiterated their support for the Province's place within the UK, this support is explicitly conditional on a majority of the Northern Ireland population wishing to maintain this status quo. Second, the Anglo-Irish Agreement of 1985 allowed the government of the Republic of Ireland a formal consultative role in the internal affairs and administration of the Province, This arrangement was subsequently strengthened by the role of the Dublin government in brokering the 1998 Belfast, or Good Friday, Agreement, and by the institutions of North–South cooperation put in place by that agreement. Northern Ireland is, therefore, more loosely incorporated into the federal United Kingdom state than Wales; this is nicely summed up in the fact that Bryant's useful sociological overview of the post-devolution state of the nations (2006) leaves out Northern Ireland altogether.

The two territories differ further in the ways that their populations are constituted with respect to ethnicity. The six counties of Northern Ireland are shared by two relatively clear-cut ethnic populations, Catholics and Protestants, who have a long history of violent conflict, the origins of which go back nearly four centuries to English subjugation of the native northern Irish and the colonization of their lands. The population of recent migrants is still relatively small.

In Wales, the situation is more complex, and less conflictual. In terms of recent history, major immigration began in earnest in the nineteenth century, as a consequence of the industrialization of the south Wales coal valleys. As discussed in Chapter 3, labour was drawn in from elsewhere in Britain, from Ireland, and from as far away as the Mediterranean. Partly because many people from rural Wales shared in the experience of migration to the Valleys, partly because of the role of the organized labour movement in forging a new, distinctly working-class, communal life in south Wales, and partly because the new migrants had to assimilate culturally in order to work underground and in the metal works (many, for example, learned to speak Welsh), sharp and conflictual ethnic differentiation did not occur – although the resultant distance between North and South Walians should not be underestimated. Over successive generations, an authentically Welsh population of sorts – about which more later – has been formed in south Wales, a population with a diversity of antecedents. The most recent waves of immigration have occurred in the last three decades or so: first, an influx of relatively affluent outsiders – typically monoglot English speakers – into rural, Welsh-speaking areas of north and west Wales (Day, 1989; Symonds, 1990), and second, a diversity of other migrants, from asylum seekers to citizens of the expanding European Union. Although this in-migration has sown the seeds of some conflict, to which I shall return, it is unlikely to produce anything resembling the Northern Irish situation in terms of substantial, mutually hostile ethnic blocs.

The final difference between the two territories is in the history and nature of their nationalist political movements. As someone who grew up in Northern Ireland and who lived, subsequently, in south Wales, one of the first differences that I noticed was in the rhetorical and actual politics of nationalism. Putting to one side, for the moment, Finlayson's argument (1996) that the Ulster Protestant cause is a nationalist ideology, and accepting the more limited definition of the situation held by most – if not all – local actors, in Northern Ireland, the nationalist objective, despite the *de facto* acceptance of the present status quo on which the Good Friday Agreement rests, is the reunification of the island. Between the late 1960s and the turn of the millennium, and intermittently before that, the most important means to this end – a situation that the current 'peace process' and arms decommissioning appears to have changed – has been armed struggle.

In Wales, by contrast, the promotion and defence of Welsh culture – symbolized most sharply by the Welsh language – and, since the inauguration the National Assembly for Wales following the 1997 referendum, the further development of a distinct devolved administration and distinctly Welsh policies are the dominant items on the nationalist agenda. Outright self-government comes a poor third. The legitimate tactic for achieving these goals in Wales is constitutional democratic politics, a limited degree of direct action and protest having apparently faded out of the picture since legislative devolution. Because means and ends are never easily distinguishable in politics – and this is perhaps peculiarly the case with nationalism – these differences lead me to question the degree to which the two nationalist movements, in Northern Ireland and in Wales, can be regarded, despite recent changes of tactics, as even varieties of the same phenomenon. I will return to the comparison between nationalism in Northern Ireland and Wales in Chapter 10.

The violence of politics

At the level of the strikingly obvious, Northern Ireland differs from Wales in that it has, for approaching forty years, been the site of a complex and bloody struggle among various ethnically organized, armed political movements and the British state. That armed struggle has been one of the defining realities of nationalist politics in Northern Ireland does not, however, mean that the use of violence is a consensual strategy, embraced and supported by all those who might identify themselves as nationalists.

Among the Catholic public élite in Northern Ireland there is a broad spectrum of opinion concerning the role and acceptability of violence. The hierarchy of the Roman Catholic Church, the confessional community of the nationalist section of the population, has been unequivocal in its condemnation and rejection of political violence, a stance which was underlined by the incumbency, between 1990 and 1996, of Archbishop Cahal Daly, a vociferous critic of paramilitary organizations, as Catholic Primate of All Ireland. The public pronouncements of individual priests with republican or nationalist sympathies have often complicated this generalization, as has the issue of whether or not the sacraments or a religious funeral should be available to unrepentant 'terrorists', but the overall picture has been consistent.

A similar stance with respect to violence is adopted by the, overwhelmingly Catholic, Social Democratic and Labour Party (SDLP). For many years the only political voice of constitutional nationalism, advocating the reunification of Ireland via democratic process – presumably when either the Catholic population becomes a majority in Northern Ireland, enough of the Protestants change their mind, the British parliament has a change of heart, or, more recently, the ongoing process of European unification renders the problem solved through irrelevance – the SDLP has no choice. It must oppose violence, although it has a long tradition of association with various forms of non-violent extra-parliamentary action. In purely political terms it also has little choice. To embrace violence would be to render itself indistinguishable in many respects from its main rival for Catholic votes, the republican Sinn Féin.

The other major 'collective actor' at this level is the republican movement (a historical identification, deriving from its past advocacy of a particular kind of government in what was then the Irish Free State), specifically the Provisional Republican movement: Sinn Féin – which may be translated from the Irish as 'Ourselves Alone' – a political party, and the Provisional IRA (Irish Republican Army), a paramilitary organization. This dual-pronged strategy was for many years publicly represented in the slogan 'the ballot box and the Armalite', the latter being a useful American assault rifle. Here, times have been changing, and rather rapidly. While the Provisional movement was historically clear about the legitimacy of violence, to force British withdrawal from the Province and to protect the Catholic population from the security forces and from Protestant paramilitary organizations, the Belfast Agreement of 1998 signalled a significant new direction. While this has not been uncontroversial – witness the, sometimes exceedingly violent, 'hold out' refusal of the Real IRA, the Continuity IRA and Oglaigh na hEireann to accept the situation – Sinn Féin is now committed to democratic politics as the only way forward, decommissioning of the IRA's weaponry is reportedly complete, the legitimacy of the police has been recognized, and early May 2007 saw the establishment of cooperation in government with Ian Paisley's Democratic Unionist Party.

Public political debate within the nationalist community, has, therefore, always been characterized by the interplay of a range of opinions about the legitimacy of violence. What, however, of the ordinary members of that community, the constituency to which nationalist politicians must appeal? In the north Belfast Catholic enclave studied by Frank Burton in the early 1970s (Burton 1978), support from the community for the use of violence by the Provisionals was shifting, situational and conditional. The defensive role – at a time of vicious interpersonal sectarian attacks in this part of Belfast, in effect an organized campaign of civilian assassination on the part of Loyalist paramilitaries – was seen as legitimate. Offensive violence was seen as considerably more problematic. Within the area there was considerable public tension between the Catholic Church and the republican movement. By the early 1980s, when Jeff Sluka undertook field research in Divis Flats, a Catholic area of west Belfast, this tension had increased considerably (Sluka 1989). Public support in the area for the 'armed struggle' as the means of securing a united Ireland was substantial; more than half the people surveyed by Sluka expressed views of this kind. The urban nationalist community's experience of the Northern Irish 'troubles', in particular specific episodes such as the H-Blocks hunger strike, appears to have led to increased, consolidated and less equivocal support for violence as a political option (although it must also be remembered that many people in these same communities are still led by their religious faith to a rejection of violence).

The situation in urban Catholic neighbourhoods at the time of writing – with the experience of more than a decade relatively free of serious violence – can only be guessed at. The large votes for Sinn Féin in Catholic west Belfast, in the 'peace process' elections held at the end of May 1996 and since, can be interpreted in at least two ways: as an endorsement of the new role of negotiation and constitutional politics, and as a recognition of the historical role of the party as the defender, by whatever means, of the Catholic community. Nor has local violence stopped altogether: 'interface' friction (Byrne 2005; Shirlow and Murtagh 2006: 81–100) and 'community punishments' (Shirlow and Murtagh 2006: 52) continue. There are other unresolved conflicts and issues, too, not least how to come to terms with decades of loss and conflict, internal as well as external, and how to memorialize local and national struggles in a new and changing context (Ardoyne Commemoration Project 2002; Rolston 2003).

In rural communities, the research literature – which is typically social anthropological – suggests a rather different picture: of Catholics and Protestants continuing to interact as well as possible despite the 'troubles', of an implicit rejection of violence, of a degree of harmony and coexistence (e.g. Buckley 1982; Bufwack 1982; Donnan and McFarlane 1983; Glassie 1982). Given that some of the most violent areas of the province are rural – near the border with the Republic – and that the IRA for a long time now has been waging an intermittent campaign in rural areas against part-time members of the security forces (who are, almost by definition, Protestant and who live 'in the community'), this may seem somewhat surprising. It is in part a reflection of the locations chosen for anthropological field studies; in part a reflection of the period during which most of them were undertaken, relatively early on in 'the troubles'; in part the product of face-to-face fieldwork, which, perhaps, overexposes the researcher to the civilities of everyday life; and in part a testimony to the enduring residual power of a consensual model of the social world in much anthropological thinking.

It is also, of course, in part an accurate reflection of a dimension of rural life in Northern Ireland. My concern here is not to deny that there is an important truth in this comforting picture of country folk living their everyday lives as uneventfully as they can manage. But it does seem likely that the picture – particularly in the current climate – is more complex. Certainly, research during the late 1980s in County Tyrone, in a community near the border (Hamilton *et al.* 1990: 39–56), suggests a situation closer to that which exists in Belfast or Derry: conditional support among Catholics for the Provisional IRA's campaign and conflict between this support and Catholicism and 'moderate' constitutional nationalism (see also Kelleher 2003). More recent research focusing on the specifics of the borderlands (Donnan 2005), paints a picture of communities that have not been able to manage the 'troubles' by withdrawing into residential segregation, in which local social relationships and livelihoods have been ravaged by violence, and for whom the intimately familiar local countryside has been redrawn as a landscape of loss and pain, defeat and victory, and obstinately difficult memory.

Finally, with respect to nationalist opinion in both urban and rural areas of Northern Ireland it cannot be emphasized too strongly that support for, or rejection of, the 'armed struggle' has been, and is, related to enthusiasm for Irish unity in complex ways that shortage of space precludes me from exploring here. Irish nationalism does *not* necessarily translate into either acceptance of, or support for, violence (in much the same way that support for the union with Britain does not necessarily translate into sectarianism). Nor should it be forgotten that waxing and waning Catholic support for violence can only be understood in the context of the violence of the state security forces and Protestant paramilitary organizations. With the benefit of hindsight, the present 'troubles' in Northern Ireland had their immediate historical roots in the violent and inept repression of the (largely Catholic) Civil Rights Movement by the (Protestant) Stormont regime in the late 1960s. And one popular image of the conflict that must be rejected is that of the British Army and security forces as disinterested mediators or referees, standing between two 'tribal' factions: it has been a three-cornered struggle, with, as revealed by the 2007 Police Ombudsman's Report on collusion between members of the Royal Ulster Constabulary – as it then was – and loyalist paramilitaries, an ambiguous relationship between the state security forces and loyalist Protestants.

Moving across the water to Wales, one of the most obvious features of Welsh nationalism is the more or less complete rejection of violence against persons. There is a sporadic history of extra-parliamentary activity in support of the nationalist political agenda, particularly by Mudiad Amddiffyn Cymru (MAC, Movement for the Defence of Wales) and the Free Wales Army in the 1960s (Clews 1980), and there were three deaths as a result of explosions at the time of the Investiture of the Prince of Wales in 1969. However, violence against English people or their representatives – as opposed to their property – quickly vanished as even a fringe element in the tactics of Welsh nationalism. Meibion Glyndŵr (The Sons of Glyndŵr) continued the tradition of direct action during the 1980s, and into the 1990s, with an incendiary campaign focused on absentee-owned second homes and the estate agents who sold them. The explicit focus – although it was a fine line, given that letter bombs were sometimes used – was on attacks on property. Within this framework of direct action, public debate was aroused, for example, by the remarks of the Anglican cleric and poet R.S. Thomas in 1990, to a meeting of Cyfamodwyr y Cymry Rhydd (The Covenanters of the Free Welsh), calling for a campaign of 'non-violent night attacks' on the homes of English people in Welsh-speaking districts.[1] The constant quest seemed to be for a rhetoric and a method to legitimize direct action.

Organizations such as these have always represented, in terms of the numbers of people involved, a tiny fraction of the broad church of opinion that is Welsh nationalism. Nor were they representative of a wider strand of opinion, although there can be little doubt that the issue of second homes remains one about which many people hold strong views, leading to some ambiguity about the Meibion Glyndŵr campaign. Although both have a history of resort to extra-parliamentary direct action, Plaid Cymru (the parliamentary political party of Welsh nationalism) and Cymdeithas yr Iaith Gymraeg (the Welsh Language Society), the two main institutional expressions of Welsh nationalism, are unequivocal in their rejection of the use of violence of any kind. In an anthropological study of nationalism in north Wales, the absence of any debate about the legitimacy of violence is striking (C.A. Davies 1989).

Nor is it just that violence hardly represents an option. It is explicitly rejected both on pragmatic grounds, as a likely obstruction to the movement's goals, and on moral grounds, in reflection of the strong thread of Christian pacifism which has always existed within Welsh nationalism (Evans 1973; Rees 1975). The furore aroused by R. S. Thomas's advocacy of non-violent direct action, referred to above, is a good indication of the depth of feeling on the issue. The overwhelming majority of the nationalist political constituency in Wales do not regard violence, particularly where life and limb are concerned, as either a sensible or a proper means to achieve their goals. It is not an 'armed struggle', and it probably isn't going to become one. However, as already mentioned, at different times there has been considerable ambiguity about the 'second homes' arson campaign, reflecting an increasing shortage of homes for local young people, due to distortions in the housing market caused by affluent – and non-Welsh – absentee home owners. I will return to this in more detail below. While there was some evidence in the early 1990s to suggest that, due to the 'second homes' issue and concern about demographic threats to rural Welsh culture, opinion in Welsh-speaking areas might have been becoming more equivocal about increasingly violent direct action,[2] and some rhetoric to this effect (N. Thomas 1991: 18), it did not materialise. A long prison sentence for a Meibion Glyndŵr activist in 1993 and, probably much more to the point, the final success of the campaign for legislative devolution, combined to shift the focus of Welsh nationalism elsewhere.

The politics of language

The previous section offers a clue about where to begin any comparison of the relationship between nationalism and language in Wales and Ireland. Most of the nationalist organizations in Wales have Welsh names; this is not the case in Northern Ireland, where, of the above-ground organizations, only Sinn Féin adopts an Irish name (and even that derives from an earlier, all-Ireland historical context). The plain fact is that, whereas in Wales the Welsh language, despite a long-term trend of decline, remains a first language of daily use for a substantial proportion of the population, in Northern Ireland Irish is, effectively, dead (and it couldn't be called healthy in the Republic).

To look at Wales first, a number of indicators can be used to illustrate the contemporary status of the language (Aitchison and Carter 1999; Coupland and Ball 1989). Census figures, for example, suggest a decline in the number of Welsh speakers from about 930,000 in 1901 (50 per cent of the total population of Wales) to a little over half a million (19 per cent of the population) in 1991. At the 2001 census, the percentage of Welsh-speakers had risen slightly, to 21 per cent (Bryant 2006: 116). Since the 1970s, as a result of the work of language activists and the impact of the 1967 and 1993 Welsh Language Acts, Welsh as an everyday presence in the public domain – in official and other documents, on television and radio, and on public displays and signs of various kinds – has, however, increased in salience. All routine public interaction in Wales now takes place in an environment in which Welsh is to some extent – and no matter how superficially – obviously and unavoidably here-and-now. In terms of its distribution, while the language remains more important in everyday conversational use in *y fro Gymraeg* – the rural heartland of the north and west – in absolute numbers the majority of Welsh speakers now live in south Wales (Aitchison and Carter 1999; C.A. Davies 1990; C.H. Williams 1989). And in the south there is also everyday use: in a town like Swansea, for example, if you keep your ears open in the market on a Saturday morning you will hear Welsh spoken. It is anything but exotic.

Until 2001, the Northern Ireland census did not collect data about the Irish language (which is telling enough in itself). In 2001, 167,490 people claimed some knowledge of Irish, 9.9 per cent of the total population; 75,125 claimed to be able to speak, read and write Irish, 4.5 per cent of the population. The last native Irish speakers passed away during the 1960s and the language now survives solely by dint of formal education and activism. Surveying the then available statistics and research, the most recent and comprehensive account has concluded that:

> the death of native Irish in its last refuges in Northern Ireland in Rathlin, the Glens of Antrim and the Sperrin Mountains has not been balanced by any substantial accretion of effective second-language learners who have proved their ability to transmit Irish naturally or semi-naturally to their own offspring. (Hindley 1990: 40)

On this account, and the 2001 census statistics do not contradict it, widespread Irish speaking in Northern Ireland has probably become a lost cause. Something similar, if perhaps less emphatic, is also true for the practical, everyday status of Irish in the Republic (ibid.: 159–60).

Nonetheless, following the 1998 Belfast Agreement the situation has changed in limited respects: there are more Irish-medium schools and nurseries, nods in the direction of the public use of Irish by government departments, in official documents etc., and increased Irish-medium broadcasting. The Education (Northern Ireland) Order 1998 places a responsibility on the state 'to encourage and facilitate the development of Irish-medium education'. Following the Agreement, Foras na Gaeilge was established as an all-Ireland body to promote Irish, replacing the Republic's Bord na Gaeilge. However, despite the undoubted symbolic political importance of these changes, in terms of the number of people who can speak Irish well and who use it in their daily lives, they are still few in the broad scheme of things, and their opportunities to do so are limited (O'Reilly 1999).

The contrast is striking. Welsh, although in some decline over the last century, remains an important language of everyday life and there are grounds for qualified optimism about its future. Irish in Northern Ireland – and throughout the rest of Ireland, outside *Gaeltacht* areas (where the situation is not encouraging) – appears to be a language in terminal decline, for which the best that can be hoped is a degree of fringe preservation by enthusiasts. The roots of the different trajectories of these two Celtic languages lie in earlier history, but one of the important points to recognize is that *if* there are grounds for guarded optimism with respect to Welsh, this is in a large part due to long-standing campaigns of activism in the twentieth century and, indeed, earlier (Jones 1973). This activism is an integral part of the nationalist movement in Wales. It would not be overemphasizing its importance to suggest that the language issue has, in fact, been the central, uniting theme of Welsh nationalism (Morgan 1971: 170–2). Cymdeithas yr Iaith Cymraeg, the Welsh Language Society, is one of the key institutional expressions of nationalist sentiments and ambitions (Davies 1973).

It is not insignificant that the two major nationalist political achievements in Wales have been the first Welsh Language Act, the result in 1967 of a sustained and controversial campaign of non-violent direct action and disruption, and the establishment of the Welsh language television station, S4C, Sianel Pedwar Cymru or Channel Four Wales, the latter in the face of public opposition from no less a person than the then Prime Minister, Margaret Thatcher (C.A. Davies 1989: 37–58). The National Assembly, opened in 1999, owed its establishment not to nationalist activism – although electoral threats at the margins may have had some influence – but to New Labour's 1997 manifesto commitment to limited constitutional reform throughout the United Kingdom, and that probably had more to do with Scottish politics than Welsh.

To further underline the centrality of culture and language to the politics of nationalism in Wales, one has only to consider the issues that have been salient during the last two decades. The first of these is the 'second homes' problem, which has been an issue for some time, although its salience may be becoming more pointedly local than national (Bollom 1978; Gallent *et al.* 2003). The concern here is that people living outside rural, Welsh-speaking areas are buying up properties in these areas for use as occasional holiday homes, at what are for them low prices but which are unaffordable for many local people. The nationalist objection to this trend derives from the shortage of affordable rural housing: the price distortions it produces in local housing markets in *y fro Gymraeg* mean that local young people struggle to afford to live in their home areas. This, together with rural unemployment, produces emigration and a loss to the area of Welsh speakers. Second homes, and the estate agents who sell them, were thus the main targets of Meibion Glyndŵr's arson campaign.

Migration and housing are also at the heart of a second focus of concern: the immigration into *y fro Gymraeg* of non-Welsh speaking people, whether they be young families seeking a rural idyll and the 'good life', or retired people who have sold a house in a more expensive area of the UK and bought a cheap retirement home in rural Wales (Day 1989; Fevre *et al.* 1999; Symonds 1990). The arrival of relatively affluent, house-buying incomers is a further constraint on local housing markets and the ability of locals to maintain an active presence in them. The demographic structure of whole areas also alters, with the presence of many more elderly people putting pressure on health and social provision. The younger migrants and their children alter the character of school populations (and these kinds of problem are not peculiar to Wales; for a discussion of the Scottish situation, see Jedrej and Nuttall 1996). It is also worth pointing out that the community conflicts that this trend generates may be as much to do with class and relative affluence as with nation, culture and language (Charles and Davies 1997).

It is this which has produced the third significant issue: Welsh language education policies. With the shift during the 1980s in the balance of rural school populations in north and west Wales from mainly Welsh-speaking to, in some areas, mainly English-speaking, the issue of whether education should be in the medium of Welsh has provoked conflict among parents and community members. In Dyfed, for example, this has, in part, found expression in conflict within local government between the Labour Party and Plaid Cymru. While all schoolchildren have to learn Welsh, education in the medium of Welsh can be a step too far. In other places, however, particularly in the south-east, it has been, largely middle-class and often monolingual Anglophone, parent pressure that has led to the establishment of Welsh-medium education. In part, at least, this reflects not nationalist values but a common belief, not necessarily well founded, that Welsh-medium education is better resourced and 'better' (Gorard 2000). Since the National Assembly opened for business in May 1999, while language issues have been prominent, not least with respect to the workings of the Assembly itself (Williams 2004), it is true to say, perhaps because much had already been achieved in the two Welsh Language Acts and the 1987 Education

Act, that it is in other areas that distinctively Welsh policies on education have been pursued (Rees 2004).

All three issues – holiday homes, immigration, and education – are manifestations of the same problem: the perceived threat to Welsh culture, and its most visible and important manifestation, the language. How, nationalists argue, is Welsh culture to be maintained, let alone promoted, if the only arbiter of policy is the market, whether for labour or for houses? This is the central essence of the nationalist political agenda and, incidentally, goes to the heart of one aspect of the difficult relationship between nationalism and the Welsh labour movement: there is still much work to be done in constructing a satisfactory image of 'real' Welshness which admits the majority who do not speak Welsh (Bowie 1993; Giles and Taylor 1978). Nor is cultural differentiation quite as simple as this anyway. One ethnographic study has looked at different *kinds* of 'Welshness', focusing on the 'Valley Welshness' of the ex-mining and steel-producing communities of the valleys of south Wales, as distinct from from the 'British Welshness' of the borders and the southern coastal margin, and the 'Welsh Welshness' of the north and west (Roberts 1999). Bryant's discussion of the variety of 'contemporary constructions' of Wales – from y *fro Gymraeg* to 'Modern Wales' – is also to the point here (2006: 124–49), and resonates with Day and Thompson's argument (1999) that 'Welshness', like any other identity, is always locally constructed and experienced. Which brings the discussion back to Barth's point about 'the cultural stuff'. It may not be stretching the point to suggest that the sharing of a common ethnic boundary – with and against the English – is among the most important factors constitutive of Welshness, of whatever variety.

Although the language, and its defence, has been the unifying framework of Welsh nationalism, language and culture were never the only items on the nationalist agenda. After the defeat of the nationalist option in the 1979 referendum on self-government, the way forward for nationalists seemed to lie within Europe, as the overall framework in which a degree of local political autonomy could be achieved (Rees 1990). This changed in the 1990s, although due more to movement within the Welsh Labour party and, indeed, the wider Labour Party's concerns about preserving the integrity of the United Kingdom, than to the success of nationalist campaigning. While Plaid Cymru retains its long-term commitment to greater independence, as the official opposition in the National Assembly since 1999 it has settled down to pursuing its cultural goals within the new framework of limited legislative devolution.

In Northern Ireland, by contrast, the Irish language is a relatively minor issue. It serves some symbolic purpose – it may be heard, for example, from the platform at the annual conference, the Árd Fheis, of the Provisional movement – and, as described above, there have been changes, which should not be underestimated, that testify to the language's symbolic significance for nationalists (O'Reilly 1999). However, the defence and promotion of the Irish language is peripheral – at best – to the central demands of nationalism in Northern Ireland. Despite Sinn Féin's pragmatic and politically astute participation in the current political settlement, with respect to limited local devolution, complete Irish freedom from Britain remains the objective. This is, what's more, as true for the SDLP as for Sinn Féin (and, indeed, in terms of practical politics, as time goes on, given the apparent republican commitment to constitutional politics only, the gap between the two parties narrows).

This is not to say that culture and language are irrelevant within Irish nationalism. They clearly have a place; there is, if nothing else, too much symbolic capital and mileage in the issues for the republican movement for it to be otherwise (O'Reilly 1999). There is also a long history of 'cultural nationalism' in Ireland (Hutchinson 1987); with its centre of gravity in Dublin, however, this slipped down the order of priorities once the Irish nation-state – minus the six northern counties – was established in 1921. While Irish-Gaelic culture continues to do useful service rhetorically, it is no longer central to nationalist objectives, whether they derive from north or south of the border. With the sophisticated development of tourism, the importance of international economic links, and the ongoing Europeanization and globalization of social life in the Republic, Irish culture – or, rather, the invented tradition of Riverdance, Guinness and the like – has become more of a successful marketing phenomenon than a matter for struggle.

Some explanatory options

I have compared two constituent territories of the United Kingdom, each part of the 'Celtic fringe', each institutionally integrated into the UK in different ways and to different degrees, and each possessing well-defined and supported nationalist movements. In Northern Ireland, although there are indications that this is changing, violence has long been part of the rules of engagement with the British state; in Wales, this is emphatically not the case. Wales, despite devolution, remains relatively uncontroversially part of the UK state, and the most important political issues, which serve to unify the competing strands of nationalist opinion, are culture and language. In Northern Ireland, by contrast, cultural issues are relatively insignificant when compared to the central nationalist objective: freedom from British rule.

How are we to understand these differences? The social science literature on nationalism is an obvious place to turn for inspiration. One of the most celebrated and influential contributions to the debate has been Ernest Gellner's *Nations and Nationalism* (1983). In his account, nationalism, as a self-conscious political ideology concerned with the self determination of 'nations', is a product of the nineteenth-century rise of industrial society, with its linked requirements of cultural-linguistic homogeneity and a workforce generically educated for participation in a modern economy. Here the stress is on the relationship between an industrial system and a literate, national 'high' culture. Benedict Anderson, in his discussion of the 'imagined political communities' which are nations (1983), adopts a perspective that is in important respects similar to Gellner's, although his emphasis is on industrial *capitalism,* rather than the more general 'industrial society', and upon the homogenizing potential of print technologies for the creation of national self-consciousness.

One of the few authors to have examined comparatively the situation in Wales and Ireland is Michael Hechter, in *Internal Colonialism* (1975). In that book, and more clearly in a subsequent paper on 'ethnoregionalism' (Hechter and Levi 1979), Hechter relates the development of different kinds of ethnoregional – in this context, nationalist – movements to different configurations of ethnically structured divisions of labour. In other words, what matters is how different ethnic or national groups are incorporated into the economy and into the stratification system, producing either a *hierarchical* or a *segmented* cultural division of labour (an analysis which has much in common with the notion of *ranked* and *unranked* systems of ethnic stratification: Horowitz 1985). Within the economistic framework that he proposes, Hechter also acknowledges the role of cultural differentiation and the behaviour of the state in producing nationalistic political movements.

In the analyses of Gellner, Hechter and Anderson, economic factors are, in one way or another, central. Anthony Smith, by way of contrast, has put forward an 'ethnosymbolic' model, in which culture and the power of symbols are most significant (Smith 1981, 1986, 1991, 1999, 2003; see also, Hutchinson 1994). Smith's emphasis is on group identification as a complex bundle of cultural processes – as, in fact, ethnicity – that precedes the modern ideology of nationalism and, paradoxically perhaps, encourages its continued vitality at a time when, according to other authors (Gellner 1983: 110–22; Hobsbawm 1990: 163–83), its vision and seductive attraction ought to have been on the wane. Kedourie's argument (1985) is even more idealistic than Smith's: for him, nationalism is a political philosophy in its own right – not 'a reflection of anything else' (be it economic or cultural) – with its power rooted in nineteenth-century political history.[3]

In the first instance, Gellner, Anderson and Smith, between them, laid out the ball court for social science debates about nationalism: on the one hand, models of nationalism that are rooted in economic factors and emphasize the modern nation-state project; on the other, the assertion of deeper historical roots in ethnicity and an emphasis on culture, ideology and/or values. Increasingly, however – and the first edition of the present book, published in 1997, was part of this trend – these debates have been superseded by a varied range of theoretical syntheses that recognize the historical and contemporary relationships between ethnic and national identification, acknowledge the centrality to modernity of nationalist projects, and are clear that 'one-size-fits-all' models of nationalism do no justice to the diversity of political movements and conflicts that are called, by themselves or others, 'nationalist' (e.g. Breuilly 1985, Calhoun 1997; Day and Thompson 2004; Eriksen 2002, Llobera 1994, McCrone 1998; Thompson 2001; B. Williams 1989). In particular, there is a growing recognition that, bearing in mind the specifics in each context of history, politics, ethnicity and economics, it may be more appropriate to talk about nationalism*s* than nationalism.

With respect to the specificities of relationships between localities and their regional or national institutional contexts, I want to suggest that, in addition to economic and cultural factors – and as the previous chapters have emphasized, these are *extremely* important for our understanding of Northern Ireland, for example – politics and the state, particularly long-term processes of state formation, must be placed at the centre of models of nationalism. In particular, drawing on Max Weber's classic account of the rise and nature of the nation-state (1978: 54–6, 901–26) and Anthony Giddens's more recent discussion of the importance of 'internal pacification' in state formation (1985: 172–97), I propose to look at two linked historical processes that are central to any understanding of why nationalism in Northern Ireland is so different to nationalism in Wales. These are the incorporation of each territory into the United Kingdom state, and the attempt by that central state to monopolize violence in each territory (and, correspondingly, the degree to which violence has been removed from the political domain).

Northern Ireland and Wales compared (again...)

To look first at processes of state integration, Wales was finally formally politically united with England in 1536. Before that, integration, built upon the accession of the Welsh Tudor dynasty to the English throne, following Henry Tudor's victory at the battle of Bosworth Field in 1485, had been effective rather than constitutionally recognized. Before that again, the last major Welsh rebel against Anglo-Norman suzerainty, Owain Glyndŵr, had been defeated in 1408, and before that again, by 1283 Edward I had subdued the kingdoms of Gwynedd and Deheubarth. Not only is the political unity of England and Wales long-standing, it is legitimized by the role of the Tudors in the establishment of the modern English state and by their contribution to modern images of the continuity and the role of the English monarchy. The use of the title Prince of Wales for the male heir to the throne is indicative of the perceived stability of the Union.

Some of these constitutional arrangements gradually changed during the twentieth century. First, a range of specifically Welsh public and governmental agencies came into being, pre-eminent among them the Welsh Office, created in 1964 and run by the Secretary of State for Wales, a ministerial post of cabinet rank. Barry Jones (1988) has argued persuasively that the degree of autonomy from London that these institutions possessed was often limited, as was the extent to which they penetrated and established a legitimate relationship with Welsh civil society. Criminal law and the justice system, for example, remained, as still today, within a unified jurisdiction, England and Wales. Second, as part of a UK-wide process of constitutional change (Deacon 2006; ESRC 2006), and following a Welsh referendum in 1997 in which the devolved option only narrowly passed the electoral test, limited legislative devolution was granted, in the shape of the National Assembly of Wales, which opened in 1999. Many of the powers of the Welsh Office passed to the Assembly. Despite this new degree of Welsh institutional devolution and specialization, the unity of the United Kingdom remains the overarching and axiomatic political reality for most Welsh people; nationhood is largely a matter of culture and identity.

Northern Ireland is a wholly different case. Apart from the period between 1800 and 1921, Ireland has never been an institutionally integral part of the British polity. Irish history since the arrival of the Normans in 1169 has been a history of more or less violent attempts to impose or maintain British control, and more or less violent resistance to that control. The north of the island proved particularly obdurate and remained the heart of Gaelic Irish culture; so much so that, as discussed in Chapter 7, in the sixteenth century the English adopted a policy of dispossessing the indigenous Catholic Irish population by force, replacing them with immigrant Protestant Scots and English settlers. This settlement – the Plantation – is the reason why there are in Northern Ireland today two mutually antagonistic ethnic populations, and the reason why they are nominally identified in religious terms as Catholic and Protestant.

The province of Northern Ireland was established as part of the United Kingdom in 1921, in reflection of the, often violently expressed, determination of the Protestant population not to join the rest of Ireland in its newly won freedom from British rule. Many Catholics in the north, perhaps the majority, did not accept the legitimacy of the partition of the island. Between 1921 and 1972 the Province was a semi-independent member of a federal United Kingdom, with its own parliament, governing its internal affairs largely in the interests of Protestants. Following the *force majeure* imposition in 1972 of direct rule from London – the result of renewed serious violence, the perceived inability of the local administration to deal with it (let alone deal with it even-handedly), and the likelihood of ever-increasing British military involvement – and the collapse in 1974, in the face of loyalist resistance, of the power-sharing Northern Ireland Executive, the Province has remained substantially apart from the rest of the UK. It is legislatively distinct, with completely different systems of local government, public service administration and justice.

Northern Ireland has also been part of the UK's late-twentieth century constitutional reforms. The difference is, however, that devolution has been an integral part of the 'peace process'. And this difference is not minor: between its establishment in 1999 and 2007, the Northern Ireland Assembly was suspended more often than it was in session, as a result of conflict and lack of trust between the two main parties, the Democratic Unionists (DUP, led by Ian Paisley) and Sinn Féin. The problem did not seem to be public rejection of devolution. Finally, in May 2007, Sinn Féin having jumped the final hurdle, recognizing the legitimacy of the new Police Service of Northern Ireland, and following new Assembly elections, the DUP agreed to lead a power-sharing Executive including Sinn Féin.

The other significant difference is that Northern Ireland's membership of the UK is constitutionally conditional upon the continued assent to the status quo of a numerical majority of the population. There is nothing conditional about the unity of the rest of the Kingdom. Furthermore, following the 1985 Anglo-Irish Agreement and the 1998 Belfast Agreement, not only does the government of the Republic of Ireland have a formally defined – although locally contentious – consultative role in the Province's affairs, but some matters are, ideally at least, increasingly dealt with by cross-border bodies.

In terms of state integration, therefore, Wales is strongly and securely a part of the United Kingdom, firmly tied in to the legislative and administrative order. Nor are the law and the institutions of government the only relevant considerations here. Drawing on Linda Colley's analysis (1992) and Bryant's recent overview (2006), Wales and the Welsh have been able to maintain their distinctiveness in the context of a relatively recently constructed *British* identity – which remains in place, in increasingly diversified forms that reflect the growing differentiation of the Scots, uncertainties about the distinct place of England in the new scheme of things, and anxieties about multi-cultural diversity (Curtice 2005; Kiely *et al.* 2005; McCrone 2002; McCrone and Kiely 2000) – the creation of which must be counted among the successes of the state-building project which followed the 1707 Act of Union. Northern Ireland, by contrast, is a peripheral and weakly integrated member of the UK, part of the greatest failure of that project and perhaps its greatest victim:

British state-penetration of Ireland was therefore, at best, formally accomplished no earlier than 1801. Yet it remained incomplete and persistently illegitimate. Ireland was never treated as if it were just like England or the rest of Britain ... the programme of plantations meant that the ethnic politics of the island could not develop on the model of the English, Welsh or Scots: cultural autonomy within a wider political union ... the processes which encouraged ethnic integration and nation-building elsewhere in early modern Europe were mostly absent from the relationships between the two largest islands of the nineteenth-century UK. (O'Leary and McGarry 1996: 73, 75)

The unity of the Kingdom, when viewed from this point of view, begins to appear as imagined as, of course, it is. However, with respect to Tom Nairn's celebrated argument about the 'break-up' of Britain (1981), for example, the account offered here suggests two things: the 'twilight of the British state' that Nairn diagnosed decades ago looks these days more like an obstinate northern midsummer glow than a prelude to pitch darkness, and the origins of the crisis, such as it is, are to be sought farther back in time than he looked, in the oldest origins of the state itself.

The strength or weakness of political integration is, as one might expect, relevant to the issue of the state's monopolization of violence. In Wales, following Glyndŵr's defeat in 1408, the state monopolization of violence was more or less total. Such major interruptions of the state's capacity to guarantee public order as there were – the Civil War, for example – were conflicts within the state of England and Wales, the legitimacy of which was not in doubt. In the nineteenth century there was violent class-based conflict and disorder – the Rebecca Riots of 1842–3 and the earlier Chartist rising in Newport, for example – but this was largely similar to contemporary events in England. There was no peculiarly Welsh problem of public order. From the mid-nineteenth century onwards, politics in Wales has been largely – bearing in mind the General Strike of 1926 and the miners' strike of the early 1980s – governed by rules that do not allow for violence. The military has long since withdrawn from politics, in Wales as in England.

Northern Ireland, once again, is different. In Ireland violence has never been – and is not fully yet, north or south of the border – successfully monopolized by the state. Since the first arrival of the Normans, every century has been marked by uprisings against the English or British state. More to the point, the state has been ethnically partisan. After 1921 it only managed to achieve a partial monopolization of violence in Northern Ireland by authorizing informal Protestant violence in the shape of a local, paramilitary police force. For fifty years, the state in Northern Ireland was, effectively, the Protestant population, and its rule was based on direct coercion or its threat.

Violence remains a key item in the repertoire of political options in Northern Ireland; it is an integral part of the rules of the political game, even the current game, in which agreements to renounce violence are key to negotiating positions. The current 'peace process' notwithstanding, at least three of the major parties to the current situation – Protestants, Catholics, and the British state – depend in part upon violence and the means of violence, whether explicitly or implicitly, in commission or de-commission, as the means to their particular ends.

Which brings us, once again following Max Weber, to an important distinction, between *power* and *authority* (Smith 1960: 15–33). Power is basically the capacity to make other people do what one wants them to do, most typically through the use of coercion. Authority is the legitimate and delegated right to command obedience. Power is rooted, ultimately, in the use of force; authority in law and custom. In Wales, for a very long time now, the state has been legitimate and so has its authority. Most of the spectrum of nationalist politics operates within the framework of this overall legitimacy. In Northern Ireland, however, the legitimacy of the state is problematic for the Catholic nationalist population (and since 1972 and direct rule, this has also been true for a significant number of Protestants). Politics in Northern Ireland are thus a matter of power rather than authority, at least with respect to the basic questions of the nature, form and functions of the state, and violence remains one of the recognized possibilities with respect to political action. The transition from power to authority is, in fact, what is at stake in the current 'peace process'.

What about culture and language, however? Once again, the key to understanding the situation seems to be the history of territorial integration into the state. The Welsh gave up armed struggle against England very early on in the history of its incorporation into Britain. As a consequence, Wales was subject to a less direct and repressive form of control and government than either Ireland or Scotland. This arguably created the social and economic space within which Welsh language and culture – not being sufficiently dangerous, perhaps – could survive. Whereas in Ireland and Scotland, indigenous culture and the Gaelic languages became identified with Catholicism[4] and political rebellion in post-Reformation geo-political struggles, in Wales the language eventually became identified with Protestant non-conformity. This may have been a threat to the established Church, but it wasn't a threat to the state (the campaign to disestablish the Anglican Church in Wales eventually succeeded in 1919). During the nineteenth century, and this once again is a reflection of the two countries' differing relationships with the central state, there was the Great Famine in Ireland – which, with the benefit of hindsight was the biggest single blow to Gaelic Irish culture – and massive industrialization in South Wales, something which brought a late flowering of Welsh culture to the coal valleys. Just as the Famine would have been unthinkable in Wales, so industrialization was out of the question for the south and west of Ireland.

The north of Ireland was, by the nineteenth century, if not altogether Anglicized, culturally distinct in its local mixture and cross-fertilization of Gaelic Irish, Anglo-Irish, English and Scottish cultures. The Plantation, two centuries earlier, had seen to that. Throughout Ireland, the state's control was more repressive and more severe than anywhere on the British mainland. In the north, where industrialization did occur – although not on anything like the scale of south Wales – it was largely in Belfast and its hinterland. The Irish language did not survive the migration to the eastern seaboard in search of employment. There was neither the social nor the economic space available to facilitate any late recovery for a language and a culture which had been marginalized -at best – by the Plantation, undermined by the Penal Laws in the eighteenth century, and dealt a final blow by famine and rural social dislocation in the nineteenth century.

The suggestion is, therefore, that the conditions which facilitate the survival of a minority language are bound up with the way in which the linguistic homeland becomes integrated into a central state. Further, part of the structure of integration will be mechanisms and institutions of social control; some of these may be specifically aimed at discouraging the indigenous language and culture. This latter occurred more severely in Ireland than in Wales.

Comparing the nationalist movements of Wales and Northern Ireland, it is clear that the differences between them with respect to their capacity for the use of violence and their emphasis on language and culture are, in large part, a reflection of the history of each territory's integration into the British state.[5] Where the language of a peripheral territory has survived it is, *ipso facto* perhaps, likely to be a substantial item on the political agenda of any nationalist movement; where it has not survived in any major way, it is unlikely to offer a focus for popular support. So much at least seems obvious. Similarly, where the process of internal pacification, which Giddens has characterized as a central aspect of modern nation-state formation, has been successfully extended to the periphery, violence is unlikely to form part of the nationalist struggle. Where violence remains among the array of local political possibilities, it will, necessarily almost, be used.

A number of things can be said in closing. It appears, for example, that organized nationalist *movements* cannot be looked at in isolation. Their character and development, as ideological expression of the aspirations of peripheral minority peoples or dominant metropolitan populations, is inextricably bound up with historical processes of modern nation-state formation. In discussions of local-level identities and movements that are, in whatever sense, definable as nationalist, it is, therefore, not possible to limit the scope of analysis to that local level. The local has to be understood alongside, and analytically integrated into, the regional, the national and, these days, the supra-national (even the global). Nor is it possible to ignore an, often substantial, history of contact and state integration. Nationalist movements are not things unto themselves, and their history is shared with other peoples and places within a context of metropolitan expansion, power and the struggle for control.

Putting the historical politics of state formation at the centre of our understanding of nationalism, should not, of course, be at the expense of attending to economic and cultural factors. As I hope this comparison of Northern Ireland and Wales suggests – and it is also the implication of the previous discussions of Northern Ireland – this cannot possibly be the case. I am suggesting a middle-of-the-road argument – which resonates with the varied recent approaches of authors such as Calhoun (1997), Day and Thompson (2004), Llobera (1994) and McCrone (1998) – that that any analysis of nationalism must, within an appropriately historical framework, take proper account of political, cultural and economic factors. Anything else will be partial (and probably in both senses of that word). As examples of properly three-dimensional analyses of nationalism, I can recommend O'Sullivan See's comparison of Northern Ireland and Quebec (1986), Ruane and Todd's historical account of Northern Ireland (1996), or Brubaker *et al.*'s local study of a Romanian town (2006).

Reviewing the comparative case studies, the question may be asked: to what extent are we actually talking about the same phenomenon in Wales and Northern Ireland? The legitimacy of the central state is central to any answer we might offer to this question. The fact that each 'nationalist' movement has recourse to essentially nineteenth-century rhetorics of self-determination does not make them the same thing (and much the same could, I suspect, be said about the various nationalisms which have emerged in eastern and central Europe and the Balkans). In Wales the struggle is over culture and language and the state is, for the overwhelming major- ity of the nationalist population, a legitimate institution, if one whose further reform they seek. In Northern Ireland, the struggle, for most nationalists, is *about* the state. Their minimum goal is its transformation; at most they seek its dissolu- tion into an authentically Irish state (and, what is more, a kind of state somewhat different to the existing Republic of Ireland).

The state's legitimacy – which is, after all, at the heart of whatever generic polit- ical philosophy of nationalism it may be possible to identify – is wholly different in Wales and Northern Ireland. Is it, then, sensible to subsume nationalism in each place under the same conceptual umbrella? The fact that theorists such as Gellner and Hobsbawm so confidently predicted nationalism's demise, only to be contra- dicted by the unravelling of the geo-political framework of the Cold War in Europe, invites a similar observation: nationalism is dead, long live nationalisms. I will explore this further in Chapter 10.

Before going on to that, a few more words about ethnicity and the cultural stuff. Elsewhere in this book I have raised the question of how to differentiate ethnicity from one of its most reactive allotropes, nationalism. The answer – to which I will also return, and in detail, in Chapter 10 – seems to definitively implicate processes of nation-state formation in nationalism. But those processes are also involved in the construction of differences *between* nationalisms. Nationalism in this sense might be thought to have its own array of allotropes. And these differences reflect not only the negotiation, exchange and imposition involved in political processes (of state creation, or whatever) across the boundaries between groups; they also reflect differences of culture.

Culture and political processes are reciprocally entailed in each other. If we accept, for example, that collective propensities to use violence are 'cultural' – inasmuch as they involve hierarchies of moral judgement and ideology – then they are, in part at least, emergent aspects of the histories of state integration that I have been discussing (cf. Brown 1975). The choice of political strategy – whether to resort to violence or not, for example – is not only defined by interests, circum- stance and situation. Nor are interests in any straightforward sense 'culture-free' (whatever that might mean: Cornell and Hartmann 1998: 86–9; Jenkins 2006b: 394). Northern Ireland's long-standing political history, in which violence – employed by the state and by allies and opponents of the state – has been a locally legitimate or accepted means to whatever end is in sight, is also a political culture, with respect to the specification of those means and ends. Which is *not* to characterize Northern Ireland and the present 'troubles' as a 'culture of violence' – as if that might actually explain anything – and to dismiss or blame the locals accordingly. It *is* to insist that the local cultural contents of ideologies of ethnic identification such as nationalism or ethnicism are not independent of either ongoing politics – within local, regional and national networks of power and authority – or histories of relationships with Others.

Finally, it has been suggested that a nationalism whose primary objectives are couched in terms of 'culture', and a nationalism that has self-government in its sights, are rather different phenomena (cf. Hutchinson 1994). Fair enough. But it is not quite that simple. What do they have in common? Is each not, after all, a mat- ter of culture? And don't nationalists in Northern Ireland and Wales face a similar problem: how to create a sense of shared collective identity in populations that, for historical reasons, can see their differences *from* each other more clearly than their similarities *with* each other? How, in the first instance, are nationalists themselves to create that sense of shared identity in their own breasts? How to create, if you like, a new and authentic national ethnic identity out of two (or more) 'old' ones, whose authenticity is sanctioned by shared history and the consequential opposi-tional realities of everyday life? Aren't these political problems about culture? In this sense, the distinction between the cultural-ideological *content* of ethnic iden-tity and the political processes that produce its *boundaries* is a distraction from the reality that each feeds off the other in an ongoing internal–external dialectic of col-lective identification. And ends and means are never easy to disentangle.

10 Nations and Nationalisms

The political spectrum that we call 'nationalism' is broad and diverse. Recognizing this, John Hall has suggested that, 'no single, universal theory of nationalism is possible. As the historical record is diverse, so too must be our concepts' (1993: 1). Anthony Smith is in agreement: 'the complexity of the empirical issues ... rules out the possibility of uncovering law-like regularities or sweeping generalisations in this field' (1994: 392). Craig Calhoun has reached the same conclusion:

> Nationalism is a rhetoric for speaking about too many different things for a single theory to explain it – let alone to explain each of those different movements, cultural patterns, state policies or other projects shaped in part by the rhetoric of nationalism. (1997: 8)

To round out this unusual display of consensus, referring the point back to the theoretical roots in common of most social science discussions of nationalism, Brubaker *et al.* remark that:

> The great range and heterogeneous causal texture of the phenomena grouped under the rubrics of ethnicity and nationalism, emphasised already by Max Weber, render problematic any efforts to construct a general theory. (2006: 357fn.)

That a unified hegemonic theory of nationalism seems to be out of the question, confounded by the variety and complexity of the observable realities in the 'real world', does not, however, mean that we should abandon model-building and theorizing. Nor can we – or should we – relativize the notion of nationalism altogether. If the concept is to retain any analytical value, the varieties of whatever-it-is-that-we-persist-in-calling-nationalism must also have something in common. Although they are probably not the only common threads, two, in particular, stand out: first, ethnicity, defined as individual and collective identification which draws upon a repertoire of perceived differences and similarities defined in cultural terms (Connor 1978; B. Williams 1989), and, second, political membership and participation conceived as *citizenship* (Verdery 1993: 38). Although they are closely related, the first has deep historical roots while the second, although not completely lacking a long history, is more modern.

Nationalism in this view is historically and locally variable, and bound up with ethnicity. Taking these propositions together, the basic anthropological model of ethnicity has a great deal to offer historical and sociological accounts of nationalism (Brubaker *et al.* 2006; Eriksen 2002). This is particularly true if we emphasize the social constructionist aspects of the model: that ethnicity is perpetually defined and redefined by social actors in the course of interaction, and that the membership of ethnic groups, their boundaries and the 'cultural stuff' on which they draw are all, to some considerable extent, variable. This Barthian transactional approach starts from the point of view of actors themselves and emphasizes the situational contingency of ethnic identity. While Barth's later discussions of ethnic diversity and pluralism (1983, 1984, 1989) still focus on interaction and negotiability, something else also emerges: ongoing 'streams of tradition' or 'universes of discourse' in which individual actors differentially participate, and which – despite the use of imagery which suggests movement and practice – possess a degree of stability over time. History combines with the give-and-take of the moment in the social construction of ethnic boundaries and identities. To paraphrase someone else – from a different tradition – actors may make their own identities, but they do not do so in circumstances of their own choosing.

Ethnicity and nationalism

It is a tribute to the solidity of intellectual boundaries that for many years, 'The remarkable congruence between theories of nationalism and anthropological theories of ethnicity' was overlooked, to the extent that, 'the two bodies of theory have largely developed independently of each other' (Eriksen 2002: 99). In Chapter 6 I argued that one way to understand nationalism, and other -isms such as localism, communalism, regionalism and racism, is to regard them as ideologies of ethnic identification. They are more-or-less structured bodies of knowledge that make claims about how the world is, and how it ought to be, organized along ethnic lines. Allotropes of the general phenomenon of ethnicity (or, to be more exact, ethnicism), they are historically and locally specific. There is thus no equation of nationalism with ethnicity: first, not all things ethnic are ideological, and second, nationalism differs from other ethnic ideologies and is defined by the specific historical conditions of its emergence.

As a relatively recent reflection of the gradual move of human societies into self-reflexive history which is a concomitant of literacy (Goody 1977), nationalism is an aspect of the growth of ever more complex political units, based, to some degree, on notions of ethnic and cultural commonality (however much, pace Benedict Anderson, imagined). As an ethnic identification which, more than most, is explicitly socially constructed and orchestrated as a historical project, 'the nation' is actually a fine example of Barthian transaction and negotiation at work: 'nationalism can be thought of as a specimen of the big family of we-talks' (Bauman 1992: 678). Similarly, Smith suggests that ethnicity offers 'a potent model for human association which has been adapted and transformed, but not obliterated, in the formation of modern nations' (A.D. Smith 1986: x; see also 1994: 382), and Llobera argues that to make a bid for nationhood, 'the first thing you must have is a reservoir of ethnic potential' (1994: 214). Nationalism is rooted in, and is one expression of, ethnic attachments, albeit, perhaps, at a high level of collective abstraction. The 'nation' and 'national identity' or 'nationality' are, respectively, varieties of ethnic collectivity and ethnicity, and are likely to be historically contingent, context-derived, and defined and redefined in negotiation and transaction. This proposition applies as much to symbolic or ideological content (nationalism) as it does to group boundaries and membership (national identity, nationality, citizenship).

Not everyone agrees with this. Hobsbawm, for example, argues that nationalism and ethnicity are 'different, and indeed non-comparable, concepts' (1992: 4): in this view nationalism is a recent and programmatic political philosophy, while ethnicity expresses authentic or primordial group identity, rooted in the distinction between insider and outsider. Ethnicity may be 'one way of filling the empty containers of nationalism', but, for Hobsbawm, there is no necessary relationship between the two (see also 1990: 63ff.). Although Anderson (1983) and Gellner (1983) each recognizes a connection between ethnicity and nationalism, they also share, with each other and with Hobsbawm, an understanding of political modernization as the triumph of the nation-state and of nationalism as a specific philosophy of political legitimacy with eighteenth- and nineteenth-century roots in the cultural homogenization produced by industrialization and the bureaucratic state. Thus, nationalism is the product of industrialization and bureaucratic government (Gellner); of the convergence of capitalism and the information technology of printing (Anderson); of all these things *plus* the French Revolution's recasting of political membership as citizenship (Hobsbawm). Viewed in this light, nationalism is the modern new broom that sweeps ethnicity clean out the door of the nation-state.

Many more authors could be cited to make the same point. To differing degrees, they offer a similarly functionalist argument: nationalism provided an ideological means, following the collapse of feudalism and absolutism, for the modern incorporation of élites and masses into a shared political space, the nation-state. However much it may incorporate a sense of *we-ness*, nationalism for these authors marks a distinctively modern break with a traditional past characterized by ethnic fragmentation and small-scale communalism. It is both a consequence of and a cure for the disenchantment produced by the rationalization of modern industrial society.

The functionalism of this argument is not, however, its main weakness. The model of nationalism as a modern replacement for, or supersession of, ethnicity, appropriate to the demands of the industrialized social world of nation-states, depends upon definitions of nationalism and ethnicity that are more constraining than may be defensible. The definition of ethnicity that is implied is certainly more limited and more limiting than Barth's broad notion of 'the social organization of culture differences' (which, if it *is* what we mean by ethnicity, must include nationalism within its scope). Nor is the difficulty simply definitional: ethnicity is conceptualized, even if only implicitly, as historically and culturally 'Other', creating in the process two problems. Historically, the argument tends towards tautology: nationalism is what supersedes ethnicity, which is what precedes nationalism. Culturally, we are left with no authentic place within modern nation-states for ethnicity, other than as axiomatic homogeneity, on the one hand, or an immigrant or peripheral presence, on the Other.

A further criticism is that this school of thought takes modernity's view of itself – as radically discontinuous with what went before – too much at face value, overemphasizing the centrality to nationalism of the *modern* (nation-)state. If we accept the absolute modernity of nationalism, what are we to make, for example, of the argument (Runciman 1958: 280–1) that the 'nascent spirit of nationalism' was encouraged by the attempts of the late thirteenth century Papacy to undermine the power of the Hohenstaufen Emperors? Or Moore's characterization (1987: 136) of European rulers of the same period as a 'new order', proclaiming a 'moral fervour' that found an expression in the emergence of a number of nation-states? Reynolds has, perhaps, articulated the question most clearly:

> The fundamental premise of nationalist ideas is that nations are objective realities, existing through history … It seems normally to be taken for granted that the nation-states of today are the true nations of history and that only they can ever have inspired loyalties which deserve to be called nationalist … The trouble about all of this for the medieval historian is not that the idea of the permanent and objectively real nation is foreign to the middle ages, as so many historians of nationalism assume, but that it closely resembles the medieval idea of the kingdom as comprising a people with a similarly permanent and objective reality. Not all the kingdoms of the middle ages, however, were destined to become modern states, and if we start from nationalist assumptions we are in danger of prejudging the relative solidarity of those which did and those which did not. (Reynolds 1984: 251, 252)

This critique is supported by Llobera's suggestion (1994) that the beginnings of European nationalism emerged in the early Middle Ages, only to be stalled by the rise of absolutism. Furthermore, to the European examples one can add Duara's recent argument (1993) that the concepts of 'nation' and 'nationalism' are applicable to the study of pre-modern China.

It is, however, necessary at least to take seriously the view that 'nationalism, as ideology and movement, is a wholly modern phenomenon' (A. D. Smith 1986: 18). One should certainly beware of the anachronistic use of words such as 'nation' and 'nationalism', which did not, apparently, achieve common currency in their *modern* usages until the late nineteenth century (Østergård 1992a: 17). However, that nationalism is a *wholly* modern phenomenon is not self-evident. There is a *prima facie* case for arguing that ideologies and politics that are recognizably nationalist, and identities which can be described as national, predate the rise of 'classical' nationalism from the late eighteenth century onwards (cf. also A. D. Smith 1986, 1994). If so, this has implications for the study of modern nationalism. To return to an earlier comment, one way out of the impasse may be to recognize the historical interplay of ethnicity and notions of citizenship – which, we should perhaps remind ourselves, can claim a genealogy extending back to Ancient Greece – in the evolution of ideologies of identification.

If nationalism is an ideology of ethnic identification, and therefore approachable via the basic anthropological model of ethnicity, we should be as much concerned with how nationalisms and nationalists define themselves – and how they are defined by other actors – as with how we as social scientists should define them. This avoids substituting 'the reality of the model' for 'the model of reality' (Bourdieu 1977: 29) and offers a flexible approach which, instead of fixing the notion too firmly in the post-Enlightenment political landscape of western Europe – as one might socialism, for example – is catholic in its recognition of ethnic identifications as, in some contexts, national(ist) and their ideological and symbolic expressions as nationalism(s). The boundary between 'ethnicism' and 'nationalism' thus becomes indeterminate, lying somewhere along a continuum of gradual change within historically evolving traditions or universes of discourse.

This argument, that nationalism may be less definitively modern than is commonly accepted,[1] differs from Anthony Smith's thesis about the ethnic origins of nations (1986) in that I do not wish to draw too sharp a line between ethnicism and nationalism. I disagree with other aspects of his work too, such as the distinction he draws between 'ethnic nationalism' and 'territorial nationalism' (1991: 82). From my perspective, *all* nationalisms are, in some sense, 'ethnic'. I appreciate the point he is trying to make and its importance, but I would prefer to distinguish between nationalisms that claim territory on the basis of putative common ethnicity and those that attempt to construct ethnic commonality within an already-occupied territory.

These points aside, however, my argument owes much to Smith. There are two reasons for emphasizing the possibility of pre-modern nationalisms. First, I want to loosen the entailment of nationalism in the nation-state. To define a phenomenon wholly in terms of what may, at least arguably, be its historical consequence seems to risk a misunderstanding. Second, following from this, I want to explore the possibility that the goals of nationalism are not exhausted by the project of the ethnically exclusive or culturally homogeneous nation-state (cf. Hutchinson 1994).

The first move in this argument is to offer a minimal heuristic definition of nationalism. Thus nationalism is an ideology of ethnic identification which:

- is historically and situationally contingent;
- characterizes the politics of complex societies (states but not necessarily nation-states);
- invokes culture and ethnicity as criteria of membership and participation in the polity; and
- claims a collective historical destiny for the polity and/or its ethnically defined members.

This model may appear not only too complex, but also unhelpfully vague – which destiny? historical according to whom? how and by whom are such claims defined and pursued? etc. – but I hope that its utility will become more apparent in the comparative discussion of cases which follows.

The full spectrum of nationalist possibilities is not, therefore, likely to be captured by a definition such as Gellner's (1983: 1):

a theory of political legitimacy, which requires that ethnic boundaries should not cut across political ones, and, in particular, that ethnic boundaries within a given state ... should not separate the power-holders from the rest.

There are phenomena which are either rhetorically constructed as 'nationalism', or which an observer can ostensibly identify as such, which do not fall within such a model.

The second move is, instead of talking about nationalism – in anything other than the most abstract or general of senses – to talk about nationalism*s*. This is not, of course, a novel suggestion. Other authors have typologized nationalisms (e.g. Alter 1989; Breuilly 1985; Brubaker 1996; Day and Thompson 2004; Hall 1993; McCrone 1998; Smith 1991), typically within a framework that, first, distinguishes, whether explicitly or implicitly, between *nationalism-in-general* and specific historical instances of *nationalist movements* (Smith 1991: 79–80), and, second, classifies the latter as 'liberal', 'civic', 'ethnic', or whatever. My proposal is different; its definition of nationalism-in-general is looser, covering a wider range of phenomena. It is as much concerned with *similarities* between nationalisms and other social phenomena as with *differences* between them. Nor are the historical instances that I am interested in examining and comparing necessarily organized *movements*.

Nationalism in three countries

This chapter continues the comparative project begun by the investigation of nationalisms in Northern Ireland and Wales in Chapter 9. That discussion focused on language, violence and the history of the integration of each region into the United Kingdom state. In Northern Ireland the objectives of contemporary nationalisms are the reunification of Ireland and the removal of British government. In Wales, by contrast, secession is an insignificant nationalist project compared to the protection and promotion of Welsh culture – particularly the Welsh language – and the economic and social development of the areas in which that culture retains its vigour.

Northern Ireland and Wales also differ with respect to the kinds of political action that are perceived as legitimate by nationalists. In each place a gulf separates constitutional nationalists, who pursue their goals through electoral means, from those who advocate the use of force. In Northern Ireland, however, armed struggle still has considerable legitimacy in the eyes of a large number of nationalists, whereas for the great majority of Welsh nationalists even modestly violent direct action is bitterly controversial. These different nationalist discourses reflect different regional histories and experiences of incorporation into the British state. As a consequence, it is possible to argue that the nationalisms of each region are, in some senses, qualitatively different phenomena (although both can legitimately claim to be nationalist).

I will return to these issues. For the moment they provide the context for the argument that follows, and indicate its antecedents. In this chapter the scope of comparison has been extended to include Denmark as well as Northern Ireland and Wales. The choice of cases reflects, in the first instance, my own research experience of these countries, rather than any extrinsic logic of comparison. But so does my scepticism about existing theories of nationalism: in their different ways, Wales, Northern Ireland and Denmark did not seem to 'fit' the analytical models to which I first turned in order to understand them.

But as case studies they are particularly appropriate for this discussion. They are integral, if peripheral, elements of modern European industrialized society, the conventionally recognized birthplace of nationalism. Northern Ireland and Wales are each part of a nation-state political system, while Denmark constitutes one in its own right. All have long histories of political change available for inspection. If, therefore, their nationalisms can be shown to differ significantly from each other and from the 'state modernization and industrialization' model, that will be telling support for my argument. In the context of these comparative intentions, I want to pose an apparently simple question: what is the nature of nationalism in each of these countries? This entails a further, deceptively simple, question – does nationalism exist in each of these countries? – that requires us to remember the definitional criteria of nationalism outlined above. Moving from the more to the less straight-forward, I will begin with Wales.

Wales

Wales has been an integral part of the British – and before that the English – state since the so-called Act of Union of 1536. But it remains culturally and politically distinct. Having been spared the depopulation of the Highland Clearances or the Irish Great Famine, Wales is linguistically the most 'Celtic' strand in the United Kingdom's 'Celtic fringe', with approximately 20 per cent of its population still speaking Welsh. Although representing a history of decline, this is significantly higher than the equivalent figures for speakers of Scots Gaelic or Irish. From the late eighteenth century Wales, like other European cultural peripheries, experienced a romanticist 'revival' of 'folk' culture, sponsored and invented by an urban élite brought into being by industrialization (Morgan 1983). Under the aegis of non-conformist Liberalism, the seeds of nationalism were sown. Medieval classics such as the *Mabinogion* found a new audience as the *eisteddfod* movement campaigned to create a publicly respectable voice for a language which still, at that time, dominated rural and working-class life. Today, despite centuries of in-migration the Principality retains a cultural identity which, elusive as its definition might be, can legitimately be called 'Welsh'.

Economically, Wales – particularly south Wales – is part of the metropolitan British economy. Its first industrial revolution, beginning in the eighteenth century, was characterized by the interdependence of coal mining and metal manufacture in the southern valleys. Here there developed a characteristic working-class communal life: culturally and linguistically Welsh, Nonconformist in religion and politically socialist. This economic strength eventually turned – with mass unemployment in the 1930s, post-1945 restructuring, and the return of recession in the 1970s – to decline, only partially arrested by recent inward investment and U.K. and European subsidies.

Due to the antiquity and nature of its incorporation into the British state, Wales is institutionally less autonomous or distinct than, for example, Scotland. It has political distinctiveness, however, in terms of the politics of party. Wales has been characterized for the last century and a half by movements with strong links to religious Nonconformity: first Liberalism and then, from the early 1900s, the socialism of 'the Labour Ascendancy' (Morgan 1981: 272–303). As much as anything, Wales differs from England politically in that Conservatism has always been a minority affiliation.

Although nationalism in Wales can be traced back – in the agitation for the dis-establishment of the Anglican state Church – into the nineteenth century, not until the twentieth was there a nationalist *movement*. The Welsh Nationalist Party was founded in 1925, and was renamed Plaid Cymru in 1945. It won its first seat in the British parliament in 1966. At the time of writing it returns three members to Westminster, one to the European parliament, and is the official party of opposition in the National Assembly of Wales. While its support remains strongest in *y fro Gymraeg*, the Welsh-speaking rural west and north, it also has significant representation in south Wales. From its beginnings, the Blaid has emphasized cultural issues (language and education), economic development and political devolution within the United Kingdom as the best way to represent Welsh interests. Secession or independence have always been marginal to the party's platform. Its commitment to non-violent electoral politics increasingly emphasizes the Assembly and Europe as the most significant political arenas.

Although it is the dominant political voice of Welsh nationalism, Plaid Cymru remains a minority party in Wales, electorally. Its 'left-leaning' oppositional vision of the political future of Wales has always competed with the articulation of class conflict and communitarianism offered by the Labour Party. Since the Welsh Labour Party can now claim to have delivered devolution, and even shows signs of enthusiasm for the Assembly, this competition has sharpened. The Blaid also competes with the other major voice of nationalism in Wales, Cymdeithas yr Iaith Gymraeg (the Welsh Language Society), founded in 1962. Using non-violent direct protest, in judicious combination with lobbying, the latter's achievements include state funding for Welsh language education and the statutory definition of Welsh as having 'equal validity' in Wales.

Welsh is everywhere: road signs, toilets, train timetables, in the bank, and so on. There is a Welsh language television station, Sianel Pedwar Cymru (S4C), and a modest but locally significant Welsh-medium cultural production industry. During the early 1990s Cymdeithas was at the forefront of protests about new Welsh language legislation and what it saw as the continued reluctance of government to grant Welsh full official status. Demographically, the decline in the number of Welsh speakers may have been arrested. Reflecting the impact of education and job opportunities, increasingly the future of the language appears to lie not in *y fro Gymraeg*, but in the industrialized and urbanized south-east (C.A. Davies 1990).

Although there is no room for an account of the gains and losses of Welsh nationalism (see C.A. Davies 1989), there are some things to add. First, not all nationalist actions have been non-violent, as discussed in Chapter 9. There is also the prospect of an anti-nationalist backlash. There have been – to date unsuccessful – cases in north Wales in which individuals have had recourse to the 1976 Race Relations Act in response to their rejection under local authority Welsh language hiring policies. In Dyfed, national legislation permitting schools to opt out of the state education system facilitated a campaign by English-speaking parents, many of whom were recent in-migrants, against the County Council's Welsh language schooling policies. These kinds of conflict, and the undoubted existence of a strand of authoritarian and exclusionary linguistic-nationalist rhetoric, have inspired, and coloured, an academic debate about the relationship between Welsh nationalism and racism (Borland *et al.* 1992; Denney *et al.* 1991; C. Williams 1995, 1999; G. Williams 1994) that, in some respects, resembles debates about sectarianism and racism in Northern Ireland.

Hostility to nationalism is not, however, confined to 'non-Welsh' immigrants. Many Welsh people feel excluded, patronized and devalued by the language movement. This is compounded by class antagonisms: in the south-east, Welsh has become identified with middle-class speakers, often working in the public sector. As discussed in the previous chapter, there is a serious problem – for Welsh nationalists not least of all – with respect to the relationship between the language and authentic Welsh identity. Plaid Cymru consistently attempts to construct a vision of Welshness which while inclusive of English speakers is sufficiently exclusive to serve as a model of national identity (and attract votes). Local electoral alliances with the Green Party have provided examples of this in practice. Such a vision of the creative interplay that is possible between similarity and difference is vital, if only because a nationalism which is wholly identified with Welsh – and remember that it is with respect to the language that nationalism has had its greatest impact – is, in modern Wales, doomed to perpetual minority status:

> The issue of language has ... given rise from the early part of this century down to the present to a crisis in identity ... English-speaking Welshmen spiritedly and justifiably counter that ... they too are a distinctively 'Welsh' people. (Howell and Baber 1990: 354)

There is thus an everyday problem to do with 'national identity' and the 'nation'. What qualifies people for membership in the nation and an authentic Welsh national identity? And who licenses authenticity? Howell and Baber go on to list the attributes, other than the Welsh language, which distinguish the Welsh:

> their separate history, instinctive radicalism in religion and politics, contempt for social pretentiousness, personal warmth and exuberance, sociability, love of music and near obsession with rugby ...

Leaving aside the gendered nature of this particular construction of Welshness, and its romantic partiality, only one item on the list has any analytic potential: the idea of a separate history. But this history is an 'invented tradition' (Hobsbawm and Ranger 1983), a 'myth to live by' (Samuel and Thompson 1990). That invention is still under way and still evolving.

Even as a social construct, a separate history is, for Wales, problematic. There cannot be *one* history (although see Davies 1993). And separate from what? The answer, of course, is England. But Wales has never been isolated. As discussed in Chapter 3, its history, even as a nationalist mythical charter, is one of engagement with its neighbours and participation in a variety of streams of tradition and universes of discourse. Wales is, and has probably always been, a 'plural society', characterized internally by diversity and, in its external relations, open and much-trampled cultural boundaries. The question for nationalism is how to integrate this plurality of voices into a Welsh national identity. The National Assembly, at least in principle, offers a powerful arena in which this process may be able to develop.

As I also argued in Chapter 3, to describe Wales as a plural society is not actually to say very much. Europe – like most of the rest of the world – has always been a tangled thicket of cultural pluralism. This is one of the things which nationalisms, in their imagination and invention of consistency, often seek to deny. The irony for Welsh nationalism is that such a denial is only possible at the cost of political success. The public articulation of a narrow Welsh identity, rooted in ancestry and language, is not just the pursuit of a chimera. It is also politically unwise. If, as a consequence, Plaid Cymru is attempting to define Welshness in terms of common territorial location, shared economic and social problems, a sense of difference that is not exclusively linguistic, and a 'European future',[2] that need not disqualify it as nationalism.

Northern Ireland

Nationalism in Northern Ireland must, first, be seen within the all-Ireland framework. It claims that context for itself, and it is part of a longer history than the eighty-six year life of the six-county northern state. But the history of Ireland is also the history of its relations with England. Irish nationalism evolved as resistance to English rule, and was in the first instance inspired by an English political tradition (Boyce 1991: 388).

The relationship with 'across the water' has changed many times. From the twelfth to the early seventeenth centuries, Ireland was an insecurely possessed English colony, with large areas remaining under Irish control. Subsequently, Ireland in the seventeenth century was a frontier (part colony, part periphery), in the eighteenth century a separate kingdom within a federal polity, and in the nineteenth superficially integrated into the British state. The Anglo-Irish Treaty of 1921 partitioned the island into the Irish Free State and Northern Ireland. The northern state was an uneasy product of the refusal of Ulster Protestants to accept government by a Catholic majority. In 1972 this state was, effectively, closed down and reopened under the direct control of Westminster. The 1985 Anglo-Irish Agreement and the 1998 multi-party Belfast Agreement (the 'Good Friday Agreement') have further modified the picture: the former acknowledged and formalized the interest in the north's affairs of the government of the Republic of Ireland, the latter established cross-border agencies in some fields and allowed the republican movement to begin to participate in the north's administration. Northern Ireland's membership of the United Kingdom remains insecure, contingent upon the consent of its electorate.

And as the relationship with Britain has changed, so too nationalism in Ireland has appeared in different guises: the 'embryonic ethnic nationalism' of Gaelic Ireland at the end of the Tudor period; an Anglo-Irish 'national identity based on religion and love of the *patria*', developing into 'intimations of nationalism' by the seventeenth century; nationalism as 'a fully formed and articulated sentiment in the Ireland of the Protestant ascendancy in the last quarter of the eighteenth century'; the revived Catholic national identity of the nineteenth century, forged out of a 'nationalism of the Catholic democracy' and 'the resurgence of Gaelic ethnic nationalism' (Boyce 1991: 19). Although Boyce's view might be contested by historians of a more nationalist bent, it supports my argument about the historical contingency of nationalisms. Apropos the modernity of nationalism, one can point to the late seventeenth- and early eighteenth-century debate about the nature of the Irish nation – although the term found only rare use – and who belonged to it (Connolly 1992: 114–24). As significant as the contested identities to which this debate attests is the fact that, at a relatively early period, it took place at all.

The twentieth century saw more change. The Republic of Ireland won its independence by violence; the northern Protestants vetoed their inclusion in that independence by the same means. Republicans in the north made their way to the negotiating tables – not least at the 1998 multi-party talks – by using violence, in the first instance, and by promising to cease violence, in the second. In the south, nationalism is the political common ground: *all* politicians in the Republic are, in some sense, nationalists. Nationalism is also, however, something of an embarrassing irrelevance: there is little evidence that politicians or voters in the south *want* the six counties 'back'. The 1985 Anglo-Irish Agreement, the 1998 Belfast Agreement and the current 'peace process', taken together, can in part be read as an ongoing attempt to forestall that scenario by the gradual establishment of some kind of joint sovereignty that will prove bearable – if not wholly acceptable – to all parties. In most respects, 'normal politics' is the order of the day in the contemporary Republic of Ireland.

In Northern Ireland, partition had deep roots in violent conflict between the British (before that the English) state, the Catholic Irish and a population – settled in Ireland for many centuries – identifying itself variously as Ulster Protestant, British or Scots-Irish. Cultural and political differences between the Irish and the descendants of the settlers found, and still find, powerful expression in religion. As I suggested in Chapter 8, although essentially political, the Northern Irish conflict is symbolized and reinforced by an important religious dimension.

Partition reinforced a further ethnic identification, with the new state of Northern Ireland. This Ulster identity, although claiming an ancient Gaelic province as its own,[3] was Protestant, new – rooted in the north's development as the industrialized region of Ireland and northern anti-Home Rule agitation during the previous thirty years – and distanced from both the Irish and the English. The latter distance increased in subsequent decades, as successive British governments allowed the internal affairs of the Province to slip ever further beyond their oversight and Ulster Unionists were happy to let them.

For most of the period[4] between partition and the present 'troubles' northern nationalists were torn between refusing to recognize the new state and striving to improve the Catholic lot (Phoenix 1994). Nationalist political participation was discouraged by the stance of Unionism, the Protestant party of government in Northern Ireland for an unbroken fifty years. Northern Catholic politicians had to choose between a dangerous and uncertain military strategy (which would attract little Catholic support but would invite a repressive response from the state), remaining aloof from the Unionist state and waiting for history to deliver the millennium of Irish unity, or attempting, under unfavourable conditions, to improve the socio-economic position of the minority.

These options reflect two political traditions: gradualist constitutional 'nationalism' and physical-force 'republicanism' (Ruane and Todd 1992: 189). In Northern Ireland, republican nationalism was represented by Sinn Féin, allied to the Irish Republican Army (IRA), and constitutional nationalism first by the Nationalist Party – until 1969 – and subsequently by the Social Democratic and Labour Party (SDLP). In reflection of the old conflicts of the post-independence Civil War, the same distinctions can be observed in the politics of the Republic of Ireland, although the official legitimacy of nationalism there makes for more complexity. The poles of republican and constitutional nationalism are represented by Sinn Féin and Fine Gael, respectively, with Fianna Fail occupying a shifting position which is usually towards the constitutional end of the spectrum.

The differences between modern nationalisms re-emerged in the early 1960s in the campaign to redress the electoral, social and economic grievances of Catholics. The Civil Rights Movement, and Protestant reaction to it, led to escalating violence, the introduction of the British Army, and the dissolution of the local parliament and the assumption of direct rule from London in 1972. In 1969 resurgent nationalist violence split republicanism into the Official and Provisional movements, reflecting a shift in the centre of gravity of republicanism to the north, a retreat from the socialism which had been influential within the movement, and a return to physical force and a Gaelic cultural tradition. These developments were associated with a new, working-class militant republicanism in Belfast and elsewhere. The Provisional movement – as represented by Sinn Féin – is now the authentic voice of a large constituency of northern Catholics (and has moved to the constitutional end of the spectrum). Constitutional nationalism reorganized into the SDLP, absorbed some of the civil rights activists, and forged a new strategy after the Anglo-Irish Agreement of 1985, relating directly to Dublin and London. Although it aspires to Irish unity, the SDLP's nationalism is compromised these days by its relationship with establishment politics in Dublin. Sinn Féin's participation in electoral politics in the Republic adds further complexity to the picture, increasing the urgency with which the Dublin political establishment desires a solution in the north, to take the issue out of the limelight and disarm the republican threat in the south.

This account suggests some observations. Irish history, first, is a history of nationalisms – both Irish and British – rather than nationalism. Nor – as I suggested in Chapter 9 – is it easily shoehorned into the frameworks proposed by Anderson, Gellner or Hobsbawm. The problem, for example, with Coakley's argument (1990) that Irish nationalism in some senses conforms to the European norm and is in some senses deviant, is its presumption of both *an* Irish nationalism and a *typical* European model. Furthermore, nationalism of various hues is of considerable antiquity in Ireland. There are few reasons to confine our recognition of Irish nationalism to the nineteenth century and since. As discussed in Chapter 7, Ruane and Todd's model (1996), in which five 'dimensions of difference' have interacted with each other during a long history, offers more nuanced possibilities for understanding the complexities of Irish nationalism.

Which brings me to 'streams of tradition', *pace* Barth. Notions of shared history require caution: history is both the circumstances in which men and women make themselves (and make more history), and the myths and inventions by which they live. Too little can be made of history, and too much. If there are today *two* nationalist traditions in Northern Ireland then we must explain them with reference to more than history (unless one regards what happened every yesterday as history, in which case all social science is history). It was despite the mutual enmities of the past and the present that the leaders of Sinn Féin and the SDLP, calculating the odds about the future, held the private talks which produced a joint submission to the Dublin government, the Anglo-Irish Downing Street Declaration of December 1993, the paramilitary cease-fires of 1994 and the subsequent 'peace process'. Without this process the multi-party talks that led to the 1998 Agreement would never have happened.

History, tradition and current politics combine, in Northern Ireland as in Wales, in questions of identity. Are Protestants, for example, Irish? Leaving aside the nationalist rhetoric which insists that they are, the answer is complex. Survey evidence suggests that there has been a change in identification. In 1968 three identities were important in Northern Ireland: 'British', 'Irish' and 'Ulster'. By 1978 this had polarized into 'British' (most Protestants) and 'Irish' (most Catholics), a state of affairs that had apparently changed little ten years later (Moxon-Browne 1991: 29);

however, as Moxon-Browne observed, Protestants appeared to know what they were *not* better than what they *were*, depending upon with whom they were contrasted. By the time of the 2003 Northern Ireland Life and Times survey,[5] the multi-dimensional profile had changed to 'British' (49 per cent, largely Protestant), 'Northern Irish' (33 per cent, evenly split between Protestants and Catholics), 'Irish' (30 per cent, overwhelmingly Catholic) and 'Ulster' (11 per cent, overwhelmingly Protestant). Apart from reinforcing the theme of this book, that identifications and their meanings may change as circumstances change, the safest conclusion is that it is, as yet, difficult to know what data such as these might mean in terms of practical politics (see also Todd *et al.* 2006).

Ulster Protestants, to return to the discussion of Chapter 7, have two Others. Do they feel quite as British as the British? How do they identify themselves as against the English? And how do the *other* British identify them? Nor do we know what the difference is between middle-class Unionism and working-class loyalism (analogues of constitutional and republican nationalism). As social anthropology insists, 'it's not as simple as that', particularly in rural districts (McFarlane 1986). Nor is it clear that 'Irishness' is the same in the north as in the south. Etcetera.

The 2003 survey data indicate that most northern Irish Catholics and Protestants share no common national identity, and that Protestant identifications are the more ambiguous. Some aspects of this ambiguity – this 'crisis of identity' – have been discussed in Chapter 7. There is, however, more that can be said. Witness, for example, the attempts by the Ulster Defence Association – a now illegal Protestant paramilitary organization – and others to invent a new history and mythology of and for the Ulster Irish (Bruce 1992: 233–36; Buckley 1989). Witness, too, the social science disagreement about whether Protestant ethnic chauvinism – sectarianism – is a form of racism (Brewer 1992; Clayton 1996: 50–83; Miles 1996; Nelson 1975). And if not racism, what? Nationalism? Ethnicism? Does a Protestant nationalism make sense? It made sense, after all, in eighteenth-century Ireland. But if it were to make sense, in what terms – given the locally definitive Catholic appropriation of nationalist rhetoric – would Protestants make their case?

Although they might see themselves as *British* nationalists, Protestant Ulster nationalism is at the moment an unlikely prospect, despite Finlayson's insistence to the contrary (1996). His argument requires us to overlook the self-identification of most Ulster Protestants *and* to redefine nationalism. This surely is too much to expect. At the heart of the problem is the nature of the Protestant claim to a 'historical destiny'. In denying themselves an Irish future in 1921, and accepting a reluctant and conditional incorporation by Britain, they arguably wrote themselves out of history for fifty years. When they re-emerged in the late 1960s, as oppressors of the Catholic minority and an embarrassment to the rest of the United Kingdom, their moment had passed. In the light of the successive false dawns offered by the 1998 multi-party Agreement and various attempts to make the Assembly work, the return of that moment still looks to be some way off. That Protestants remain neither fully Irish nor fully British does, as Mitchell suggests (2003), allow a chink of light through the hatches that are so tightly battened down on their insecure imaginings of community. However, as McKay (2000) reminds us, it leaves many of them, at least for the time being, 'unsettled', seeking a destiny as well as an identity.

Denmark

On the face of it, there is no nationalism in Denmark. A lack of nationalist movements has, in fact, been identified as a general characteristic of Nordic societies
(Elklit and Tonsgaard 1992). Although this absence may reflect their own tight definition of nationalist movements,[6] for Elklit and Tonsgaard it indicates the solution
through other kinds of politics of ethno-national grievances which could otherwise
foment movements of this kind. Not everyone, of course, takes this view. Eriksen,
for example, suggests (2002: 100–3) that weak nationalism has been influential in
the history of the Nordic peoples – in his example, Norway, in particular – and
a similar thesis runs through the contributions to Tägil's collection on nation-
building (1995).

The absence or weakness of nationalist movements is widely held to be part of a
Nordic political style that emphasizes conflict avoidance and the promotion of
consensus. The most cursory look at Denmark illustrates the point: it is difficult to
find anything that would identify itself, or might be identified by others, as a
nationalist political party *per se*. The major party of the extreme right that focuses,
increasingly successfully, on immigration and similar issues – Dansk Folkeparti,
The Danish People's Party – is perceived, by most of its opponents, as racist rather
than specifically nationalist. Yet this is despite Denmark's progressive loss of once-
substantial peripheral territories (Borish 1991: 28–37). It is despite invasion and
occupation by Germany three times between 1848 and 1945. It is despite incorporation into a much-enlarged European Union of which many Danes, perhaps the
majority, are deeply suspicious and fearful (Buch and Hansen 2002). It is despite
increased unemployment. It is despite recent immigration from southern Europe
and the Middle East, increased popular ethnic intolerance (Enoch 1994; Gundelach
2002: 119–27; Hervik 2004; Wren 2001), and a hardening of political attitudes on
immigration that has united the broad middle ground of Danish party politics and
resulted in ever more restrictive policies in this respect (Østergaard Nielsen 2003).
And it is despite a contemporary European political climate in which nationalism
has regained much of its potency. Any one of these might provide the catalyst for
a nationalist political party. But there is none.

Understanding nationalism's apparent absence, no less than its presence,
demands recourse to history. The development in Denmark of a characteristically
Nordic political style is only part of the explanation (and something which itself
requires explanation). Three other themes in recent history are significant (Jones
1986: 59–151; Østergård 1992b: 63–83). First, contraction and international decline
produced a political territory that, with the notable and complicated exception of
the southern border region, is a *relatively* homogeneous linguistic and cultural unit
(Jenkins 2005). Second, the reaction to contraction was a rapid and non-violent
process of modernization, taking Denmark from late absolutism in the early nineteenth century to the foundation of a precocious social-democratic welfare state by
the early twentieth (Jespersen 2004: 58–82). Finally, this process does not seem to
have been underwritten by industrialization – Denmark remains among the least
industrialized of northern European states – but by land reform, the modernization
of agriculture and a corporatist political strategy based on egalitarianism.

Hvad udad tabes, det skal indad vindes – 'What is lost outwards, shall be won
inwards' – was the motto of the Danish Heath Society, which in the nineteenth

century promoted the cultivation of hitherto infertile land. It is paradigmatic of an acceptance of constraints, and a resolve to overcome them, which was central to modern Danish nation-building. Inward looking and reconstructive, within a culturally homogeneous polity, that process is crucial to understanding why there appear to be no nationalist movements in Denmark today.

But the detail of everyday life suggests a different picture. Take, for example, the white cross on the red field of Dannebrog, the Danish flag. Many Danish houses have a flagpole in the garden, from which the flag is flown to mark the whole range of domestic festivals and rites of passage. Those households lacking a flagstaff may display instead a small portable version on a wooden base. At Christmas, miniature paper Dannebrog, which are sold in every supermarket, may adorn the tree, and a birthday cake is incomplete without at least one. Dannebrog has even become essential to consumerist marketing strategies in Denmark. 'Flying the flag' is central to the symbolization of Danish national and civic culture; in the process, family celebrations become more than simply domestic (Jenkins 2006a: 374–8).

A comparative perspective brings this into focus. In Northern Ireland, flags – on the one hand the Union Flag, the Ulster flag or various loyalist paramilitary flags, on the other the Republic's tricolour – are part of ethnic boundary maintenance and a recognized element in the rituals of confrontation of the annual 'marching season' (Bryan 2005). In Britain, a private citizen flying the Union Flag runs the risk of being diagnosed as eccentric, at best, or racist and fascist, at worst. The latter is certainly what is symbolized by the Union Jack T-shirt of the English football fan abroad.

Dannebrog painted on the face of a Danish football supporter, however, symbolizes something different; certainly not the xenophobia which informs much British political discourse, even in the mainstream, and from which the English football fan draws a sense of his place in history. But what *does* it signify? And what does it mean when Danes tell you, with unselfconscious pride, that Queen Margrethe II's line of descent extends back more than a millennium to Gorm the Old, the oldest royal line in Europe? Or, to return to the flag, what should we make of its myth of origin, which has it dropping from heaven as a gift from God to King Valdemar II during a battle in 1219? Although Danes acknowledge the invention of this particular tradition, 'even so it is considered the oldest of present-day European flags' (Jacobsen 1986: 23). Here it is possible to have one's traditional national cake and eat it.

The recipe for that cake is the usual mixture of contradictions. Insofar as one can generalize, Danes like to appear to be understated in their national pride, modesty and restraint being important components of a relatively consensual model of 'proper' Danishness. They celebrate the fact that Denmark is a small country, *et lille land*. Østergård, a perceptive local commentator, calls this 'lilliput-chauvinism' (1992b: 56) or 'humble assertiveness': 'We know we are the best, therefore we don't have to brag about it.' (1992c: 170). However, there is also defensiveness: although it is 'bad form' to be a nationalist, 'intrinsic nationalism surfaces immediately for-eigners start criticising anything Danish' (Østergård 1992c: 169). Despite the public framing of the controversy within Denmark as a matter of freedom of the press, outraged national chauvinism was certainly part of the Danish reaction to the international furore during 2006–7 about the 'Muhammad cartoons' published by the Danish newspaper *Jyllands-Posten*. In this context, the national and international political climate since 9/11 has encouraged the assertive appropriation of

Dannebrog by the anti-immigrant, anti-Islamic right: the annual meetings of the Danish People's Party, for example, feature platforms dominated by flags.

Thus, if it is not too much of a conundrum, defining features of 'Danish nationalism' may be, on the one hand, a refusal to acknowledge itself as nationalism and, on the other, assertive national chauvinism. Accepting this characterization, what are its other distinguishing features? Much depends on context: the Danes are, if nothing else, abundantly supplied with a classificatory hierarchy and choice of Others. In the Scandinavian or Nordic context a distancing rhetoric comes into play: ethnic jokes and stereotypes are common, touching on the most mundane areas of daily life (Linde-Laursen 1993). These only make sense, however, within a commonly recognized cultural, linguistic and political affinity, particularly with Sweden and Norway. Important as national-ethnic boundaries and identities are, the shared 'imagined community' of Scandinavia (Gerholm and Gerholm 1990; Gullestad 1989) is a resource that can be drawn upon to make regional sense of similarity and difference. Although the distances involved, greater linguistic differences, and more distant histories, mean that a shared Nordic identity remains an as yet unrealized political project (Götz 2003), it is nonetheless a 'symbolic construction of community' that makes a degree of 'cultural' sense to all parties (Sørensen and Stråth 1997).

The broader European context is more ambiguous. The distinction between Scandinavia and Europe is just one of the fault lines that structure that ambiguity: is Denmark European or Scandinavian? The conventional answer to this question, 'something of each', leaves unbroached the even more interesting question of why Scandinavia, or the Nordic countries, might not be considered part of Europe (Hansen and Wæver 2001). Nor has the admission of Sweden to the EU clarified the matter; Norway remains outside. These ambiguities came to a head in a prolonged political struggle within Denmark over ratification of the 1992 Maastricht Treaty and European unification (Heurlin 1994; Skovgaard-Petersen 1994). They have subsequently resurfaced every time there is another European referendum (Buch and Hansen 2002; Haahr 2003).

After two referenda in 1992 and 1993, and only by a very narrow margin, the Danish political establishment achieved the 'yes' to European Union that it wanted. The reasons which informed the votes of those who were uncertain and opposed in 1992 were complex: distrust of centralization, defence of 'Danish democracy', a desire to preserve the Danish welfare state, fear of immigration, and dissatisfaction with the Danish political elite, all figured (Jenkins 2000b). These came together in a fear of reduced sovereignty (Lyck 1992; Sørensen and Væver 1992), which can only be understood in the historical context outlined earlier. There was also a cultural context, in which the perception of Denmark as *et lille land*, vulnerable to cultural and linguistic domination, played a part (Christensen 1994).

There is, however, another European context, and another fault line. Europe begins in Germany. Denmark has been invaded by Germany three times in modern history; the last time is a living memory. Influential in the modern construction of Danish identity was the question of Slesvig and Holstein, resolved by plebiscite in 1920 after a campaign in which Danes and Germans used stereotypes of the other to define themselves (Adriansen 1992). And here the contrast between Northern Ireland and Denmark becomes most obvious. The 1920 campaign about partition in southern Denmark was fought with posters and speeches; in Ireland in 1920 the matter was settled by guns and bloodshed. Today in the south of Denmark, a substantial minority of *hjemme tyskere* ('home Germans'), Danish citizens who are linguistically German, ensures the continuing vitality of the issue, as does the presence of a linguistically Danish minority in Germany (Østergård 1995). The differences between the two countries in terms of size and affluence further feeds Danish distrust. If Danish nationalism exists, it is for many Danes, depending perhaps upon generation and geography, articulated as much in opposition to Germany as anything else.[7] Anti-German feeling certainly figured in the 1992 EU referendum campaign (Jenkins 2000b).

And there are many other things against which Danish national identity can be defined: immigrants, Americanization, etc. One of the things that has been most striking is the level of recent collective scrutiny within Denmark of the nature of *danskhed* (Danishness). A range of issues have problematized what had previously been taken for granted if not consensual (Gundelach 2002; Harbsmeier 1986; Østergård 1992d). Among the most interesting epiphenomena of this debate are specifications of the qualities of Danish national character, whether by Danes – 'individualism, solidarity, faith in authority and discipline' (Østergård 1992b: 21) – or, more controversially within Denmark, by outsiders: privatized, individualized, suppressed and collectivized, according to Reddy (1993: 130–56).

As well as EU referenda campaigns and local perceptions of the presence of immigrants and refugees, this debate reflects other issues. The most important concerns the future of the *danske vej*, the 'Danish way' (Østergård 1992b: 63), the social experiment which since the mid-nineteenth century has attempted to blend capitalism with equality into a historical destiny which Denmark has chosen for its own: the nation as 'a social laboratory' (Manniche 1969). Rooted within an agrarian populist political tradition that is both egalitarian and libertarian, 'This is the ultimate Danish discourse: Everyone is in the same boat' (Østergård 1992e: 14). As this core component of national identity has come under pressure, not least from consumerism, affluence, increasing social stratification within Denmark and the pressures on the public welfare purse of a greying population (Greve 2004), so too has *danskhed* come into question.

Among the reasons I began to look systematically at the Danish case was the fact that conventional wisdom in the social science literature about nationalism didn't help me to understand the place. Initially, as an intermittent anthropological tourist, I was fairly sure that there was *some* kind of nationalism going on – people cannot, after all, spend as much time waving and flying their flag as Danes do without being, in some sense, nationalists – but I was unsure how best to make sense of it. Now, after a more systematic look and proper field research, there remain questions to be asked about Danish nationalism. Is it *really* nationalism? And, if so, what are my reasons for identifying it as such?

In the first place – and it is not quite as trivial as it might sound – what I have described is, *in some respects*, identified as nationalism by *some* Danes. It is a contested description in Denmark, but it can be found sufficiently often to be credible. In the second, it is possible to offer a plausible definition of nationalism that is sufficiently broad to include the Danish case, but sufficiently focused to exclude cognate ideologies of ethnic identification. By this definition, the conditions for, and components of, nationalism are an ideology of ethnic identification (*danskhed*), ethnic criteria of political membership (Danish citizenship, which is contested for immigrants, particularly Muslims), a state context (*Danmark*), and a claim to a collective historical destiny (*den danske vej*).

The notion of ideology implies structure and organization as a body of knowledge of how the world *is* and how it *should* be. This is the '-ism' in nationalism. Is what I have been talking about sufficiently organized to qualify? The answer is 'yes' and 'no'. 'No', in the relative absence of nationalist *movements* or *parties*. 'Yes', in the existence of an extensive and explicit universe of discourse, a stream of tradition, which identifies, and identifies *with*, Denmark in terms of national character and historical destiny. This is the weak ideology of Danish nationalism, and it is showing signs of perhaps weakening further. The debate about *danskhed*, and the concern about threats to the *danske vej*, reveal a dissensus about how the world is, and how it should be, that is antagonistic to the certainties of nationalism. In the resolution of this uncertainty, Danish nationalism is being redefined.

Identity, ideology and the everyday

Danish nationalism, as I have described it, is an everyday and very ordinary matter, rather than a structured nationalist movement. The recent literature offers some suggestively homologous notions that may help us further understand the Danish situation. Emphasizing the everyday, Linde-Laursen talks about the 'nationalization of trivialities' (1993), the way in which national communities that are culturally very close in many respects, Danes and Swedes in this case, 'do' everyday life – washing the dishes, for example – differently, and use these distinctions as boundary markers denoting much larger imagined differences of hygiene and proper behaviour. In similar terms, Wilk contrasts:

> official, planned, government policies of nationalism and unofficial, unplanned, nonpolitical ideas and practices of nationalism which are outside the power, reach or interest of the state. (1993: 296)

A broadly homologous distinction has been drawn by Eriksen (1993a) between 'formal nationalisms', ideologies of ethnic identification that are part of the institutional and political organization of the modern nation-state, and 'informal nationalisms', that are rooted in the daily round of civil society. Both exist in the context of the nation-state and may complement or oppose each other. When Duara (1993: 14) contrasts the 'discursive meaning' of the nation, located in ideology and rhetoric, with its 'symbolic meaning' – to be found in 'cultural practices ... such as rituals, festivals, kinship forms, and culinary habits' – he also appears to address the same issues. More recently again, Michael Billig has explored in some depth a notion of 'banal nationalism' – as opposed to 'hot nationalism' – that speaks to a similar set of concerns:

> the ideological habits which enable the established nations of the West to be reproduced ... these habits are not removed from everyday life, as some observers have supposed. Daily, the nation is indicated, or 'flagged' in the lives of its citizenry. Nationalism, far from being an intermittent mood in established nations, is the endemic condition. (Billig 1995: 6)

Most recently, Brubaker *et al.*'s exploration of the relationship between 'everyday ethnicity' and nationalism in a Romanian town (2006) is clearly mining a similar seam. Not the least important thing about these converging arguments and models is that they underline the ethnic character of nationalisms, and the importance of experience and the 'cultural stuff' in their everyday social construction.

In this context, the distinction between *nationalism* and *national identity* (Smith 1991, 1994) may be helpful: the latter is the ethnicity to which nationalist ideological identification refers. Borneman, writing about Berlin, makes a similar point when he differentiates *nationalism*, as a public ideology of identification with the state, from *nationness*, which is an implicit practical sense of being the kind of person, or living the kind of life, appropriate to membership in that state: 'a subjectivity, not contingent upon an opinion or attitude, but derived from lived experience within a state' (Borneman 1992: 352). This is another allusion to everyday civil society and the symbolic meaning of the nation.

National identity or nationness can exist in the absence of nationalism (and Ulster Protestants may be a case in point); nationalism without some kind of national identity is unthinkable. In Northern Ireland and in Wales, for example, the politics of authentic national identity are at the heart of organized nationalism and its ideologies and also distinct from it, threaded in and out of the banal routines of living in 'cultural stuff' such as religion and language. It is from the everyday and the banal that Billig's 'hot nationalism' draws its sustenance. To take these ideas further, national identity is to nationalism as unofficial, informal, everyday nationalism is to the official and the formal. Informal, unofficial nationalism and national identity, if this argument is correct, are similar, if not actually the same thing. And the existence of formal, organized nationalism does not mean the absence of the informal, the unofficial, or the banal. Quite the reverse.

Nor should it be thought that everyday life is somehow free from ideology. Here we return to the 'cultural stuff' again. Everyday life is fundamentally ideological: in religion, in discourses about the various yardsticks of deviance – normality, respectability, propriety, morality (Jenkins 1998a) – in child-rearing wisdom, in folk history, in models of gender and sexuality, in the building-block categories of language. And, which is what interests me here, in discourses about ethnicity and its allotropes: locality, community, region, nation, 'race'. These are all bodies of knowledge that make claims about the way the social world *is* and about the way it *ought* to be. Everyday ideology may not be formally structured and organized, but it has pattern and it matters in people's lives.

If Borneman, Eriksen and Wilk, in particular, are correct in locating distinctions of this kind within the broader relationships between the state and civil society, then much will depend upon the nature and history of that relationship in any specific case. In Denmark, for example, where a strong state and civil society have evolved side by side along the *danske vej*, informal (or unofficial or banal) nationalism draws the formal symbols of the state – because, as Østergård reminds us, Dannebrog, despite its domestication, 'actually symbolises the power of the monarchy and the state' (1992a: 22) – into the intimate settings of daily life. In the process it becomes difficult to know where state and civil society begin and end in Denmark, and informal nationalism to some extent fills the space created by the relative absence of official state nationalism.

These distinctions – between formal-official and informal-unofficial national-ism, between the discursive and the symbolic meanings of the nation, between hot and banal nationalism, between state and civil society – resonate with the arguments advanced in this chapter. As a convergent set of ideas produced by different authors, writing about different places, from different points of view, they offer the beginnings of a useful framework for understanding different nationalisms and the differences between them. They also remind us of the importance of maintaining a historical perspective. The relationship between state and civil society is, in any given case, the product of history. Nationalisms, ideologies of ethnic identification of a particular kind, are streams of tradition, universes of political discourse located within history. And as local political narratives, they are also social productions, by means of which people make sense of and live in a complex and changing contemporary world.

These case studies suggest that there is more to nationalism than is allowed by the 'state modernization and industrialization' model. Although comparison of this kind cannot 'prove' or 'disprove' anything, it supports a more flexible theoretical framework that is concerned with nationalism*s* rather than nationalism. Of course, the reader may doubt whether the case studies actually represent comparable phenomena. Certainly, they document very different histories and situations. In part, this is precisely my point. While each can legitimately be described as referring to 'nationalism', the differences between them are sufficiently significant to suggest that nationalism is a broad church with many mansions under its roof.

In Wales the nationalist tradition is recent and more or less unified, focusing on culture and language within a pragmatic acceptance of an existing constitutional status quo. Although it has its roots in nineteenth-century Romanticism, Wales during that period was already an integral part of a centralized state. Processes of economic or political modernization do not seem to have been central to the formation of Welsh nationalism.

In Northern Ireland, by contrast, constitutional and republican nationalisms, divided against themselves, are aspects of a tradition of resistance to rule from and by Britain which extends back to the early modern period and beyond. That tradition, however, has been discontinuous, adopted by different groups at different times in the pursuit of different ends. Taking account of the various historical expressions in Ireland of British nationalisms complicates the situation even further.

Danish nationalism is different again: implicit and elusive, a low-key ideology of everyday discourse rather than a matter of organized politics. Existing in a social and political context that in many senses refuses to legitimize nationalist *movements*, it reflects Denmark's history of relationships with its neighbours and is an expression of faith in the Danish experiment in welfare state capitalism and social democracy. The complexities of the Danish case stem not only from the variability of nationalism but also from its subtleties and its relationships to other locally dominant political ideologies (social democracy and welfarism, in particular).

Yet, allowing for these differences – in degree of organization, strength or weakness of ideology, political goals and objectives, and practical strategies and tactics – these are all nationalisms. First, they are all, in some respect, identified as nationalism by the relevant locals. This is one of the reasons why a degree of scepticism about the possibility of Ulster Protestant nationalism is indicated. Second, it is possible to formulate a definition of nationalism broad enough to include them all, but capable of differentiating nationalism from racism, ethnicism or regionalism, for example (although the boundaries between them will always be located along continua of degrees of difference and distance). In each case it is possible to identify the conditions for and components of nationalism which I defined earlier: an *ideology or ideologies of ethnic identification, historical contingency and variation*, a *state context, ethnic criteria of political membership* and a claim to a *collective historical destiny*.

Historical destiny may seem an odd notion – even dated or anachronistic – to introduce into the argument (and perhaps Eriksen's 'future orientation' [1993b] might sound less worrying). To some, mindful of the terrible ends to which notions of history and destiny can be bent, its use may appear irresponsible. But it is crucial. One distinguishing feature of nationalisms is their appeal to the past – an ethnic-national history embodied in such things as myths of origin, royal genealogies or cultural romanticism – in the construction of a collective project for the future. This is the inspiration for Benedict Anderson's evocation (1983: 147) of Walter Benjamin's imagery of the 'angel of history': looking back, in nostalgia and anger, but irresistibly propelled forward at the mercy of progress. Nationalism differs from Benjamin's angel, however, in that it does not present its back to the future in futile resistance to change. It is, rather, actively in the business of moving forward, in pursuit of the historical destiny that it claims for itself. Perhaps a more appropriate image is Anderson's other description of nationalism, as Janus-headed (1983: 144), simultaneously looking ahead and behind.[8]

The future towards which nationalism looks is not, however, as tightly circumscribed as some commentators argue. The collective project need not be independence, secession, or any of the other political goals that may come to mind most readily under the sign of nationalism. It may be cultural preservation and promotion, as in Wales, or the creation and preservation of a particular kind of society, as in Denmark. And, as in both cases and in Northern Ireland, there may be important subsidiary concerns too. If literacy gave people, in history, a different kind of past, it also created for them the possibility of the future as a project. Nationalism was among the results. As social scientists we must continue to talk about nationalism in an abstract ideal-typical sense. We can only do so, however, in full recognition of the limitations of such a discourse. The 'real' world is full of nationalism*s*.

Rethinking Ethnicity

I began this book by arguing that although the basic social anthropological model of ethnicity has for a long time been the most useful analytical framework available, its potential has not been fully explored or appreciated. The 'rethinking ethnicity' of the title is my attempt to do some of that exploration and to encourage that appreciation. In the process, I do not, however, lay claim to dramatic innovation. The rethinking that I have done is just that: thinking again about what others have thought about before, building upon what they have done, occasionally rescuing or renovating overlooked insights, developing hints and suggestions into something more substantial, and putting together things that may not, hitherto, have been connected.

The 'basic anthropological model' is a series of loosely linked propositions, thus:

- ethnicity is a matter of 'cultural' differentiation (bearing in mind that identity is always a dialectic between similarity and difference);
- ethnicity is a matter of shared meanings – 'culture' – but it is also produced and reproduced during interaction;
- ethnicity is no more fixed than the way of life of which it is part, or the situations in which it is produced and reproduced; and
- ethnicity is both collective and individual, externalized in social interaction and the categorization of others, and internalized in personal self-identification.

In emphasizing social construction and everyday practice, acknowledging change as well as stability, and allowing us to recognize individuality in experience and agency as well as the sharing of 'culture' and collective identification, they remain fundamental to a rounded understanding of ethnicity.

These propositions do not amount to all there is to be said. Developments and themes have emerged in the course of previous chapters that are worth restating in closing. If some of them were put on the agenda by Fredrik Barth in 1969, only to be subsequently sidelined, that is more, rather than less, reason to attend to them now.

And the first of these themes is just such an issue. The axiomatic preoccupation with 'groupness' in many studies of ethnicity, post-*Ethnic Groups and Boundaries*, has encouraged the continuing reification of ethnic groups and, particularly, their boundaries. This is a serious problem in that it undermines the analytical vision of the human world consistently promoted by Barth himself; a vision of social life as perpetual coalition, fission and negotiation; of collective forms as emergent patterns generated by the ongoing ins and outs of individuals interacting. Social groups are not 'things'.

Another problem is at least as serious. The preoccupation with definite bounded groups focuses largely – if not totally – on their collective self-identification. This arguably obstructs our better understanding of processes of ethnic identification in

all of their complexity. The focus on group identification rather than social categorization is not simply an 'empirical' oversight. It is, if one can use such a word,
simply wrong. If ethnic identification is understood as a dialectical process of
mutually implicated internal and external definition, then categorization must
be included in our analyses, and social categories as well as groups be counted
legitimate – and necessary – as building blocks for our arguments. Even if we
acknowledge the analytical centrality of group identification – a reasonable enough
point of view, given that some self-conscious 'group-ness' is necessary for active
collective identification – it is impossible to understand how groups are constituted without a full appreciation of social categorization. There are no groups,
ethnic or otherwise, without categorization.

Nor does this line of argument apply only to collective identifications. Any
identification – and ethnicity and its allotropes are not exceptions – must mean
something to individuals before it can be said to 'exist' in the social world. The
collective cannot be 'real' without the individual. With respect to individual meanings and experience, primary socialization is an obvious place to begin. Entering
into ethnic identification during childhood is definitively a matter of categorization:
we learn who we are because, in the first instance, other people – whether they be
co-members or Others – tell us. Socialization is categorization. It cannot be otherwise. What is more, categorization continues to contribute in a significant fashion
to individual identification throughout adult life. Being categorized is a necessary
and foundational part of the individual development and ongoing production and
reproduction of group identifications; it is at the heart of the individual meaning
and experience, and the power and force, of ethnic identification. Without categorization, there are no socialized individuals.

To recognize that categorization – as I have defined it – is a vital element in our
models of the social construction of ethnicity is to place issues of power and com-
pulsion – and resistance – at the heart of what we do, rather than uncomfortably
regarding them with our peripheral vision. The corner of our analytical eye will not
do. If for no other reason, this is because the capacity to define for Others – in the
shape of consequences – what it means for them to be identified in a particular way
is part of our group identification and our experience of membership. To put
Others in their place is necessarily to claim a place for ourselves (and vice versa).

This also speaks to the particular need – political as much as intellectual – to
engage with the difficult relationship between ethnicity and 'race'. Anthropology
has recently, and for too long, neglected this matter. Although 'race' is an allotrope
of ethnicity, they are somewhat different social phenomena. Historically speaking,
ethnic identity is probably ubiquitous; 'race' is not. With respect to individual
identification, the two are qualitatively different. Ethnic identity is the more general, the more basic; it is also the more likely to be embedded in the everyday contexts of 'culture'-in-common such as language and religion. This does not mean,
however, that it is more significant. 'Race' is likely to be at least as consequential
as ethnicity in everyday experience, and historically it has been an organizing principle of domination almost without parallel. Identifications of 'race' are typically
rooted in categorization rather than group identification, in ascription and imposition rather than subscription, in the external rather than the internal moment of
identification. Power in this context is the capacity to determine for Others, not just
the consequences of identity, but also their nominal identification itself.

The distinction between the nominal and the virtual is basic to the understanding of ethnic – and other – identities which I am proposing. It is homologous to the group-category distinction but not precisely the same. The nominal is the name: English, Welsh, Ulster Protestant, Irish, Danish, etcetera. Nominal identities are often hierarchically segmentary; individuals may thus participate in a plurality of nominal ethnic (or similar) identities. One can be Danish and a 'home German', Welsh and a *gog;* British and Welsh. In fact, to be a 'home German' one must be Danish, to be a *gog* one must be Welsh, and so on.

The virtualities of identification are constituted in consequences and everyday experience. The hierarchical and segmentary organization of the nominal – the classificatory intersection of the communal, the local, the ethnic, the national, the 'racial' – is, at least in part, to be understood in terms of virtual identification. The practical entailments of communal identification are, for example, different from those of local identity; local identification has different consequences from national identity; and so on.

The relationship between the nominal and the virtual is thus always a matter of specifics, to be discovered. Nominal and virtual may be in harmony with each other or they may not. The virtualities of the same nominal identification can differ from situation to situation. The name may stay the same – 'Welsh', for example – even though the experience of being Welsh may change dramatically; conversely, the experience may stay relatively stable while the name changes. Both name and experience may change. Individuals may share a nominal identity, but that may mean very different things to them in practice, it may have different consequences for their lives; they may 'do' it differently. And so on across a wide range of possibilities. The virtualities of experience are likely to be central to processes of change; they are certainly likely to be less stable than the nominal. In times of flux, the relationship between the nominal and the virtual may contribute a useful image of continuity; it is just as likely, however, to sow the seeds of confusion and conflict.

Although the nominal and the virtual can be distinguished for analytical purposes, in everyday social reality they are chronically implicated in each other. This brings us back to the consequences of identification by others. My argument here can be understood as in some respects a collective version of the labelling model of individual identification developed within symbolic interactionism. It is a loosely specified processual model of the way in which what goes on at and across the boundary affects the 'cultural content' of identity. Our 'cultural stuff' will, even if only in part, reflect our interactions with Other(s): how those Others categorize and behave towards us, how they label us. Nor is this all. Our categorizations of Others, and the routines that we evolve for dealing with them, are also intrinsic to our 'cultural' repertoire. Social interaction at and across the boundary will necessarily involve categorizations: of 'us' by 'them', and of 'them' by 'us'. Whose categorizations are the more influential, and the balances that are struck between group identification and categorization, are ongoing open questions, emerging out of history and past experience, located within power relations in the here-and-now, and constitutive of the ongoing situation. Whose definition of the situation counts, nominally and virtually, impinges upon the (external) interactional boundary and (internal) 'cultural content'. Taking categorization seriously means taking the cultural stuff seriously too.

The 'cultural stuff' is undeserving of neglect for other reasons. Logically and substantively, similarity and difference are mutually entailed in identification. Difference cannot exist without similarity, and vice versa. If we are to focus on the social construction of cultural differentiation then we also have to take into account the social construction of cultural similarity (which suggests that we should pay attention to the cultural content of identity). Difference and similarity are each imagined; neither is imaginary; both come together in ethnicity. For difference to be socially marked, there has to be something upon which to seize as its marker, no matter how minor, no matter how arbitrary (no matter how imaginary?). For similarity to be identified there has to be something in common. To follow Max Weber and recognize ethnicity as a principle of collective social organization, in the context of group identification, for example, there probably has to be at least mutual intelligibility of behaviour. Even in the context of categorization, the criteria of identification have to possess at least some social relevance: they have to be differences that make a difference to someone. There are local limits to how arbitrary the social construction of identities can be.

This means that we must also take seriously the fact that ethnicity means something to individuals, and that when it matters, it can *really* matter. This doesn't, in any sense, mean swallowing the primordialist line. It suggests a focus on 'culture' and the everyday constitution of ethnicity, during primary socialization and subsequently. Some kinds of 'cultural stuff' – religion, or language, perhaps – may be of greater affective and personal consequence than others. In principle, it is possible to mobilize around any marker of differentiation – which end of a boiled egg is the right one to open, for example – and the logic of symbolism allows that anything can be signified in this way. In terms of everyday realities, however, some things may be more emotable than others. And, whether one accepts this or not, the character of the 'cultural content' of being an X or a Y is likely to influence the character of the interaction between Xs and Ys (the 'cultural' acceptability of violence as a means for the pursuit of ends is one obvious illustration that comes to mind).

Re-emphasizing the 'cultural content' of ethnicity offers a further way to differentiate among ethnicity and its allotropes: locality, community, national identity, nationality (which is not quite the same thing), and 'race'. They are about somewhat different things, 'culturally'. And so are their respective ideological expressions. Thus looking at content allows us to distinguish, for example, nationalism and racism, or to differentiate between nationalisms and racisms. This is no more than we might expect given that these are fundamentally ideological: ideology, perhaps before it is anything else, is a matter of 'culture'. The 'cultural stuff' concerned is not, what is more, just a matter of elite 'culture', of 'culture with a capital C'. It is also inescapably a matter of everyday banal social reality. At least in part, the ordinariness of life fuels the extra-ordinariness of collective mobilization and conflict.

Another theme has been implicit in my approach to the comparative discussions of Northern Ireland, Wales and Denmark. I have leaned heavily on history, albeit an amateur's history, dependent upon secondary sources and commentaries, in order to understand these places. A historical perspective is vital if we are to understand the differences between ethnicity and 'race', or between different nationalist impulses. And without taking the long view we can only take the 'cultural stuff' somewhat for granted. The here-and-now of the ethnographic present that is rightly so beloved by anthropologists is – and must remain – one basic datum of our theorizing and exploration. History, however, must be the other.

These issues and themes come together in the recognition that, although ethnic identity is socially constructed, it is not infinitely variable, malleable or negotiable. It may be deeply founded in the more than half forgotten experiences of primary socialization. It is constrained and shaped by its necessary dependence upon the categorization of Others. Its potential is always an immanent emergent property of its 'cultural content' and history. And it all depends upon how much it matters – in terms of costs and benefits if nothing else – to those whose everyday lives are its making, remaking and unmaking.

That there are limits to the plasticity of ethnicity, as well as to its fixity and solidity, is the founding premise for the development of an understanding of ethnicity that permits us to appreciate that although it is imagined it is not imaginary; to acknowledge its antiquity as well as its modernity. Rethinking demands that we should strike a balanced view of the authenticity of ethnic attachments. Somewhere between irresistible emotion and utter cynicism, neither blindly primordial nor completely manipulable, ethnicity and its allotropes are principles of collective identification and social organization in terms of 'culture' and history, similarity and difference, that show little signs of withering away. In itself this is neither a 'good thing' nor a 'bad thing'. It is probably just very human. It is hard to imagine the social world in their absence.

Notes

Chapter 2 From Tribes to Ethnic Groups

1. For further discussion of whether the Nuer are really the Dinka (and vice versa), see the correspondence pages of *Man* (n.s.) 8 (1973), Burton (1981), and Southall (1976). Hutchinson's recent study (1995) brings the issue up to date in the context of the warfare of the last two decades or more.
2. I have placed the word 'race' in inverted commas to signify that it is a contested concept, whose meaning may not be taken for granted. In my own usage it refers simply to folk 'racial' categorization, and no other meaning should be presumed for it.
3. It is moot whether 'ethnic set' – a broad social field within which ethnic categories are significant classificatory and organizational themes – should actually be included in Handelman's typology.
4. For a discussion of local Hutu–Tutsi 'racial' classifications in Rwanda, see Maquet (1972); see Banks (1996: 164–5) and de Waal (1994) for discussions of more recent, and more anthropologically troubling, aspects of this conflict; see Prunier (1997) for a general account of the genocide.
5. The work of Bruce Kapferer (1988) is particularly relevant to the topic under discussion.

Chapter 3 Myths of Pluralism

1. Gluckman's work, of course, owed much to Coser and Simmel.
2. And not *just* anthropologists: see Saggar (1996).
3. Among the major sources for this discussion, Volumes 2–5 of the *Glamorgan County History* (Cardiff: University of Wales Press, various dates) stand out, for those who want to follow up in great detail, and with respect to only one part of the region, many of the points made in the first half of this section. John Davies's single-volume history of Wales (1993) is indispensable, as is the survey of contemporary issues edited by Dunkerley and Thompson (1999). See Rees (1990) for a political argument that complements in some respects my discussion here. The interested reader can also consult the collection to which the original paper on which this section is based formed the tailpiece (Jenkins and Edwards 1990).
4. This is a reference to Gwyn Alf Williams's *When Was Wales?* (1985) and his thesis that Wales only existed as a nation between the collapse of the Roman Empire and the emergence, as part of the imperialist project, of the British nation.

Chapter 4 Ethnicity etcetera

1. This can, for example, be seen in the pages of the Royal Anthropological Institute's magazine *Anthropology Today*. The, mainly anthropological, contributions to *Identities*, a new journal edited in the United States, also illustrate the increasing comfort of the discipline with change and conflict. There is still a way to go, however.
2. Among other such conceits are the notions that childhood was unknown in earlier times, or that reflexive self-identity is a distinctively modern phenomenon.

Chapter 7 Majority Ethnicity

1. This in itself may seem to be an odd choice of words: haven't Protestants, after all, always been a minority within Ireland? I am, however, referring here to the fact that until the Reformation, the Irish and their conquerors were adherents to the same universal Catholicism.
2. Although it is valid enough, this is of course the kind of generalization to which one has to resort in a short discussion, and there is considerable variation in this pattern.
3. I have summarized the debate about the extent and impact of discrimination in the decades leading up to the 'troubles' elsewhere (Jenkins 1988: 318–19).
4. Among the 'other things' to which I am referring, the Protestant sense of the legitimacy of their own loyalist political violence was undermined, as it was taken outside the law by paramilitary organizations, and, particularly, as it was manifest in the bloodthirsty assassination campaigns of the 1970s.
5. Lest I am even further misunderstood, to say this is not to join Allen Feldman, for example, in objectivizing murder; in reducing extreme violence and death to acts of communication: 'Stiffing [i.e. murder] is a graphic act, and the stiff is a political text whose original script of ethnic-spatial symmetry has been effaced by wounding and death. The corpse, its blood, its wounds are quasi-organic signs of a tactile and political contiguity with the other' (Feldman 1991: 78).

Chapter 8 The Cultural Stuff

1. Reported in the *Guardian*, 28 July 1984.

Chapter 9 Violence, Language and Politics

1. Reported, for example, in the *Guardian*, 17 September 1990.
2. This claim was made in a BBC Cymru-Wales documentary in the *Week In – Week Out* series broadcast on 25 May 1993, on the basis of an opinion poll undertaken for the programme by Beaufort Research, Cardiff, in the counties of Dyfed and Gwynedd. I am grateful to both these organizations for making available to me the survey findings.

3. The utter idealism of Kedourie is perhaps most delightfully summed up in his char-acterization (1985: 147) of Gellner's argument as 'similar to Marxism'.
4. I recognize that is a major oversimplification of a complex picture, historically and today: see, for example, Ennew (1980).
5. The discussion also suggests that, whatever the 'cultural' and linguistic similarities which exist between the 'Celtic' peoples of the European maritime periphery, their different histories of incorporation into the relevant metropolitan nation-states (i.e. the UK and France) will discourage the emergence of the 'pan-Celtic' nationalist movement proposed by Berresford Ellis (1985).

Chapter 10 Nations, Nationalisms

1. Another way of putting this – and arguably a better one – might be to suggest that our notions of where modernity started might require some revision (along with our ideas about the medieval). So also might our concepts of 'the state'.
2. For what that alternative might be, see D.E. Thomas (1991).
3. Albeit minus the three Ulster counties of Donegal, Monaghan and Cavan which, in reflection of the demography of ethnicity (and political loyalties), became part of the Free State.
4. Apart from sectarian riots, there were two minor northern campaigns by the Irish Republican Army, a clandestine nationalist organization, illegal on both sides of the border, during the Second World War and in the 1950s (Bardon 1992: 581–6, 604–12).
5. For summaries of the relevant data from the Life and Times survey, see: www.ark. ac.uk/nilt/2003/Political_Attitudes/ ID.html and www.ark.ac.uk/nilt/2003/Political_ Attitudes/ID.html#religion
6. National movements are defined as: 'the efforts of ethnonational groups which can-not be identified with the state to restructure or reshape existing state arrangements' (Elklit and Tonsgaard 1992: 83). Although this is, as the authors admit, a restrictive definition, it is probably less so than Gellner's.
7. In this context, one wonders what the basis might have been for Mann's confident assertion about the European Union, that 'the polls show that negative national stereotypes have almost vanished' (1993: 131).
8. An image that has also been used by Tom Nairn (1981: 329–63).

Sources and Acknowledgements

This book derives to a greater or lesser extent from pieces that have been written over a period of more than twenty years. I have accumulated along the way too many debts of gratitude to those who have read and commented on my work to mention them individually in a context such as this. They have all been thanked in the original publications and those thanks remain on record and heartfelt. I am grateful to the editors, publishers and learned societies concerned, for their support in the past, and, where appropriate, their permission to draw upon – for nothing has simply been reprinted – the following pieces. The italics in parentheses after each piece indicate the chapter or chapters in this book where its remains, or bits of them, now lie buried:

'Ethnicity and the rise of capitalism in Ulster', in R. Ward and R. Jenkins (eds), *Ethnic Communities in Business: Strategies for Economic Survival*. Cambridge University Press, 1984: 57–72 [7].

'Northern Ireland: in what sense "religions" in conflict?', in R. Jenkins, H. Donnan and G. McFarlane, *The Sectarian Divide in Northern Ireland Today* (Royal Anthropological Institute Occasional Paper No. 41), London, Royal Anthropological Institute, 1986: 1–21 [8].

'Social anthropological models of inter-ethnic relations', in J. Rex and D. Mason (eds), *Theories of Race and Ethnic Relations,* Cambridge, Cambridge University Press, 1986: 170–86 [2, 3].

'International perspectives', in R. Jenkins and A. Edwards (eds), *One Step Forward? South and West Wales towards the Year 2000,* Llandysul, Gwasg Gomer, 1990: 151–60. Swansea, Social Science Research Institute [3].

'Violence, language and politics: nationalism in Northern Ireland and Wales', *North Atlantic Studies,* 3, 1 (1991): 31–40. Aarhus, Centre for North Atlantic Studies [9].

'Rethinking ethnicity: identity, categorization and power', *Ethnic and Racial Studies,* 17 (1994): 197–223 [5].

'Nations and nationalisms: towards more open models', *Nations and Nationalism,* 1 (1995): 369–90. London, Association for the Study of Ethnicity and Nationalism [10].

'"Us" and "them": ethnicity, racism and ideology', in R. Barot (ed.), *The Racism Problematic: Contemporary Sociological Theories on Race and Ethnicity,* Lampeter, Edwin Mellon Press, 1996: 69–88 [6].

'Ethnicity etcetera: anthropological points of view', *Ethnic and Racial Studies,* 19 (1996): 807–22 [1, 4].

'Categorization: identity, social process and epistemology', *Current Sociology*, 48, 3 (2000): pp. 7–25 [5].

'Telling the forest from the trees: local images of national change in a Danish town', *Ethnos*, 71 (2006): 367–89 [1].

'When politics and social theory converge: group identification and group rights in Northern Ireland', *Nationalism and Ethnic Politics*, 12 (2006): 389–410 [2].

Bibliography

ADAM, H. 1972. *Modernizing Racial Domination,* Berkeley: University of California Press.

ADAM, H. and GILIOMEE, H. 1979. *Ethnic Power Mobilized: Can South Africa Change?* New Haven: Yale University Press.

ADRIANSEN, I. 1992. 'Dansk og tysk spejlet i hinanden', in U. Østergard (ed.), *Dansk Identitet?* Aarhus: Aarhus Universitetsforlag.

AHMED, A. and SHORE, C. 1995. 'Introduction: is anthropology relevant to the contemporary world? in A. Ahmed and C. Shore (eds), *The Future of Anthropology: Its Relevance to the Contemporary World,* London: Athlone.

AITCHISON, J. and CARTER, H. 1999. 'The Welsh language today', in D. Dunkerley and A. Thompson (eds), *Wales Today,* Cardiff: University of Wales Press.

AKENSON, D. H. 1973. *Education and Enmity: The Control of Schooling in Northern Ireland 1920–50,* Newton Abbot: David and Charles.

ALLEN, I. L. 1990. *Unkind Words: Ethnic Labeling from 'Redskin' to 'WASP,'* New York: Bergin and Garvey.

ALTER, P. 1989. *Nationalism,* London: Edward Arnold.

AMIT, V. (ed.) 2000. *Constructing the Field: Ethnographic Fieldwork in the Contemporary World,* London: Routledge.

ANDERSON, B. 1983. *Imagined Communities: Reflections on the Origin and Spread of Nationalism,* London: Verso.

ANDERSON, E. 1978. *A Place on the Corner,* Chicago: University of Chicago Press.

ANDERSON, M. and FIENBERG, S. E. 2000. 'Race and ethnicity and the controversy over the US census', *Current Sociology,* 48 (3): 87–110.

ANTHIAS, F. 1992. 'Connecting "race" and ethnic phenomena', *Sociology,* 26: 421–38.

Ardoyne Commemoration Project 2002. *Ardoyne: The Untold Truth,* Belfast: Beyond the Pale.

BACK, L. and SOLOMOS, J. (eds), 2000. *Theories of Race and Racism: A Reader,* London: Routledge.

BAKER, S. E. 1973. 'Orange and Green Belfast: Belfast, 1832–1912', in H.J. Dyos and M. Wolff (eds), *The Victorian City: Images and Reality,* London: Routledge and Kegan Paul.

BALIBAR, E. 1991. 'Racism and nationalism', in E. Balibar and E. Wallerstein, *Race, Nation, Class: Ambiguous Identities,* London: Verso.

BALZER, M. M. 1999. *The Tenacity of Ethnicity: A Siberian Saga in Global Perspective,* Princeton: Princeton University Press.

BANKS, M. 1996. *Anthropological Constructions of Ethnicity: An Introductory Guide,* London: Routledge.

BANTON, M. 1967. *Race Relations,* London: Tavistock.

BANTON, M. 1983. *Racial and Ethnic Competition,* Cambridge: Cambridge University Press.

BANTON, M. 1986. 'Epistemological assumptions in the study of racial differentiation', in J. Rex and D. Mason (eds), *Theories of Race and Ethnic Relations,* Cambridge: Cambridge University Press.

BANTON, M. 1988. *Racial Consciousness,* London: Longman.

BANTON, M. 1998. *Racial Theories,* 2nd edn, Cambridge: Cambridge University Press.

BARDON, J. 1992. *A History of Ulster,* Belfast: Blackstaff.

BARKER, M. 1981. *The New Racism: Conservatives and the Ideology of the Tribe,* London: Junction.

BARNES, J. A. 1954. 'Class and committees in a Norwegian island parish', *Human Relations,* 7: 39–58.

BARTH, F. 1959. *Political Leadership among Swat Pathans,* London: Athlone.

BARTH, F. 1966. *Models of Social Organization* (RAI Occasional Paper No. 23), London: Royal Anthropological Institute.

BARTH, F. 1969a. 'Introduction', in Barth 1969b.

BARTH, F. (ed.), 1969b. *Ethnic Groups and Boundaries. The Social Organization of Culture Difference,* Oslo: Universitetsforlaget.

BARTH, F. 1981. *Process and Form in Social Life: Collected Essays of Fredrik Barth,* Vol. 1, London: Routledge and Kegan Paul.

BARTH, F. 1983. *Sohar: Culture and Society in an Omani Town,* Baltimore: Johns Hopkins University Press.

BARTH, F. 1984. 'Problems in conceptualising cultural pluralism, with illustrations from Sohar, Oman', in D. Maybury-Lewis (ed.), *The Prospects for Plural Societies,* Proceedings, American Ethnological Society, Washington, DC.

BARTH, F. 1989. 'The analysis of culture in complex societies', *Ethnos, 54*: 120–42.

BARTH, F. 1994. 'Enduring and emerging issues in the analysis of ethnicity', in H. Vermeulen and C. Govers (eds), *The Anthropology of Ethnicity: Beyond 'Ethnic Groups and Boundaries',* Amsterdam: het Spinhuis.

BATLEY, R. 1981. 'The politics of administrative allocation', in R. Forrest, J. Henderson and P. Williams (eds), *Urban Political Economy and Social Theory,* Aldershot: Gower.

BAUMAN, Z. 1989. *Modernity and the Holocaust,* Cambridge: Polity.

BAUMAN, Z. 1990. *Thinking Sociologically,* Oxford: Basil Blackwell.

BAUMAN, Z. 1992. 'Soil, blood and identity', *Sociological Review,* 40: 675–701.

BAUMANN, G. 1996. *Contesting Culture: Discourses of Identity in Multi-ethnic London,* Cambridge: Cambridge University Press.

BAUMANN, G. 1999. *The Multicultural Riddle: Rethinking National, Ethnic and Religious Identities,* New York: Routledge.

BAX, M. 1976. *Harpstrings and Confessions: Machine-Style Politics in the Irish Republic,* Assen: van Gorcum.

BECHER, T. 1989. *Academic Tribes and Territories: Intellectual Enquiry and the Cultures of Disciplines,* Milton Keynes: Open University Press.

BECKER, H. S. 1963. *Outsiders: Studies in the Sociology of Deviance,* New York: Free Press.

BECKETT, J. C. 1966. *The Making of Modern Ireland, 1603–1923,* London: Faber and Faber.

BECKETT, J. C. 1973. 'Introduction', in W.H. Crawford and B. Trainor (eds), *Aspects of Irish Social History, 1750–1800,* Belfast: HMSO.

BENEDICT, R. 1983. *Race and Racism,* London: Routledge and Kegan Paul (first published 1942).

BENHABIB, S. (ed.) 1996. *Democracy and Difference: Contesting the Boundaries of the Political,* Princeton: Princeton University Press.

BENTLEY, G. C. 1987. 'Ethnicity and practice', *Comparative Studies in Society and History,* 29: 24–55.

BERRESFORD ELLIS, P. 1985. *The Celtic Revolution: A Study in Anti Imperialism,* Talybont: Y. Lolfa.

BEW, P., GIBBON, P. and PATTERSON, H. 1979. *The State in Northern Ireland 1921–1972,* Manchester: Manchester University Press.

BHAT, A., CARR-HILL, R., OHRI, S., THE RADICAL STATISTICS RACE GROUP, 1988. *Britain's Black Population: A New Perspective,* 2nd edn, Aldershot: Gower.

BILLIG, M. 1995. *Banal Nationalism,* London: Sage.

BLAKEY, M. L., DUBINSKAS, F., FORMAN, S., MacLENNAN, C., NEWMAN, K. S., PEACOCK, J. L., RAPPAPORT, R., VELEZ-IBANEZ, C. G. and WOLFE, A. W. 1994. 'A Statement to the profession', in S. Forman (ed.), *Diagnosing America: Anthropology and Public Engagement,* Ann Arbor: University of Michigan Press.

BLUM, A. 2002. 'Resistance to identity categorization in France', in D. I. Kertzer and D. Arel (eds), *Census and Identity: The Politics of Race, Ethnicity and Language in National Censuses*, Cambridge: Cambridge University Press.

BOAL, F. W., KEANE, M. C. and LIVINGSTONE, D. N. 1997. *Them and us? Attitudinal Variation Among Churchgoers in Belfast*, Belfast: Institute of Irish Studies.

BOAS, F. 1940. *Race, Language and Culture*, New York: Free Press.

BOISSEVAIN, J. 1968. 'The place of non-groups in the social sciences', *Man* (n.s.) 3: 542–56.

BOLLOM, C. 1978. 'Attitudes towards second homes in rural Wales', in G. Williams (ed.), *Social and Cultural Change in Contemporary Wales*, London: Routledge and Kegan Paul.

BOON, J. A. 1982. *Other Tribes, Other Scribes: Symbolic Anthropology in the Comparative Study of Cultures, Histories, Religions and Texts*, Cambridge: Cambridge University Press.

BORISH, S. M. 1991. *The Land of the Living: The Danish Folk High Schools and Denmark's Non-violent Path to Modernization*, Nevada City: Blue Dolphin.

BORLAND, J., FEVRE, R. and DENNEY, D. 1992. 'Nationalism and community in North West Wales', *Sociological Review*, 40: 49–72.

BORNEMAN, J. 1992. *Belonging in the Two Berlins. Kin, State, Nation*, Cambridge: Cambridge University Press.

BOURDIEU, P. 1977. *Outline of a Theory of Practice*, Cambridge: Cambridge University Press.

BOURDIEU, P. 1984. *Distinction: A Social Critique of the Judgement of Taste*, London: Routledge and Kegan Paul.

BOURDIEU, P. 1990. *The Logic of Practice*, Cambridge. Polity.

BOWIE, F. 1993. 'Wales from within: conflicting interpretations of Welsh identity', in S. Macdonald (ed.), *Inside European Identities*, Oxford: Berg.

BOYCE, D. G. 1991. *Nationalism in Ireland*, 2nd edn, London: Routledge.

BOYD, A. 1969. *Holy War in Belfast: A History of the Troubles in Ireland*, Tralee: Anvil.

BOYD, R. and RICHERSON, P. J. 2005. *The Origin and Evolution of Cultures*, New York: Oxford University Press.

BRAH, A. 1996. *Cartographies of Diaspora: Contesting Identities*, London: Routledge.

BREUILLY, J. 1985. *Nationalism and the State*, amended edn, Manchester: Manchester University Press.

BREWER, J. D. 1992. 'Sectarianism and racism, and their parallels and differences', *Ethnic and Racial Studies*, 15: 352–64.

BREWER, J. D. and HIGGINS, G. I. 1998. *Anti-Catholicism in Northern Ireland 1600–1998: The Mote and the Beam*, Basingstoke: Macmillan.

BREWER, J. D. and HIGGINS, G. I. 1999. 'Understanding anti-Catholicism in Northern Ireland', *Sociology*, 33: 235–55.

BRODY, H. 1986. *Maps and Dreams: Indians and the British Columbia Frontier*, 2nd edn, London: Faber and Faber.

BROWN, R. M. 1975. *Strain of Violence: Historical Studies of American Violence and Vigilantism*, New York: Oxford University Press.

BRUBAKER, R. 1996. *Nationalism Reframed: Nationhood and the National Question in Europe*, Cambridge: Cambridge University Press.

BRUBAKER, R. 2002. 'Ethnicity without groups', *Archives Européenes de Sociologie*, 43: 163–89.

BRUBAKER, R. 2003. 'Neither individualism nor "groupism"', *Ethnicities*, 3: 553–7.

BRUBAKER, R. 2004. *Ethnicity without Groups*, Cambridge, MA: Harvard University Press.

BRUBAKER, R. and COOPER, F. 2000. 'Beyond "identity"', *Theory and Society*, 29: 1–47.

BRUBAKER, R., LOVEMAN, M. and STAMATOV, P. 2004. 'Ethnicity as cognition', *Theory and Society*, 33: 1–34.

BRUBAKER, R., FEISCHMIDT, M., FOX, J. and GRANCEA, L. 2006. *Nationalist Politics and Everyday Ethnicity in a Transylvanian Town*, Princeton: Princeton University Press.

BRUCE, S. 1986. *God Save Ulster! The Religion and Politics of Paisleyism*, Oxford: Clarendon Press.

BRUCE, S. 1992. *The Red Hand: Protestant Paramilitaries in Northern Ireland*, Oxford: Oxford University Press.

BRUCE, S. 1994. *The Edge of the Union: The Ulster Loyalist Political Vision*, Oxford: Oxford University Press.

BRUCE, S. and ALDERDICE, F. 1993. 'Religious belief and behaviour', in P. Stringer and G. Robinson (eds), *Social Attitudes in Northern Ireland: The Third Report*, Belfast: Blackstaff.

BRYAN, D. 2000a. *Orange Parades: The Politics of Ritual, Tradition and Control*, London: Pluto.

BRYAN, D. 2000b. 'Drumcree and "The right to march": Orangeism, ritual and politics in Northern Ireland', in T. G. Fraser (ed.), *The Irish Parading Tradition: Following the Drum*, Basingstoke: Macmillan.

BRYAN, D. 2005. 'Flags and Identity in a 'New' Northern Ireland'. ESRC Research Programme on Devolution and Constitutional Change Briefing Paper No. 34, see: www.devolution.ac.uk/Briefing_papers.htm).

BRYANT, C. G. A. 2006. *The Nations of Britain*, Oxford: Oxford University Press.

BRYSON, L. and McCARTNEY, C. 1994. *Clashing Symbols: A Report on the Use of Flags, Anthems and Other National Symbols in Northern Ireland*, Belfast: Institute of Irish Studies.

BUCH, R. and HANSEN, K. M. 2002. 'The Danes and Europe: from EC 1972 to Euro 2000', *Scandinavian Political Studies*, 25: 1–26.

BUCKLAND, P. 1980. *James Craig*, Dublin: Gill and Macmillan.

BUCKLEY, A. D. 1982. *A Gentle People: A Study of a Peaceful Community*, Cultra: Ulster Folk and Transport Museum.

BUCKLEY, A. D. 1989. '"We're trying to find our identity": uses of history among Ulster Protestants', in E. Tonkin, M. McDonald and M. Chapman (eds.), *History and Ethnicity*, London: Routledge.

BUCKLEY, A. D. (ed.) 1998. *Symbols in Northern Ireland*, Belfast: Institute of Irish Studies.

BUCKLEY, A. D. and KENNY, M.C. 1995. *Negotiating Identity: Rhetoric, Metaphor and Social Drama in Northern Ireland*, Washington, DC: Smithsonian Institution Press.

BUFWACK, M. S. 1982. *Village without Violence*, Cambridge, MA: Schenkman.

BULMER, M. and SOLOMOS, J. (eds) 1999. *Racism*, Oxford: Oxford University Press.

BURLEIGH, M. and WIPPERMANN, W. 1991. *The Racial State: Germany 1933–1945*, Cambridge: Cambridge University Press.

BURTON, F. 1978. *The Politics of Legitimacy: Struggles in a Belfast Community*, London: Routledge and Kegan Paul.

BURTON, J. W. 1981. 'Ethnicity on the hoof: on the economics of Nuer identity', *Ethnology*, 20: 157–62.

BYRNE, J. 2005. *Interface Violence in East Belfast during 2002: The Impact on Residents of Short Strand and Inner East Belfast*, Belfast: Institute for Conflict Research.

CAIRNS, E. 1992. 'Political violence, social values and the generation gap', in P. Stringer and G. Robinson (eds), *Social Attitudes in Northern Ireland: The Second Report*, Belfast: Blackstaff.

CALHOUN, C. 1997. *Nationalism*, Buckingham: Open University Press.

CALHOUN, C. 2003a '"Belonging" in the cosmopolitan imaginary', *Ethnicities*, 3(4): 531–53.

CALHOUN, C. 2003b 'The variability of belonging', *Ethnicities*, 3(4): 558–68.

CARRITHERS, M. 1992. *Why Humans Have Cultures: Explaining Anthropology and Social Diversity*, Oxford: Oxford University Press.

CECIL, R. 1993. 'The marching season in Northern Ireland: an expression of politico-religious identity', in S. Macdonald (ed.), *Inside European Identities*, Oxford: Berg.

CHAPMAN, M. 1992. *The Celts: The Construction of a Myth*, Basingstoke: Macmillan.

CHARLES, N. 1990. 'Women – advancing or retreating?', in R. Jenkins and A. Edwards (eds), *One Step Forward? South and West Wales towards the Year 2000*, Llandysul: Gwasg Gomer.

CHARLES, N. and DAVIES, C. A. 1997. 'Contested communities: the refuge movement and cultural identities in Wales', *Sociological Review*, 45: 416–36.

CHRISTENSEN, J. G. 1994. 'Sprog og kultur i europæisk integration', in J. Liep and K. Fog Olwig (eds), *Komplekse liv. kulturel mangfoldighed i Danmark,* Copenhagen: Akademisk Forlag.

CICCHETTI, D. and BEEGHLEY, M. (eds) 1990. *The Self in Transition: Infancy to Childhood,* Chicago: University of Chicago Press.

CICOUREL, A. V. and KITSUSE, J. I. 1963. *The Educational Decision Makers,* Indianapolis: Bobbs-Merrill.

CLARKE, D. M. 1984. *Church and State: Essays in Political Philosophy,* Cork: Cork University Press.

CLAYTON, P. 1996. *Enemies and Passing Friends: Settler Ideologies in Twentieth Century Ulster,* London: Pluto.

CLEWS, R. 1980. *To Dream of Freedom: The Struggle of M.A.C. and the Free Wales Army,* Talybont: Y Lolfa.

CLIFFORD, J. and MARCUS, G.E. (eds) 1986. *Writing Culture: The Poetics and Politics of Ethnography,* Berkeley: University of California Press.

COAKLEY, J. 1990. 'Typical case or deviant? Nationalism in Ireland in a European perspective', in M. Hill and S. Barber (eds), *Aspects of Irish Studies,* Belfast: Institute of Irish Studies.

COE, W. E. 1969. *The Engineering Industry in the North of Ireland,* Newton Abbot: David and Charles.

COHEN, A. 1974. 'Introduction: the lesson of ethnicity', in A. Cohen (ed.), *Urban Ethnicity,* London: Tavistock.

COHEN, A. P. (ed.) 1982. *Belonging: Identity and Social Organisation in British Rural Cultures,* Manchester: Manchester University Press.

COHEN, A. P. 1985. *The Symbolic Construction of Community,* London: Ellis Harwood/ Tavistock.

COHEN, A. P. (ed.) 1986. *Symbolising Boundaries: Identity and Diversity in British Cultures,* Manchester: Manchester University Press.

COHEN, A. P. 1992. 'Self-conscious anthropology', in J. Okely and H. Callaway (eds), *Anthropology and Autobiography,* London: Routledge.

COHEN, A. P. 1994. *Self Consciousness: An Alternative Anthropology of Identity,* London: Routledge.

COHEN, R. 1978. 'Ethnicity: problem and focus in anthropology', *Annual Review of Anthropology,* 7: 379–403.

COHEN, Y. A. 1969. 'Social boundary systems', *Current Anthropology,* 10: 103–26.

COHN, B. S. 1988. *An Anthropologist among the Historians and Other Essays,* revised corrected edn, Delhi: Oxford University Press.

COLLEY, L. 1992. *Britons: Forging the Nation 1707–1837,* New Haven: Yale University Press.

COLLIS, J. 2003. *The Celts: Origins, Myths and Inventions,* Stroud: Tempus.

COLLMANN, J. and HANDELMAN, D. (eds) 1981. 'Administrative frameworks and clients', special issue of *Social Analysis (9), passim.*

COLSON, E. 1953. *The Makah Indians: A Study of an Indian Tribe in Modern American Society,* Manchester: Manchester University Press.

COMAROFF, J. and COMAROFF, J. 1992. *Ethnography and the Historical Imagination,* Boulder, CO: Westview Press.

COMPTON, P. 1991. 'Employment differentials in Northern Ireland and job discrimination: a critique', in P. Roche and B. Barton (eds), *The Northern Ireland Question: Myth and Reality,* Aldershot: Avebury.

CONNOLLY, S. J. 1992. *Religion, Law and Power: The Making of Protestant Ireland 1660–1760,* Oxford: Clarendon Press.

CONNOR, W. 1978. 'A nation is a nation, is a state, is an ethnic group, is a ...', *Ethnic and Racial Studies,* 1: 378–400.

CONNOR, W. 1993. 'Beyond reason: the nature of the ethnonational bond', *Ethnic and Racial Studies,* 16: 373–98.

CORMACK, R. I. and OSBORNE, R. D. (eds) 1983. *Religion, Education and Employment. Aspects of Equal Opportunity in Northern Ireland,* Belfast. Appletree Press.

CORMACK, R. I. and OSBORNE, R. D. (eds) 1991. *Discrimination and Public Policy in Northern Ireland,* Oxford: Clarendon Press.

CORNELL, S. 1996. 'The variable ties that bind: content and circumstances in ethnic processes', *Ethnic and Racial Studies,* 19: 265–89.

CORNELL, S. and HARTMANN, D. 1998. *Ethnicity and Race: Making Identities in a Changing World,* Thousand Oaks: Pine Forge.

COSTA, J. and BAMOSSY, G. (eds) 1995. *Marketing in a Multicultural World,* London: Sage.

COUPLAND, N. and BALL, M. J. 1989, 'Welsh and English in contemporary Wales: sociolinguistic issues', *Contemporary Wales,* 3: 7–40.

CRAWFORD, W. H. 1972. *Domestic Industry in Ireland: The Experience of the Linen Industry,* Dublin: Gill and Macmillan.

CRAWFORD, W. H. and TRAINOR, B. (eds) 1973. *Aspects of Irish Social History: 1750–1800,* Belfast: HMSO.

CROTTY, R.D. 1966. *Irish Agricultural Production,* Cork: Cork University Press.

CULLEN, L. M. 1969. 'The Irish economy in the eighteenth century', in L. M. Cullen (ed.), *The Formation of the Irish Economy,* Cork: Mercier.

CUNLIFFE, B. 1997. *The Ancient Celts,* Oxford: Oxford University Press.

CURTICE, J. 2005. 'Devolution and Britishness', ESRC Research Programme on Devolution and Constitutional Change Briefing Paper no. 35, see: www.devolution.ac.uk/Briefing_papers.htm.

DAVIES, C. 1973. 'Cymdeithas yr Iaith Gymraeg', in M. Stephens (ed.), *The Welsh Language Today,* Llandysul: Gwasg Gomer.

DAVIES, C. 1990. *Ethnic Humor around the World: A Comparative Analysis,* Bloomington: Indiana University Press.

DAVIES, C. A. 1989. *Welsh Nationalism in the Twentieth Century: The Ethnic Option and the Modern State,* New York: Praeger.

DAVIES, C. A. 1990. 'Language and nation', in R. Jenkins and A. Edwards (eds), *One Step Forward? South and West Wales towards the Year 2000,* Llandysul: Gwasg Gomer.

DAVIES, J. 1993. *A History of Wales,* Harmondsworth: Penguin (Welsh language edn, 1990: *Hanes Cymru,* Allen Lane The Penguin Press).

DAVIS, J. 1975. 'Beyond the hyphen: some notes and documents on community–state relations in South Italy', in J. Boissevain and J. Friedl (eds), *Beyond the Community,* The Hague: Ministry of Education and Science.

DAY, G. 1989. '"A million on the move"? Population change and rural Wales', *Contemporary Wales,* 3: 137–59.

DAY, G. 1999. 'The rural dimension', in D. Dunkerley and A. Thompson (eds), *Wales Today,* Cardiff: University of Wales Press.

DAY, G. and REES, G. (eds) 1989. *Contemporary Wales,* 3, special issue devoted to linguistic and cultural change.

DAY, G. and THOMPSON, A. 1999. 'Situating Welshness: "local" experience and national identity', in R. Fevre and A. Thompson (eds), *Nation, Identity and Social Theory: Perspectives from Wales,* Cardiff: University of Wales Press.

DAY, G. and THOMPSON, A. 2004. *Theorizing Nationalism,* Basingstoke: Palgrave Macmillan.

DEACON, R. 2006. *Devolution in Britain Today,* 2nd edn, Manchester: Manchester University Press.

DENNEY, D., BORLAND, J. and FEVRE, R. 1991. 'The social construction of nationalism: racism and conflict in Wales', *Contemporary Wales,* 4: 149–65.

DEPARTMENT OF MANPOWER SERVICES 1974. *Industrial Relations in Northern Ireland: Report of a Review Body 1971–74,* Belfast: HMSO.

DEPARTMENT OF MANPOWER SERVICES 1979. *Northern Ireland Labour Market: A Guide in Graphs and Charts,* Belfast: DMS.

De SWAAN, A. 1990. *The Management of Normality: Critical Essays in Health and Welfare,* London: Routledge.

De WAAL, A. 1994. 'Genocide in Rwanda', *Anthropology Today,* 10 (3): 1–2.

DIKÖTTER, F. 1992. *The Discourse of Race in Modern China,* London: Hurst.

DIKÖTTER, F. (ed.) 1997. *The Construction of Racial Identities in China and Japan,* London: Hurst.

DILLON, M. and LEHANE, D. 1973. *Political Murder in Northern Ireland,* Harmondsworth: Penguin.

DOLLARD, J. 1957. *Caste and Class in a Southern Town,* 3rd edn, New York: Doubleday.

DONNAN, H. 2005. 'Material identities: fixing identities in the Irish borderlands', *Identities: Global Studies in Culture and Power,* 12: 69–105.

DONNAN, H. and McFARLANE, G. 1983. 'Informal social organisation', in J. Darby (ed.), *Northern Ireland: The Background to the Conflict,* Belfast: Appletree Press.

DONNAN, H. and WILSON, T. (eds) 1999. *Borders: Frontiers of Identity, Nation and State,* Oxford: Berg.

DOORNBOS, M. 1991. 'Linking the future to the past: ethnicity and pluralism', *Review of African Political Economy,* 52: 53–65.

DORLING, D. and SIMPSON, S. (eds) 1999. *Statistics in Society: The Arithmetic of Politics.* London: Arnold.

DOUGLAS, M. 1975. *Implicit Meanings: Essays in Anthropology,* London: Routledge and Kegan Paul.

DRESCH, P. and JAMES, W. 2000. 'Introduction', in P. Dresch *et al.* (eds), *Anthropologists in a Wider World: Essays on Field Research,* New York: Berghahn.

DRESCH, P., JAMES, W. and PARKIN, D. (eds) 2000. *Anthropologists in a Wider World: Essays on Field Research,* New York: Berghahn.

DUARA, P. 1993. 'De-constructing the Chinese nation', *Australian Journal of Chinese Affairs,* 30: 1–26.

DUNKERLEY, D. AND THOMPSON, A. (eds) 1999. *Wales Today,* Cardiff: University of Wales Press.

DUNN, J. 1988. *The Beginnings of Social Understanding,* Oxford: Basil Blackwell.

EASTHOPE, G. 1976. 'Religious war in Northern Ireland', *Sociology,* 10: 427–50.

EIDHEIM, H. 1969. 'When ethnic identity is a social stigma', in F. Barth (ed.), *Ethnic Groups and Boundaries,* Oslo: Universitetsforlaget.

ELKLIT, J. and TONSGAARD, O. 1992. 'The absence of nationalist movements: the case of the Nordic area', in J. Coakley (ed.), *The Social Origins of Nationalist Movements: The West European Experience,* London: Sage.

ELLER, J. D. and COUGHLAN, R. M. 1993. 'The poverty of primordialism: the demystification of ethnic attachments', *Ethnic and Racial Studies,* 16: 185–202.

ENNEW, J. 1980. *The Western Isles Today,* Cambridge: Cambridge University Press.

ENOCH, Y. 1994. 'The intolerance of a tolerant people: ethnic relations in Denmark', *Ethnic and Racial Studies,* 17: 282–300.

EPSTEIN, A. L. (ed.) 1967. *The Craft of Social Anthropology,* London: Tavistock.

EPSTEIN, A. L. 1978. *Ethos and Identity: Three Studies in Ethnicity,* London: Tavistock.

ERICKSON, F. 1976. 'Gatekeeping encounters: a social selection process', in P. R. Sanday (ed.), *Anthropology and the Public Interest,* New York: Academic Press.

ERIKSEN, T. H. 1991. 'The cultural contexts of ethnic differences', *Man* (n.s.) 26: 127–44.

ERIKSEN, T. H. 1993a. 'Formal and informal nationalism', *Ethnic and Racial Studies,* 16: 1–25.

ERIKSEN, T. H. 1993b. 'A future-oriented, non-ethnic nationalism? Mauritius as an exemplary case', *Ethnos,* 58: 197–221.

ERIKSEN, T. H. 2002. *Ethnicity and Nationalism: Anthropological Perspectives,* 2nd edn, London: Pluto.

ESRC 2006. *Final Report of the ESRC Devolution and Constitutional Change Programme*, see: http://www.devolution.ac.uk/final_report.htm.

EVANS, G. 1973. *Non-violent Nationalism*, New Malden: Fellowship of Reconciliation.

EVANS-PRITCHARD, E.E. 1940. *The Nuer*, Oxford: Clarendon Press.

EVENS, T.M.S. 1977. 'The predication of the individual in anthropological interactionism', *American Ethnologist*, 79: 579–97.

FARRELL, M. 1976. *Northern Ireland: The Orange State*, London: Pluto.

FAWCETT, L. 2000. *Religion, Ethnicity and Social Change*, Basingstoke: Macmillan.

FELDMAN, A. 1991. *Formations of Violence: The Narratives of the Body and Political Terror in Northern Ireland*, Chicago: University of Chicago Press.

FENTON, S. 1999. *Ethnicity: Racism, Class and Culture*, Basingstoke: Macmillan.

FENTON. S. 2003. *Ethnicity*, Cambridge: Polity.

FEVRE, R., BORLAND, J. and DENNY, D. 1999. 'Nation, community and conflict: housing policy and immigration in North Wales', in R. Fevre and A. Thompson (eds), *Nation, Identity and Social Theory: Perspectives from Wales*, Cardiff: University of Wales Press.

FINLAYSON, A. 1996. 'Nationalism as an ideological interpellation: the case of Ulster Loyalism', *Ethnic and Racial Studies*, 19: 88–112.

FIRTH, R. 1958. *Human Types: An Introduction to Social Anthropology*, New York: Mentor.

FIRTH, R. 1961. *Elements of Social Organization*, 3rd edn, London: Watts.

FLETT, H. 1979. 'Bureaucracy and ethnicity: notions of eligibility to public housing', in S. Wallman (ed.), *Ethnicity at Work*, London: Macmillan.

FOG OLWIG, K. and HASTRUP, K. (eds) 1997. *Siting Culture: The Shifting Anthropological Object*, London: Routledge.

FORMAN, S. (ed.) 1994. *Diagnosing America: Anthropology and Public Engagement*, Ann Arbor: University of Michigan Press.

FORSTER, P. G., HITCHCOCK, M. and LYIMO, F. F. 2000. *Race and Ethnicity in East Africa*, Basingstoke: Macmillan.

FOUCAULT, M. 1979. *Discipline and Punish: The Birth of the Prison*, Harmondsworth: Peregrine.

FRANK, A. G. and GILLS, B. K. (eds) 1993. *The World System: Five Hundred Years or Five Thousand?* London: Routledge.

FRASER, T. G. (ed.) *The Irish Parading Tradition: Following the Drum*, London: Macmillan.

FRIEDMAN, J. 1990. 'Being in the world: globalization and localization', in M. Featherstone (ed.), *Global Culture: Nationalism, Globalization and Modernity*, London: Sage.

FRIEDMAN, J. 1994. *Cultural Identity and Global Process*, London: Sage.

FULTON, J. 1991. *The Tragedy of Belief: Division, Politics, and Religion in Ireland*, Oxford: Clarendon Press.

FURNIVALL, J. S. 1948. *Colonial Policy and Practice*, Cambridge: Cambridge University Press.

GALLAGHER, A. M. and DUNN, S. 1991. 'Community relations in Northern Ireland: attitudes to contact and integration', in P. Stringer and G. Robinson (eds), *Social Attitudes in Northern Ireland: 1990–91 Edition*, Belfast: Blackstaff.

GALLAGHER, T. 2003. 'Education and equality in Northern Ireland', in O. Hargie and D. Dickson (eds), *Researching the Troubles: Social Science Perspectives on the Northern Ireland Conflict*, Edinburgh: Mainstream.

GALLENT, N., MACE, A. and TEWDR-JONES, M. 2003. 'Dispelling a myth? Second homes in rural Wales', *Area*, 35: 271–84.

GAMBETTA, D. and HAMILL, H. 2005. *Streetwise: How Taxi Drivers Establish their Customers' Trustworthiness*, New York: Russell Sage Foundation.

GEERTZ, C. 1973. *The Interpretation of Cultures*, New York. Basic Books.

GELLNER, E. 1983. *Nations and Nationalism*, Oxford: Basil Blackwell.

GERHOLM, L. and GERHOLM, T. 1990. 'The cultural study of Scandinavia: where are the frontiers?' *Anthropological Journal on European Cultures*, 1: 83–108.

GIBBON, P. 1975. *The Origins of Ulster Unionism*, Manchester: Manchester University Press.

GIDDENS, A. 1984. *The Constitution of Society,* Cambridge: Polity.

GIDDENS, A. 1985. *The Nation-State and Violence,* Cambridge: Polity.

GIGGS, J. and PATTIE, C. 1992. 'Wales as a plural society', *Contemporary Wales,* 5: 25–63.

GILES, H. and TAYLOR, D. M. 1978. 'National identity in south Wales: some preliminary data', in G. Williams (ed.), *Social and Cultural Change in Contemporary Wales,* London: Routledge and Kegan Paul.

GILL, O. 1925. *The Rise of the Irish Linen Industry,* Oxford: Oxford University Press.

GILROY, P. 1987. *There Ain't No Black in the Union Jack: The Cultural Politics of Race and Nation,* London: Hutchinson.

GIL-WHITE, F. J. 1999. 'How thick is blood?', *Ethnic and Racial Studies,* 22: 789–820.

GIL-WHITE, F. J. 2001. 'Are ethnic groups biological "species" to the human brain?', *Current Anthropology,* 42: 515–53.

GLASSIE, H. 1982. *Passing the Time in Ballymenone.* Philadelphia. University of Pennsylvania Press.

GLEDHILL, J. 2000. *Power and its Disguises: Anthropological Perspectives on Politics,* 2nd edn., London: Pluto.

GLICKMAN, M. 1972. 'The Nuer and the Dinka: a further note', *Man* (n.s.) 7: 586–94.

GLUCKMAN, M. 1956. *Custom and Conflict in Africa,* Oxford: Basil Blackwell.

GLUCKMAN, M. 1965. *Politics, Law and Ritual in Tribal Society,* Oxford: Basil Blackwell.

GOFFMAN, E. 1969. *The Presentation of Self in Everyday Life,* London: Allen Lane.

GOFFMAN, E. 1983. 'The interaction order', *American Sociological Review,* 48: 1–17.

GOODMAN, M. E. 1964. *Race Awareness in Young Children,* rev. edn, New York: Collier.

GOODY, J. 1977. *The Domestication of the Savage Mind,* Cambridge: Cambridge University Press.

GORARD, S. 2000. 'Underachievement is still an ugly word: reconsidering the relative effectiveness of schools in England and Wales', *Journal of Education Policy,* 15: 559–73.

GÖTZ, N. 2003. 'Norden: structures that do not make a region', *European Review of History,* 10: 323–41.

GOUDSBLOM, J. 1967. *Dutch Society,* New York: Random House.

GRAY, J. 1985. *City in Revolt: James Larkin and the Belfast Dock Strike of 1907,* Belfast: Blackstaff.

GRENIER, G. J. and PÉREZ, L. 2003. *The Legacy of Exile: Cubans in the United* States, Boston: Allyn and Bacon.

GRENIER, G. J. and STEPICK, A. (eds) 1992. *Miami Now! Immigration, Ethnicity and Social Change,* Gainesville: University Press of Florida.

GREVE, B. 2004. 'Denmark: universal or not so universal welfare state?' *Social Policy and Administration,* 38: 156–69.

GRILLO, R. D. 1980. 'Introduction', in Grillo (ed.), *'Nation' and 'State' in Europe: Anthropological Perspectives,* London: Academic Press.

GRILLO, R. D. 1985. *Ideologies and Institutions in Urban France: The Representation of Immigrants,* Cambridge: Cambridge University Press.

GRILLO, R. D. 1998. *Pluralism and the Politics of Difference: State, Culture and Ethnicity in Comparative Perspective,* Oxford: Oxford University Press.

GRIMSHAW, A. and HART, K. 1995. 'The rise and fall of scientific ethnography', in A. Ahmed and C. Shore (eds), *The Future of Anthropology: Its Relevance to the Contemporary World,* London: Athlone.

GROSBY, S. 1995. 'Territoriality: the transcendental, primordial feature of modern societies', *Nations and Nationalism,* 1: 143–62.

GULLESTAD, M. 1989. 'Small facts and large issues: the anthropology of contemporary Scandinavian society', *Annual Review of Anthropology,* 18: 71–93.

GUNDELACH, P. 2002. *Det er Dansk,* Copenhagen: Hans Reitzels Forlag.

GUPTA, A. and FERGUSON, J. (eds) 1997. *Anthropological Locations: Boundaries and Grounds of a Field Science,* Berkeley: University of California Press.

GUTMANN, A. (ed.) 1994. *Multiculturalism: Examining the Politics of Recognition*, Princeton: Princeton University Press.

HAAHR, J. H. 2003. '"Our Danish democracy": community, people and democracy in the Danish debate on the common currency', *Cooperation and Conflict*, 38: 27–47.

HACKING, I. 1990. *The Taming of Chance*, Cambridge: Cambridge University Press.

HADDICK-FLYNN, K. 1999. *Orangeism: The Making of a Tradition*, Dublin: Wolfhound.

HAGENDOORN, L. 1993. 'Ethnic categorization and outgroup exclusion: cultural values and social stereotypes in the construction of ethnic hierarchies', *Ethnic and Racial Studies*, 16: 27–51.

HALE, H. E. 2004. 'Explaining ethnicity', *Comparative Political Studies*, 37: 458–85.

HALL, J. A. 1993. 'Nationalisms: classified and explained', *Daedalus*, 122 (3): 1–28.

HALL, S. 1990. 'Cultural identity and diaspora', in J. Rutherford (ed.), *Identity: Community, Culture, Difference*, London: Lawrence and Wishart.

HALL, S. 1991. 'The local and the global: globalization and ethnicity', in A. King (ed.), *Culture, Globalization and the World-System*, London: Macmillan.

HALL, S. 1992. 'Our mongrel selves', *New Statesman and Society*, supplement, 19 June: 6–8.

HALL, S. 1996. 'Introduction: Who Needs Identity?' in S. Hall and P. du Gay (eds), *Questions of Cultural Identity*, London: Sage.

HALL, S., CRITCHER, C., JEFFERSON, T., CLARKE, J. and ROBERTS, B. 1978. *Policing the Crisis: Mugging, the State, and Law and Order*, London: Macmillan.

HAMILTON, A., McCARTNEY, C., ANDERSON, T. and FINN, A. 1990. *Violence and Communities: The Impact of Political Violence in Northern Ireland on Intra-community, Inter-community and Community–State Relationships*, Coleraine: Centre for the Study of Conflict, University of Ulster.

HANDELMAN, D. 1977. 'The organization of ethnicity', *Ethnic Groups*, 1: 187–200.

HANNERZ, U. 1969. *Soulside: Inquiries into Ghetto Life and Culture*, New York: Columbia University Press.

HANNERZ, U. 1990. 'Cosmopolitans and locals in world culture', in M. Featherstone (ed.), *Global Culture: Nationalism, Globalization and Modernity*, London: Sage.

HANNERZ, U. 1992. *Cultural Complexity: Studies in the Social Organization of Meaning*, New York. Columbia University Press.

HANSEN, L. and WÆVER, O. (eds) 2001. *European Integration and National Identity: The Challenge of the Nordic States*, London: Routledge.

HANSON, F. A. 1993. *Testing Testing: Social Consequences of the Examined Life*, Berkeley: University of California Press.

HARBINSON, J. F. 1973. *The Ulster Unionist Party 1883–1973*, Belfast: Blackstaff.

HARBSMEIER, M. 1986. 'Danmark: Nation, kultur og køn', *Stofskifte*, 13: 47–73.

HARDING, P. and JENKINS, R. 1989. *The Myth of the Hidden Economy: Towards a New Understanding of Informal Economic Activity*, Milton Keynes: Open University Press.

HARRIS, C. C. 1990. 'Religion', in R. Jenkins and A. Edwards (eds), *One Step Forward? South and West Wales towards the Year 2000*, Llandysul: Gwasg Gomer.

HARRIS, R. 1972. *Prejudice and Tolerance in Ulster: 'Neighbours' and 'Strangers' in a Border Community*, Manchester: Manchester University Press.

HARRISON, F. V. 2002. 'Unravelling "race" for the twenty-first century', in J. MacClancey (ed.), *Exotic No More: Anthropology on the Front Lines*, Chicago: University of Chicago Press.

HECHTER, M. 1975. *Internal Colonialism: The Celtic Fringe in British National Development 1536–1966*, London: Routledge and Kegan Paul.

HECHTER, M. and LEVI, M. 1979. 'The comparative study of ethno-regional movements', *Ethnic and Racial Studies*, 2: 260–74.

HELMAN, C. G. 2007. *Culture, Health and Illness*, 5th edn, London: Hodder Arnold.

HERVIK, P. 2004. 'The Danish cultural world of unbridgeable differences', *Ethnos*, 69: 247–67.

HESKIN, K. 1980. *Northern Ireland: A Psychological Analysis*, Dublin: Gill and Macmillan.

HEURLIN, B. (ed.) 1994. *Danmark og Den Europaeisk Union*, Copenhagen: Forlaget Politiske Studier.

HICKEY, J. 1984. *Religion and the Northern Ireland Problem*, Dublin: Gill and Macmillan.

HIGGINS, G. I. and BREWER, J. D. 2003. 'The roots of sectarianism in Northern Ireland', in O. Hargie and D. Dickson (eds), *Researching the Troubles: Social Science Perspectives on the Northern Ireland Conflict*, Edinburgh: Mainstream.

HILLYARD, P. and PERCY-SMITH, J. 1988. *The Coercive State: The Decline of Democracy in Britain*, London: Fontana.

HINDLEY, R. 1990. *The Death of the Irish Language: A Qualified Obituary*, London: Routledge.

HOBSBAWM, E. J. 1990. *Nations and Nationalism since 1780: Programme, Myth, Reality*, Cambridge: Cambridge University Press.

HOBSBAWM, E. J. 1992. 'Ethnicity and nationalism in Europe today', *Anthropology Today*, 8(1): 3–8.

HOBSBAWM, E. J. and RANGER, T. (eds) 1983. *The Invention of Tradition*, Cambridge: Cambridge University Press.

HOCKEY, J. and JAMES, A. 2003. *Social Identities across the Life Course*, Basingstoke: Palgrave Macmillan.

HOGG, M. A. 2004. 'Social categorization, depersonalization, and group behavior', in M. B. Brewer and M. Hewstone (eds), *Self and Social Identity*, Oxford: Blackwell.

HOROWITZ, D. L. 1985. *Ethnic Groups in Conflict*, Berkeley: University of California Press.

HOWE, L. E. A. 1985. 'The deserving and the undeserving: practice in an urban, local social security office', *Journal of Social Policy*, 14: 49–72.

HOWELL, D. L. 1994. 'Ainu ethnicity and the boundaries of the early modern Japanese state', *Past and Present*, 142: 69–93.

HOWELL, D. W. and BABER, C. 1990. 'Wales', in F. M. L. Thompson (ed.), *The Cambridge Social History of Britain 1750–1950. I: Regions and Communities*, Cambridge: Cambridge University Press.

HUG, C. 1999. *The Politics of Sexual Morality in Ireland*, Basingstoke: Macmillan.

HUGHES, E. C. 1994. *On Work, Race and the Sociological Imagination*, ed. L.A. Coser, Chicago: University of Chicago Press.

HUGHES, J. 2004. 'Attitudes towards equality in Northern Ireland: evidence of progress?' in B. Osborne and I. Shuttleworth (eds), *Fair Employment in Northern Ireland: A Generation On*, Belfast: Blackstaff Press.

HUTCHINSON, J. 1987. *The Dynamics of Cultural Nationalism: The Gaelic Revival and the Creation of the Irish Nation State*, London: Allen and Unwin.

HUTCHINSON, J. 1994. *Modern Nationalism*, London: Fontana.

HUTCHINSON, J. and SMITH, A. D. (eds) 1996. *Ethnicity*, Oxford: Oxford University Press.

HUTCHINSON, S. 1995. *Nuer Dilemmas: Coping with Money, War and the State*, Berkeley: University of California Press.

HUTSON, J. 1990. 'Rural life', in R. Jenkins and A. Edwards (eds), *One Step Forward? South and West Wales towards the Year 2000*, Llandysul: Gwasg Gomer.

HUTSON, J. 2003. 'Family farm businesses and the farming community: revisiting farm families in west Wales eighteen years on', in C. A. Davies and S. Jones (eds), *Welsh Communities: New Ethnographic Perspectives*, Cardiff: University of Wales Press.

IGNATIEFF, M. 1994. *Blood and Belonging: Journeys into the New Nationalism*, London: Vintage.

INGLIS, T. 1998. *Moral Monopoly: The Rise and Fall of the Catholic Church in Modern Ireland*, Dublin: University College Dublin Press.

IRIGARAY, L. 1993. *Je, tu, nous: Towards a Culture of Difference*, trans. A. Martin, New York: Routledge.

IRVINE, M. 1991. *Northern Ireland: Faith and Faction*, London: Routledge.

JACKSON, A. (ed.) 1987. *Anthropology at Home*, London: Tavistock.

JACOBSEN, H. S. 1986. *An Outline History of Denmark*, Copenhagen: Has.

JAMES, A., JENKS, C. and PROUT, A. 1998. *Theorizing Childhood*, Cambridge: Polity.

JAMES, S. 1999. *The Atlantic Celts: Ancient People or Modern Invention?* London: British Museum Press.

JARMAN, N. 1997. *Material Conflicts: Parades and Visual Displays in Northern Ireland*, Oxford: Berg.

JARMAN, N. 2003. 'Managing disorder: responses to interface violence in North Belfast', in O. Hargie and D. Dickson (eds), *Researching the Troubles: Social Science Perspectives on the Northern Ireland Conflict*, Edinburgh: Mainstream.

JÄRVINEN, M. and MIK-MEYER, N. (eds) 2003. *At Skabe en Klient: Institutionelle identiteter i socialt arbejde*, Copenhagen: Hans Reitzels Forlag.

JEDREJ, C. and NUTTALL, M. 1996. *White Settlers: The Impact of Rural Repopulation in Scotland*, Luxembourg: Harwood.

JENKINS, R. 1982. *Hightown Rules: Growing up in a Belfast Housing Estate*, Leicester: National Youth Bureau.

JENKINS, R. 1983. *Lads, Citizens and Ordinary Kids: Working-class Youth Life-styles in Belfast*, London: Routledge and Kegan Paul.

JENKINS, R. 1984. 'Understanding Northern Ireland', *Sociology*, 19: 253–64.

JENKINS, R. 1986a. *Racism and Recruitment: Managers, Organisations and Equal Opportunity in the Labour Market*, Cambridge: Cambridge University Press.

JENKINS, R. 1986b. 'Northern Ireland: in what sense "religions" in conflict?', in R. Jenkins, H. Donnan and G. McFarlane, *The Sectarian Divide in Northern Ireland Today* (RAI Occasional Paper No. 41), London: Royal Anthropological Institute.

JENKINS, R. 1987. 'Countering prejudice – anthropological and otherwise', *Anthropology Today*, 3(2): 3–4.

JENKINS, R. 1988. 'Discrimination and equal opportunity in employment: ethnicity and "race" in the United Kingdom', in D. Gallie (ed.), *Employment in Britain*, Oxford: Basil Blackwell.

JENKINS, R. 1998a. 'From criminology to anthropology: identity, morality and normality in the social construction of deviance', in S. Holdaway and P. Rock (eds), *Thinking about Criminology*, London: UCL Press.

JENKINS, R. 1998b. 'Culture, classification and (in)competence', in R. Jenkins (ed.), *Questions of Competence: Culture, Classification and Intellectual Disability*, Cambridge: Cambridge University Press.

JENKINS, R. 2000a. 'Categorization: identity, social process and epistemology', *Current Sociology*, 48(3): 7–25.

JENKINS, R. 2000b. 'Not simple at all: Danish identity and the European Union', in I. Bellier and T. M. Wilson (eds), *An Anthropology of the European Union: Building, Imagining and Experiencing the New Europe*, Oxford: Berg.

JENKINS, R. 2002a. *Foundations of Sociology: Towards a Better Understanding of the Human World*, Basingstoke: Palgrave Macmillan.

JENKINS, R. 2002b. 'Imagined but not imaginary: ethnicity and nationalism in the modern world', in J. MacClancey (ed.), *Exotic No More: Anthropology on the Front Lines*, Chicago: University of Chicago Press.

JENKINS, R. 2005. 'Denmark', in C. Skutsch (ed.), *Encyclopedia of the World's Minorities*, New York: Routledge.

JENKINS, R. 2006a. 'Telling the forest from the trees: local images of national change in a Danish town', *Ethnos*, 71: 367–89.

JENKINS, R. 2006b. 'When politics and social theory converge: group identification and group rights in Northern Ireland', *Nationalism and Ethnic Politics*, 12: 389–410.

JENKINS, R. 2008. *Social Identity*, 3rd edn, London: Routledge.

JENKINS, R. and EDWARDS, A. (eds) 1990. *One Step Forward? South and West Wales towards the Year 2000*, Llandysul: Gwasg Gomer.

JESPERSEN, K. J. V. 2004. *A History of Denmark*, Basingstoke: Palgrave Macmillan.

JONES, B. 1988. 'The development of Welsh territorial institutions: modernization theory revisited', *Contemporary Wales*, 2: 47–61.

JONES, D. G. 1973. 'The Welsh Language movement', in M. Stephens (ed.), *The Welsh Language Today*, Llandysul: Gwasg Gomer.

JONES, W. G. 1986. *Denmark: A Modern History*, London: Croom Helm.

KAPFERER, B. (ed.) 1976. *Transaction and Meaning*, Philadelphia: ISHI.

KAPFERER, B. 1988. *Legends of People. Myths of State: Violence, Intolerance and Political Culture in Sri Lanka and Australia*, Washington, DC: Smithsonian Institution Press.

KAPLAN, J. B. and BENNETT, T. 2003. 'Use of race and ethnicity in biomedical publication', *Journal of the American Medical Association*, 289(20): 2709–16.

KARN, V. 1983. 'Race and housing in Britain: the role of the major institutions', in N. Glazer and K. Young (eds), *Ethnic Pluralism and Public Policy: Achieving Equality in the United States and Britain*, London: Heinemann.

KAUFMAN, J. S. and COOPER, R. S. 2001. 'Commentary: considerations for use of racial/ethnic classification in etiological research', *American Journal of Epidemiology*, 154, (4): 291–98.

KAYE, K. 1982. *The Mental and Social Life of Babies: How Parents Create Persons*, Brighton: Harvester.

KEDOURIE, E. 1985. *Nationalism*, revised edn, London: Hutchinson.

KELLEHER, W. F. 2003. *The Troubles in Ballybogoin: Memory and Identity in Northern Ireland*, Ann Arbor: University of Michigan Press.

KELLY, J. 2000. 'The emergence of political parading, 1660–1800', in T. G. Fraser (ed.), *The Irish Parading Tradition: Following the Drum*, Basingstoke: Macmillan.

KERTZER, D. I. and AREL, D. (eds) 2002. *Census and Identity: The Politics of Race, Ethnicity and Language in National Censuses*, Cambridge: Cambridge University Press.

KIELY, R., McCRONE, D. and BECHOFER, F. 2005. 'Whither Britishness? English and Scottish people in Scotland', *Nations and Nationalism*, 11: 65–82.

KUPER, A. 1988. *The Invention of Primitive Society: Transformations of an Illusion*, London: Routledge.

KUPER, L. 1971. 'Political change in plural societies', *International Social Science Journal*, 23: 594–607.

KUPER, L. and SMITH, M. G. (eds) 1969. *Pluralism in Africa*, Berkeley: University of California Press.

LA FONTAINE, J. 1986. 'Countering racial prejudice: a better starting point', *Anthropology Today*, 2(6): 1–2.

LAING, R. D. 1971. *Self and Others*, Harmondsworth: Pelican.

LAMONT, M. 1992. *Money, Morals and Manners: The Culture of the French and the American Upper-Middle Class*, Chicago: University of Chicago Press.

LAMONT, M. 1995. 'National identity and national boundary patterns in France and the United States', *French Historical Studies*, 19: 349–65.

LAMONT, M. 1997. The meaning of class and race: French and American workers discuss differences', in J. R. Hall (ed.), *Reworking Class*, Ithaca, NY: Cornell University Press.

LAMONT, M. 1999. 'Above "people above"? Status and worth among black and white workers', in M. Lamont (ed.), *The Cultural Territories of Race: Black and White Boundaries*, Chicago: University of Chicago Press.

LAMONT, M. and MOLNÁR, V. 2001. 'How blacks use consumption to shape their collective identity', *Journal of Consumer Culture*, 1: 31–45.

LAMONT, M. and MOLNÁR, V. 2002. 'The study of boundaries in the social sciences', *Annual Review of Sociology*, 28: 167–95.

LANCLOS, D. M. 2003. *At Play in Belfast: Children's Folklore and Identities in Northern Ireland*, New Brunswick: Rutgers University Press.

LANE, C. 1981. *The Rites of Rulers: Ritual and Industrial Society – the Soviet Case*, Cambridge: Cambridge University Press.

LARSEN, S. S. 1982. 'The Glorious Twelfth: the politics of legitimation in Kilbroney', in A. P. Cohen (ed.), *Belonging: Identity and Social Organisation in British Rural Cultures*, Manchester: Manchester University Press.

LEACH, E. 1954. *Political Systems of Highland Burma: A Study of Kachin Social Structure*, London: Athlone.

LEACH, E. 1961. *Rethinking Anthropology*, London: Athlone.

LEE, R. M. 1981. 'Inter-religious courtship and marriage in Northern Ireland', Ph.D. thesis, University of Edinburgh.

LEE, S. M. 1993. 'Racial classifications in the US census: 1890–1990', *Ethnic and Racial Studies*, 16: 75–94.

LEMERT, E. M. 1972. *Human Deviance, Social Problems and Social Control*, 2nd edn, Englewood Cliffs, NJ: Prentice-Hall.

LENTZ, C. 1994. '"They must be Dagaba first and any other thing second ... " The colonial and post-colonial creation of ethnic identities in north-western Ghana', *African Studies*, 53(2): 57–91.

LENTZ, C. 1995. '"Tribalism" and ethnicity in Africa: a review of four decades of anglophone research', *Cahiers des Sciences humaines*, 31: 303–28.

LENTZ, C. 2000 'Contested identities: the history of ethnicity in northwestern Ghana', in C. Lentz and P. Nugent (eds), *Ethnicity in Ghana: The Limits of Invention*, Basingstoke; Macmillan.

LeESPIRITU, Y. (1992) *Asian American Panethnicity: Bridging Institutions and Identities*. Philadelphia: Temple University Press.

LÉVI-STRAUSS, C. 1952. *The Race Question in Modern Science*, Paris: UNESCO.

LEVINE, H. 1999. 'Reconstructing ethnicity', *Journal of the Royal Anthropological Institute*, 5: 165–80.

LIDDIARD, M. and HUTSON, S. 1991. 'Homeless young people and runaways – agency definitions and processes', *Journal of Social Policy*, 20: 365–88.

LIEBOW, E. 1967. *Tally's Corner: A Study of Negro Streetcorner Men*, Boston: Little, Brown.

LINDE-LAURSEN, A. 1993. 'The nationalization of trivialities: how cleaning becomes an identity marker in the encounter of Swedes and Danes', *Ethnos*, 58: 275–93.

LIPSKY, M. 1980. *Street-Level Bureaucracy: Dilemmas of the Individual in Public Services*, New York: Russell Sage Foundation.

LLOBERA, J. 1994. *The God of Modernity: The Development of Nationalism in Western Europe*, Oxford: Berg.

LOFTUS, B. 1994. *Mirrors: Orange and Green*, Dundrum: Picture Press.

LYCK, L. 1992. 'Denmark and the Maastricht agreement: perspectives for Denmark, EC and Europe', in L. Lyck (ed.), *Denmark and EC Membership Evaluated*, London: Pinter.

LYONS, F. S. L. 1973. *Ireland since the Famine*, London: Fontana.

McALLISTER, I. 1982. 'The Devil, miracles and the afterlife: the political sociology of religion in Northern Ireland', *British Journal of Sociology*, 33: 330–47.

MacCLANCEY, J. (ed.) 2002. *Exotic No More: Anthropology on the Front Lines*, Chicago: University of Chicago Press.

McCRONE, D. 1998. *The Sociology of Nationalism*, London: Routledge.

McCRONE, D. 2002. 'Who do you say you are? Making sense of national identities in modern Britain', *Ethnicities*, 2: 301–20.

McCRONE, D. and KIELY, R. 2000. 'Nationalism and citizenship', *Sociology*, 34: 19–34.

McFARLANE, W. G. 1979. '"Mixed" marriages in Ballycuan, Northern Ireland', *Journal of Comparative Family Studies*, 10: 191–205.

McFARLANE, W. G. 1986. '"It's not as simple as that": the expression of the Catholic and Protestant boundary in Northern Irish rural communities', in A. P. Cohen (ed.), *Symbolizing Boundaries: Identity and Diversity in British Culture*, Manchester: Manchester University Press.

McGLYNN, C., NIENS, U., CAIRNS, E. and HEWSTONE, M. 2004 . 'Moving out of conflict: the contribution of integrated schools in Northern Ireland to identity, attitudes, forgiveness and reconciliation', *Journal of Peace Education*, 1: 147–63.

MACKAY, H. (ed.) 1997. *Consumption and Everyday Life*, London: Sage.

McKAY, S. 2000. *Northern Protestants: An Unsettled People*, Belfast: Blackstaff.

McKERNAN, J. 1982. 'Value systems and race relations in Northern Ireland and America', *Ethnic and Racial Studies*, 5: 156–74.

MacLEOD, J. 1987. *Ain't No Makin' It: Levelled Aspirations in a Low-Income Neighbourhood*, London: Tavistock.

MAINWARING, L. 1990. 'The economy', in R. Jenkins and A. Edwards (eds), *One Step Forward? South and West Wales towards the Year 2000*, Llandysul: Gwasg Gomer.

MALEŠEVIĆ, S. 2004. *The Sociology of Ethnicity*, London: Sage.

MALINOWSKI, B. 1922. *Argonauts of the Western Pacific*, London: Kegan Paul, Trench, Trubner.

MANN, M. 1993. 'Nation-states in Europe and other continents: diversifying, developing, not dying', *Daedalus*, 122(3): 115–40.

MANNICHE, P. 1969. *Denmark: A Social Laboratory*, Oxford: Pergamon.

MANSERGH, N. 1936. *The Government of Northern Ireland*, London: George Allen and Unwin.

MAQUET, J. 1972. 'Inborn differences and the premise of inequality', in P. Baxter and B. Sansom (eds), *Race and Social Difference*, Harmondsworth: Penguin.

MARCUS, G. 1992. 'Past, present and emergent identities: requirements for ethnographies of late twentieth-century modernity', in S. Lash and J. Friedman (eds.), *Modernity and Identity*, Oxford: Basil Blackwell.

MARCUS, G. and FISCHER, M. M. J. 1986. *Anthropology as Cultural Critique: An Experimental Moment in the Human Sciences*, Chicago: University of Chicago Press.

MATZA, D. 1969. *Becoming Deviant*, Englewood Cliffs, NJ: Prentice-Hall.

MAYBURY-LEWIS, D. (ed.) 1984. *The Prospects for Plural Societies*, Washington, DC: American Ethnological Society.

MAYER, A. 1966. 'The significance of quasi-groups in the study of complex societies', in M. Banton (ed.), *The Social Anthropology of Complex Societies*, London: Tavistock.

MEAD, G. H. 1934. *Mind, Self and Society from the Standpoint of a Social Behaviorist*, Chicago: University of Chicago Press.

MEGAW, J. V. S. and MEGAW, M. R. 1998. 'The mechanism of (Celtic) dreams: a partial response to our critics', *Antiquity*, 72: 432–5.

MEGAW, M. R. and MEGAW, J. V. S. 1996. 'Ancient Celts and modern ethnicity', *Antiquity*, 70: 175–81.

MIDMORE, P., HUGHES, G. and BATEMAN, D. 1994. 'Agriculture and the rural economy: problems, policies and prospects', *Contemporary Wales*, 6: 7–32.

MILES, R. 1982. *Racism and Migrant Labour*, London. Routledge and Kegan Paul.

MILES, R. 1989. *Racism*, London: Routledge.

MILES, R. 1996. 'Racism and nationalism in the British Isles: a view from the periphery', in R. Barot (ed.), *The Racism Problematic: Contemporary Sociological Debates on Race and Ethnicity*, Lampeter: Edwin Mellon Press.

MILLER, D. (ed.) 1995. *Worlds Apart: Modernity through the Prism of the Local*, London: Routledge.

MILLER, D. 1998. *A Theory of Shopping*, Cambridge: Polity.

MILNER, D. 1975. *Children and Race*, Harmondsworth: Penguin.

MITCHELL, C. 2003. 'Protestant identification and political change in Northern Ireland', *Ethnic and Racial Studies*, 26: 612–31.

MITCHELL, C. 2006. *Religion, Identity and Politics in Northern Ireland*, Aldershot: Ashgate.

MITCHELL, J. C. (ed.) 1969. *Social Networks in Urban Situations*, Manchester: Manchester University Press.

MOERMAN, M. 1965. 'Ethnic identification in a complex civilization: who are the Lue?' *American Anthropologist*, 67: 1215–30.

MODOOD, T. 1992. *Not Easy Being British: Colour, Culture and Citizenship*, Stoke-on-Trent: Trentham Books.

MOODY, T. W. 1974. *The Ulster Question 1603–1973*, Cork: Mercier.

MOORE, R. 1972. 'Race relations in the six counties: colonialism, industrialization and stratification in Ireland', *Race*, 14: 21–42.

MOORE, R. I. 1987. *The Formation of a Persecuting Society: Power and Deviance in Western Europe 950–1250*, Oxford: Basil Blackwell.

MORGAN, K. O. 1971. 'Welsh nationalism: the historical background', *Journal of Contemporary History*, 6: 153–72.

MORGAN, K. O. 1981. *Rebirth of a Nation: Wales 1880–1980*, Oxford: Clarendon Press.

MORGAN, P. 1983. 'From a death to a view: the hunt for the Welsh past in the Romantic period', in E. Hobsbawm and T. Ranger (eds), *The Invention of Tradition*, Cambridge: Cambridge University Press.

MORGAN, V. and FRASER, G. 1999. 'When does "good news" become "bad news"? Relationships between government and integrated schools in Northern Ireland', *British Journal of Educational Studies*, 47: 364–79.

MORRIS, B. 1994. *Anthropology of the Self: The Individual in Cultural Perspective*, London: Pluto.

MOXON-BROWNE, E. 1983. *Nation, Class and Creed in Northern Ireland*, Aldershot: Gower.

MOXON-BROWNE, E. 1991. 'National identity in Northern Ireland', in P. Stringer and G. Robinson (eds), *Social Attitudes in Northern Ireland: 1990–91 Edition*, Belfast: Blackstaff.

MÜLLER-HILL, B. 1988. *Murderous Science: Elimination by Scientific Selection of Jews, Gypsies and Others, Germany 1933–1945*, Oxford: Oxford University Press.

MUNCK, R. and ROLSTON, B. 1987. *Belfast in the Thirties: An Oral History*, Belfast: Blackstaff.

MURRAY, D. 1983. 'School and conflict', in J. Darby (ed.), *Northern Ireland: The Background to the Conflict*, Belfast: Appletree.

MURTAGH, B. 2003. 'Territoriality, research and policy-making in Northern Ireland', in O. Hargie and D. Dickson (eds), *Researching the Troubles: Social Science Perspectives on the Northern Ireland Conflict*, Edinburgh: Mainstream.

NAIRN, T. 1981. *The Break-Up of Britain: Crisis and Neo-Nationalism*, 2nd edn, London: New Left Books.

NASH, J. and OGAN, E. 1990. 'The red and the black: Bougainvillean perceptions of other Papuan New Guineans', *Pacific Studies*, 13(2): 1–17.

NAZROO, J. 2001. *Ethnicity, Class and Health*, London: Policy Studies Institute.

NELSON, S. 1975. 'Protestant "ideology" reconsidered: the case of "discrimination"', *British Political Sociology Yearbook*, 2: 155–87.

NEWCOMER, P. J. 1972. 'The Nuer are Dinka: an essay on origins and environmental determinism', *Man* (n.s.) 7: 5–11.

NIENS, U., CAIRNS, E. and HEWSTONE, M. 2003. 'Contact and conflict in Northern Ireland', in O. Hargie and D. Dickson (eds), *Researching the Troubles: Social Science Perspectives on the Northern Ireland Conflict*, Edinburgh: Mainstream.

OAKES, P. 2004. 'The root of all evil in intergroup relations? Unearthing the categorization process', in M. B. Brewer and M. Hewstone (eds), *Social Cognition*, Oxford: Blackwell.

O'DONNELL, E. E. 1977. *Northern Irish Stereotypes*, Dublin: College of Industrial Relations.

O'DOWD, L., ROLSTON, B. and TOMLINSON, M. 1980. *Northern Ireland: Between Civil Rights and Civil War*, London: CSE Books.

OKELY, J. 1983. *The Traveller-Gypsies*, Cambridge: Cambridge University Press.

O'LEARY, B. and McGARRY, J. 1996 *The Politics of Antagonism: Understanding Northern Ireland*, 2nd edn, London: Athlone.

O'REILLY, E. 1992. *Masterminds of the Right*, Dublin: Attic.

O'REILLY, C. 1999. *The Irish Language in Northern Ireland: The Politics of Culture and Identity,* Basingstoke: Macmillan.

OSBORNE, B. and SHUTTLEWORTH, I. (eds) 2004. *Fair Employment in Northern Ireland: A Generation On,* Belfast: Blackstaff.

OSBORNE, R. D. 2004. 'Education and the labour market', in B. Osborne and I. Shuttleworth (eds), *Fair Employment in Northern Ireland: A Generation On,* Belfast: Blackstaff.

O'SULLIVAN SEE, K. 1986. *First World Nationalisms: Class and Ethnic Politics in Northern Ireland and Quebec,* Chicago: University of Chicago Press.

ØSTERGÅRD, U. 1992a. 'What is national and ethnic identity?' in P. Bilde, T. Engberg-Pedersen, L. Hannestad and J. Zahle (eds), *Ethnicity in Hellenistic Egypt,* Aarhus: Aarhus University Press.

ØSTERGÅRD, U. 1992b. *Europas Ansigter: Nationale stater og politiske kulturer I en ny, gammel, verden,* Copenhagen: Rosinante.

ØSTERGÅRD, U. 1992c. 'Danish identity: European, Nordic or peasant?' in L. Lyck (ed.), *Denmark and EC Membership Evaluated,* London: Pinter.

ØSTERGÅRD, U. (ed.) 1992d. *Dansk Identitet?* Aarhus. Aarhus Universitetsforlag.

ØSTERGÅRD, U. 1992e. 'Peasants and Danes: the Danish national identity and political culture', *Comparative Studies in Society and History,* 34: 3–27.

ØSTERGÅRD, U. 1995. *Dansk mindretals politik i praksis* (Arbejdspapir 24–95), Aarhus: Center for Kulturforskning.

ØSTERGAARD NIELSEN, E. 2003. 'Counting the cost: Denmark's changing migration policies', *International Journal of Urban and Regional Research,* 27: 448–54.

PAINE, R. 1974. *Second Thoughts about Barth's Models* (RAI Occasional Paper No. 32), London: Royal Anthropological Institute.

PATTERSON, H. 1980. *Class Conflict and Sectarianism: The Protestant Working Class and the Belfast Labour Movement,* Belfast: Blackstaff.

PELTO, P. J. and PELTO, G. H. 1978. *Anthropological Research: The Structure of Inquiry,* 2nd edn, Cambridge: Cambridge University Press.

PHOENIX, E. 1994. *Northern Nationalism: Nationalist Politics, Partition and the Catholic Minority in Northern Ireland 1890–1940,* Belfast: Ulster Historical Foundation.

PLECK, E. H. 2000. *Celebrating the Family: Ethnicity, Consumer Culture and Family Rituals,* Cambridge, MA: Harvard University Press.

PORTER, E. 1996. 'Culture, community and responsibilities: abortion in Ireland', *Sociology,* 30: 279–98.

PORTES, A. and STEPICK, A. 1993. *City on the Edge: The Transformation of Miami,* Berkeley: University of California Press.

PROTTAS, J. M. 1979. *People Processing: The Street-Level Bureaucrat in Public Service Bureaucracies,* Lexington, MA: Lexington Books.

PRUNIER, G. 1997. *The Rwanda Crisis: History of a Genocide,* New York: Columbia University Press.

PRYCE, K. 1979. *Endless Pressure: A Study of West-Indian Life-styles in Bristol,* Harmondsworth: Penguin.

RADCLIFFE-BROWN, A. R. 1952. *Structure and Function in Primitive Society: Essays and Addresses,* London: Cohen and West.

RAPPORT, N. 1995. 'Migrant selves and stereotypes: personal context in a postmodern world', in S. Pile and N. Thrift (eds), *Mapping the Subject: Geographies of Cultural Transformation,* London: Routledge.

RAPPORT, N. 2003. *I Am Dynamite: An Alternative Anthropology of Power,* London: Routledge.

RAUDZENS, G. 1999. *Empires: Europe and Globalization 1492–1788,* Stroud: Sutton.

REDDY, G. P. 1993. *Danes Are Like That! Perspectives of an Indian Anthropologist on the Danish Society,* Mørke: Grevas.

REES, G. 2004. 'Democratic devolution and education policy in Wales: the emergence of a national system?' *Contemporary Wales,* 17: 28–43.

REES, I. B. 1975. *The Welsh Political Tradition,* Cardiff: Plaid Cymru.

REES, I. B. 1990. 'Wales today: nation or market?' *Planet,* 79: 56–91.

REICHER, S. and HOPKINS, N. 2001. *Self and Nation,* London: Sage.

REID, A. 1980. 'Skilled workers in the shipbuilding industry 1880–1920: a labour aristocracy', in A. Morgan and B. Purdie (eds.), *Ireland: Divided Nation, Divided Class,* London: Ink Links.

REX, J. 1973. *Race, Colonialism and the City,* London: Oxford University Press.

REX, J. 1986. *Race and Ethnicity,* Milton Keynes: Open University Press.

REX, J. 1991. *Ethnic Identity and Ethnic Mobilization in Britain,* Warwick: ESRC Centre for Research in Ethnic Relations.

REYNOLDS, S. 1984. *Kingdoms and Communities in Western Europe 900–1300,* Oxford: Clarendon Press.

RICHARDS, M.P.M. (ed.) 1974. *The Integration of a Child into a Social World,* Cambridge: Cambridge University Press.

RICHERSON, P. J. and BOYD, R. 2004. *Not By Genes Alone: How Culture Transformed Human Evolution,* Chicago: University of Chicago Press.

RINGER, B. B. 1983. *'We The People' and Others: Duality and America's Treatment of its Racial Minorities,* London: Tavistock.

RIST, R. C. 1977. 'On understanding the processes of schooling: the contributions of labelling theory', in J. Karabel and A. H. Halsey (eds), *Power and Ideology in Education,* New York: Oxford University Press.

RITZER, G. 2004. *The McDonaldization of Society,* 4th edn, Thousand Oaks: Pine Forge.

ROBERTS, B. 1999. 'Welsh identity in a former mining valley: social images and imagined communities', in R. Fevre and A. Thompson (eds), *Nation, Identity and Social Theory: Perspectives from Wales,* Cardiff: University of Wales Press.

ROBERTSON, R. 1992. *Globalization: Social Theory and Global Culture,* London: Sage.

ROBERTSON, R. 1995. 'Glocalization: time–space and homogeneity–heterogeneity', in M. Featherstone, S. Lash and R. Robertson (eds), *Global Modernities.* London: Sage.

ROLSTON, B. 1991. *Politics and Painting: Murals and Conflict in Northern Ireland,* Rutherford: Fairleigh Dickinson University Press.

ROLSTON, B. 1992. *Drawing Support: Murals in the North of Ireland,* Belfast: Beyond the Pale.

ROLSTON, B. 1995. *Drawing Support 2: Murals of War and Peace,* Belfast: Beyond the Pale.

ROLSTON, B. 2003. *Drawing Support 3: Murals and Transition in the North of Ireland,* Belfast: Beyond the Pale.

ROSE, R. 1971. *Governing without Consensus,* London: Faber and Faber.

RUANE, J. and TODD, J. 1992. 'The social origins of nationalism in a contested region: the case of Northern Ireland', in J. Coakley (ed.), *The Social Origins of Nationalism. The West European Experience,* London: Sage.

RUANE, J. and TODD, J. 1996. *The Dynamics of Conflict in Northern Ireland: Peace, Conflict and Emancipation,* Cambridge: Cambridge University Press.

RUANE, J. and TODD, J. 2004. 'The roots of intense ethnic conflict may not in fact be ethnic: categories, communities and path dependence', *Archives Européenes de Sociologie,* 45: 209–32.

RUNCIMAN, S. 1958. *The Sicilian Vespers: A History of the Mediterranean World in the Later Thirteenth Century,* Cambridge: Cambridge University Press.

RUTHERFORD, J. (ed.) 1990. *Identity: Community, Culture, Difference,* London: Lawrence and Wishart.

RYLE, G. 1963. *The Concept of Mind,* Harmondsworth: Peregrine (first published 1949).

SACKS, P. M. 1976. *The Donegal Mafia,* New Haven: Yale University Press.

SAGGAR, S. 1996. 'The politics of racial pluralism in Britain: problems of evaluation', in R. Barot (ed.), *The Racism Problematic,* Lampeter: Edwin Mellon Press.

SAHLINS, M. 1972. *Stone Age Economics,* London: Tavistock.

SAHLINS, P. 1989 *Boundaries: The Making of France and Spain in the Pyrenees,* Berkeley: University of California Press.

SALES, R. 2002. 'The deserving and the undeserving? Refugees, asylum seekers and welfare in Britain', *Critical Social Policy*, 22: 456–78.

SAMUEL, R. and THOMPSON, P. (eds) 1990. *The Myths We Live By*, London: Routledge.

SCHERMERHORN, R. A. 1978. *Comparative Ethnic Relations: A Framework for Theory and Research*, 2nd edn, Chicago. University of Chicago Press.

SCHLEE, G. 1989. *Identities on the Move: Clanship and Pastoralism in Northern Kenya*, Manchester: Manchester University Press.

SCHUTZ, A. 1967. *The Phenomenology of the Social World*, Evanston: Northwestern University Press.

SCHUTZ, A. and LUCKMANN, T. 1973. *The Structures of the Life-World*, Evanston: Northwestern University Press.

SCOTT, R. A. 1970. 'The construction of conceptions of stigma by professional experts', in J. D. Douglas (ed.), *Deviance and Respectability: The Social Construction of Moral Meanings*, New York: Basic Books.

SCOURFIELD, J. and DAVIES, A. 2005. 'Children's accounts of Wales as racialized and inclusive', *Ethnicities*, 5: 83–107.

SCOURFIELD, J., DICKS, B., DRAKEFORD, M. and DAVIES, A. 2006. *Children, Place and Identity: Nation and Locality in Middle Childhood*, London: Routledge.

SEIDMAN, S. 1997. *Difference Troubles: Queering Social Theory and Sexual Politics*, Cambridge: Cambridge University Press.

SENIOR, H. 1966. *Orangeism in Ireland and Britain, 1795–1836*, London: Routledge and Kegan Paul.

SHILS, E. 1957. 'Primordial, personal, sacred and civil ties', *British Journal of Sociology*, 8: 130–45.

SHIRLOW, P. and MURTAGH, B. 2006. *Belfast: Segregation, Violence and the City*, London: Pluto.

SIDDLE, R. 2002a. 'An epoch-making event? The 1997 Ainu Cultural Promotion Act and its impact', *Japan Forum*, 14: 405–23.

SIDDLE, R. 2002b. 'Return to Uchina: the politics of identity in contemporary Okinawa', in G. D. Hook and R. Siddle (eds), *Japan and Okinawa: Structure and Subjectivity*, London: RoutledgeCurzon.

SKOVGAARD-PETERSEN, E. 1994. 'Stemmer om Maastricht', in J. Liep and K. Fog Olwig (eds), *Komplekse liv: kulturel mangfoldighed i Danmark*, Copenhagen: Akademisk Forlag.

SLUKA, J. A. 1989. *Hearts and Minds, Water and Fish: Support for the IRA and INLA in a Northern Irish Ghetto*, Greenwich: JAI Press.

SMART, B. (ed.) 1999. *Resisting McDonaldization*, London: Sage.

SMITH, A. 2001, 'Religious segregation and the emergence of integrated schools in Northern Ireland', *Oxford Review of Education*, 27: 559–75.

SMITH, A. D. 1981. *The Ethnic Revival in the Modern World*, Cambridge: Cambridge University Press.

SMITH, A. D. 1986. *The Ethnic Origins of Nations*, Oxford: Basil Blackwell.

SMITH, A. D. 1991. *National Identity*, Harmondsworth: Penguin.

SMITH, A. D. 1994. 'The problem of national identity: ancient, medieval and modern?' *Ethnic and Racial Studies*, 17: 375–99.

SMITH, A. D. 1999. *Myths and Memories of the Nation*, Oxford: Oxford University Press.

SMITH, A. D. 2003. *Chosen People: Sacred Sources of National Identity*, Oxford: Oxford University Press.

SMITH, D. J. and CHAMBERS, G. 1991. *Inequality in Northern Ireland*, Oxford: Clarendon Press.

SMITH, G. 1999. *Confronting the Present: Towards a Politically Engaged Anthropology*, Oxford: Berg.

SMITH, M. G. 1960. *Government in Zazzau 1800–1950*, London: Oxford University Press for the International African Institute.

SMITH, M. G. 1965. *The Plural Society in the British West Indies*, Berkeley: University of California Press.

SMITH, M. G. 1974. *Corporations and Society,* London: Duckworth.

SMITH, M. G. 1986. 'Pluralism, race and ethnicity in selected African countries', in J. Rex and D. Mason (eds), *Theories of Race and Ethnic Relations,* Cambridge: Cambridge University Press.

SOLOMOS, J. 1988. *Black Youth, Racism and the State: The Politics of Ideology and Policy,* Cambridge: Cambridge University Press.

SØRENSEN, H. and VAEVER, O. 1992. 'State, society and democracy and the effect of the EC', in L. Lyck (ed.), *Denmark and EC Membership Evaluated,* London: Pinter.

SØRENSEN. Ø. and STRÅTH, B. (eds) 1997. *The Cultural Construction of Norden,* Oslo: Scandinavian University Press.

SOUTHALL, A. 1976. 'Nuer and Dinka are people: ecology, economy and logical possibility', *Man* (n.s.) 11: 463–91.

SPEAR, T. and WALLER, R. (eds) 1993. *Being Maasai: Ethnicity and Identity in East Africa,* London: James Currey.

SPENCER, J. W. 2001. 'Self-presentation and organizational processing in a human service agency', in J. F. Gubrium and J. A. Holstein (eds), *Institutional Selves: Troubled Identities in a Postmodern World,* New York: Oxford University Press.

STEAD, P. 1990. 'The quest for political power', in R. Jenkins and A. Edwards (eds), *One Step Forward? South and West Wales towards the Year 2000,* Llandysul: Gwasg Gomer.

STEPICK, A., GRENIER, G., CASTRO, M. and DUNN, M. 2003. *This Land is Our Land: Immigrants and Power in Miami,* Berkeley: University of California Press.

STERN, D. N. 1985. *The Interpersonal World of the Infant: A View from Psychoanalysis and Developmental Psychology,* New York: Basic Books.

STONE, J. 2004. 'Ethnicity', in A. Kuper and J. Kuper (eds), *The Social Science Encyclopedia,* 3rd edn, London. Routledge.

STONE, M. 1981. *The Education of the Black Child in Britain,* London: Fontana.

STRATHERN, M. (ed.) 1995. *Shifting Contexts: Transformations in Anthropological Knowldege,* London: Routledge.

STUCHLIK, M. 1976. *Life on a Half Share: Mechanisms of Social Recruitment among the Mapuche of Southern Chile,* London: C. Hurst.

STUCHLIK, M. 1979. 'Chilean native policies and the image of the Mapuche Indians', in D. Riches (ed.), *The Conceptualisation and Explanation of Processes of Social Change* (Queen's University Papers in Social Anthropology, 3), Belfast: Queen's University.

SUNDAR, N. 2000. 'Caste as census category: implications for sociology', *Current Sociology,* 48 (3): 111–26.

SYMONDS, A. 1990. 'Migration, communities and social change', in R. Jenkins and A. Edwards (eds), *One Step Forward? South and West Wales towards the Year 2000,* Llandysul: Gwasg Gomer.

TÄGIL, S. (ed.) 1995. *Ethnicity and Nation Building in the Nordic World,* London: Hurst.

THOMAS, D. E. 1991. 'The Constitution of Wales', in B. Crick (ed.), *National Identities: The Constitution of the United Kingdom,* Oxford: Basil Blackwell.

THOMAS, N. 1991. *The Welsh Extremist: Modern Welsh Politics, Literature and Society,* 2nd edn, Talybont: Y Lolfa.

THOMPSON, A. 2001. 'Nations, national identities and human agency: putting people back into nations', *Sociological Review,* 49: 18–32.

THOMPSON, K. 1998. *Moral Panics,* London: Routledge.

TODD, J. 2005. 'Social transformations, collective categories and identity change', *Theory and Society,* 34: 429–63.

TODD, J., O'KEEFE, T., ROUGIER, N. and CAÑÁS BOTTOS, L. 2006. 'Fluid or frozen? Choice and change in ethno-national identification in contemporary Northern Ireland', *Nationalism and Ethnic Politics,* 12: 323–46.

TROYNA, B. and HATCHER, R. 1992. *Racism in Children's Lives: A Study of Mainly White Primary Schools,* London: Routledge.

URRY, J. 2000a 'Mobile sociology', *British Journal of Sociology*, 51: 185–203.

URRY, J. 2000b. *Sociology beyond Societies: Mobilities for the Twenty-First Century*, London: Routledge.

VAN AUSDALE, D. 2001. *The First R: How Children Learn Race and Racism*, New York: Rowman and Littlefield.

VAN DEN BERGHE, P. L. 1967. *Race and Racism: A Comparative Perspective*, New York: Wiley.

VAN DEN BERGHE, P. L. 1981. *The Ethnic Phenomenon*, New York. Elsevier.

VAN DEN BERGHE, P. L. 1986. 'Ethnicity and the socio-biology debate', in J. Rex and D. Mason (eds.), *Theories of Race and Ethnic Relations*, Cambridge: Cambridge University Press.

VAN DEN BERGHE, P. L. 1995. 'Does race matter?' *Nations and Nationalism*, 1: 357–68.

VERDERY, K. 1993. 'Whither "nation" and "nationalism"?', *Daedalus*, 122 (3): 37–45.

VERDERY, K. 1994. '"Ethnicity", nationalism and state-making. *Ethnic Groups and Boundaries: past and future*', in H. Vermeulen and C. Govers (eds), *The Anthropology of Ethnicity: Beyond 'Ethnic Groups and Boundaries'*, Amsterdam: het Spinhuis.

VERMEULEN, H. and GOVERS, C. 1994. 'Introduction', in H. Vermeulen and C. Govers (eds), *The Anthropology of Ethnicity: Beyond 'Ethnic Groups and Boundaries'*, Amsterdam: het Spinhuis.

WADE, P. 1993. '"Race", nature and culture', *Man* (n.s.) 28: 17–34.

WADE, P. 2002. *Race, Nature and Culture: An Anthropological Perspective*, London: Pluto.

WALLMAN, S. 1978. 'The boundaries of race: processes of ethnicity in England', *Man* (n.s.) 13: 200–17.

WALLMAN, S. 1979. 'Introduction: the scope for ethnicity', in S. Wallman (ed.), *Ethnicity at Work*, London: Macmillan.

WALLMAN, S. 1986. 'Ethnicity and the boundary process in context', in J. Rex and D. Mason (eds), *Theories of Race and Ethnic Relations*, Cambridge: Cambridge University Press.

WATERS, M. 1995. *Globalization*, London: Routledge.

WEBER, M. 1978. *Economy and Society*, ed. G. Roth and C. Wittich, Berkeley: University of California Press.

WHYTE, J. H. 1980. *Church and State in Modern Ireland 1923–1979*, Dublin: Gill and Macmillan.

WHYTE, J. H. 1990. *Understanding Northern Ireland*, Oxford: Clarendon Press.

WILK, R.R. 1993. 'Beauty and the feast: official and visceral nationalism in Belize', *Ethnos*, 58: 294–316.

WILLIAMS, B. 1989. 'A class act: anthropology and the race to nation across ethnic terrain', *Annual Review of Anthropology*, 18: 401–44.

WILLIAMS, C. 1995. 'Race and racism: some reflections on the Welsh context', *Contemporary Wales*, 8: 113–31.

WILLIAMS, C. 1999. 'Race, nation and identity', in R. Fevre and A. Thompson (eds), *Nation, Identity and Social Theory: Perspectives from Wales*, Cardiff: University of Wales Press.

WILLIAMS, C. H. 1989. 'New domains of the Welsh language: education, planning and the law', *Contemporary Wales*, 3: 41–76.

WILLIAMS, C. H. 2004. '*Iaith Pawb*: the doctrine of plenary inclusion', *Contemporary Wales*, 17: 1–27.

WILLIAMS, G. 1994. 'Discourses on "nation" and "race": a response to Denney *et al.*', *Contemporary Wales*, 6: 87–103.

WILLIAMS, G. A. 1985. *When Was Wales?* Harmondsworth: Penguin.

WILLIS, P. 1977. *Learning to Labour: How Working Class Kids Get Working Class Jobs*, Farnborough: Saxon House.

WILSON, T. 1955. 'Conclusions: devolution and partition', in T. Wilson (ed.), *Ulster under Home Rule*, London: Oxford University Press.

WILSON, T. 1989. *Ulster: Conflict and Consensus*, Oxford: Basil Blackwell.

WILSON, T. and DONNAN, H. (eds) 1998. *Border Identities: Nation and State at International Frontiers*, Cambridge: Cambridge University Press.

WOLF, E. R. 1994. 'Perilous ideas: race, culture, people', *Current Anthropology*, 5: 1–12.

WOODWARD, K. (ed.) 1997. *Identity and Difference*. London: Sage/Open University.

WREN, K. 2001. 'Cultural racism: something rotten in the state of Denmark?' *Social and Cultural Geography*, 2: 141–62.

Index